Studies in Social Policy

'Studies in Social Policy' is an important series of textbooks intended for students of social administration and social welfare at all levels. The books are directly related to the needs of undergraduate and postgraduate students in universities, polytechnics and similar institutions as well as vocational students preparing for careers in a variety of social and other public services. The series includes the following topics:

the roles of different public and private institutions such as social services departments and building societies in meeting social needs;

introductory guides to new technical and theoretical developments relevant to the analysis of social policy such as political theory and the newly emerging specialism of the economics of social care;

contemporary social policy issues such as the use of charges in the delivery of social welfare or the problem of determining priorities in the health and personal social services.

Studies in Social Policy

Editor: Ken Judge

Published

The Building Societies
Martin Boddy

Access to Welfare
Peggy Foster

Health Policy in Britain
Christopher Ham

Policy-making in the National Health Service
Christopher Ham

Pricing the Social Services
Ken Judge (ed.)

The Economics of Social Care
Martin Knapp

Choices for Health Care
Gavin H. Mooney, Elizabeth M. Russell and Roy D. Weir

Power, Authority and Responsibility in Social Services
Malcolm Payne

Political Theory and Social Policy
Albert Weale

Forthcoming

Low Pay and Family Poverty in Northern Ireland
John Ditch, Mike Morrissey, Pat McGinn and Richard Steele

Introducing Social Policy
Ken Judge and Roger Hampson

The Welfare State
John Macnicol

The Economics of Poverty
Alan Maynard

Health Care in the European Community
Alan Maynard and Anne Ludbrook

Power, Rationality and Social Planning
Adrian Webb and Gerald Wistow

Health Policy in Britain

The Politics and Organisation of the National Health Service

SECOND EDITION

Christopher Ham

School for Advanced Urban Studies
University of Bristol

MACMILLAN

First edition 1982
Second edition 1985

Published by
Higher and Further Education Division
MACMILLAN PUBLISHERS LTD
Houndmills, Basingstoke, Hampshire RG21 2XS
and London
Companies and representatives
throughout the world

Printed in Hong Kong

British Library Cataloguing in Publication Data
Ham, Christopher
Health policy in Britain.—2nd ed.
1. Medical policy—Great Britain
I. Title
362.1′0941   RA395.G6
ISBN 0–333–39492–5
ISBN 0–333–39493–3 Pbk

Published and distributed in the USA by:
Baywood Publishing Company Inc
120 Marine Street
P.O. Box D
Farmingdale
NY 11735

Baywood edition ISBNs:
0-89503-046-2
0-89503-047-0 pbk

To Ioanna

Contents

Figures and Tables

Preface to the First Edition

This book is based on undergraduate and postgraduate courses in health policy which I have taught at the University of Bristol. The students who have taken the courses have helped me develop my ideas, and I would like to acknowledge their assistance. In particular, I am grateful to Laurie McMahon and Andrew Wall, two former members of the M.Sc. course in Public Policy Studies at the School for Advanced Urban Studies, for commenting on an earlier draft of the book. A number of colleagues at the School also commented on draft chapters. Robin Hambleton, Michael Hill, Robin Means, Randall Smith and David Towell helped in this way, and made many useful suggestions and criticisms. My thanks are due to them. John James and John Rogers of the Department of Health and Social Security assisted me in clarifying the role of the Department and in reducing factual errors. Their help has been invaluable, though I should like to emphasise that they bear no responsibility for the judgements I have made about the Department and the processes of health policy-making within central government. Steven Kennedy of Macmillan, and Ken Judge of the University of Kent and editor of the Studies in Social Policy series, have been a source of encouragement, and both made helpful comments on the structure of the book and its detailed contents. Penny Buckland and Sue Cottrell were responsible for typing the manuscript, and did so efficiently and cheerfully. Finally, I would like to thank Ioanna Burnell for her comments on the manuscript, and for putting up with me during the writing. I alone am responsible for the final text.

Bristol   CHRISTOPHER HAM
April 1982

Preface to the Second Edition

In preparing the second edition of the book, I have concentrated mainly on updating the contents to take account of policy developments since 1982 and changes (including proposed changes) to the organisation of health services. I have also sought in one or two places to relate the discussion of theory to debates among political scientists and others about the relevance of corporatism to the British political system. Otherwise, I have let the original text stand.

The reasons for doing so are twofold. First, reviewers of the first edition in general found the analysis of the politics of health care offered in the book convincing, and this has encouraged me to believe that my general approach is sound. Second, the rationale for a book of this kind, as expressed in the Introduction, still stands. Although the literature on health services has continued to grow apace since 1982, there are very few books which attempt to offer an overall analysis of the processes of policy-making and implementation in the NHS. One of the main exceptions, Rudolf Klein's study of the politics of the NHS (Klein, 1983), is principally historical in its approach, and as such is complementary to the analysis put forward here. For these reasons I have not attempted to change the basic structure of the book, and I hope that it will remain a useful introduction to health policy for students of health services.

I have again benefitted from the comments of John James, John Rogers and Andrew Wall. Sue Cottrell prepared the manuscript, demonstrating skill with scissors and Sellotape as well as typewriter. In thanking them, I once more accept responsibility for the final text.

Bristol   CHRISTOPHER HAM
October 1984

Abbreviations

AHA	Area Health Authority
BMA	British Medical Association
CHC	Community Health Council
CPRS	Central Policy Review Staff
DGH	District General Hospital
DGM	District General Manager
DHA	District Health Authority
DHSS	Department of Health and Social Security
DMT	District Management Team
FPC	Family Practitioner Committee
GHS	General Household Survey
GP	General Practitioner
HAS	Health Advisory Service
HMC	Hospital Management Committee
JCC	Joint Consultative Committee
MAS	Management Advisory Service
MPC	Medical Practices Committee
NAHA	National Association of Health Authorities
NHS	National Health Service
PESC	Public Expenditure Survey Committee
RAWP	Resource Allocation Working Party
RCP	Royal College of Physicians
RGM	Regional General Manager
RHA	Regional Health Authority
RHB	Regional Hospital Board
RL	Regional Liaison
RTO	Regional Team of Officers
SMR	Standardised mortality ratio

Acknowledgements

The author and publishers wish to thank the following who have kindly given permission for the use of copyright material:

The Controller of Her Majesty's Stationery Office for tables from *Social Trends*, 1984; *Health Care and Its Costs*, 1983; *HM Treasury: The Government Expenditure Plans*, and data from the Black Report, *Inequalities in Health*.

The University of Chicago Press for a diagram from *A Systems Analysis of Political Life*, 1965 by David Easton.

Introduction

This book provides an introduction to health policy for students of
health services in the United Kingdom. The book is concerned
with both the substance of health policy and the process of health
policy-making and implementation. Its aim is to introduce students to the organisation of the National Health Service (NHS), its
history and development; and to the way in which policies for
health services are made and implemented in central government
and in health authorities. The book also examines the impact of
health services, and considers which groups have power over
policy-making. The main concern of what follows, then, is the
politics of health care: who decides, who benefits and who controls
health services.

The book arose out of a dissatisfaction with existing treatments
of these questions. While there is no shortage of literature on
health services and the politics of health care, the main contributions are inadequate in various ways. Descriptive accounts, for
example, often provide a wealth of information on the structure
and functions of the principal institutions and services (see, for
example, Levitt, 1979), but do not help to explain in an analytical
way how policies develop and who influences what is decided.
Equally, books which *are* analytical in focus tend to be partial
rather than comprehensive, typically using the case-study method.
Thus, they may examine a single issue (Allen, 1979), a single
decision (Willcocks, 1967), a single organisation (Eckstein, 1960),
or a single level of policy-making (Ham, 1981), rather than
considering health policy as a whole. This is not to say that
descriptive accounts and case studies have no value. On the
contrary, descriptive work contains much useful information on
which to build an analytical approach, while case studies frequently include valuable insights into specific aspects of health policy.

Both kinds of work are drawn on in the chapters which follow. What we are suggesting, though, is that there is a need to go beyond these approaches and to analyse the overall pattern of health service provision.

There are a few studies that attempt to do this. Perhaps the best example is Brown's (1975) examination of the management of health and welfare services. Brown's study has in many ways served as a model for this book. Yet since Brown's book was written, the diaries of Richard Crossman and Barbara Castle have been published, giving an inside view of policy-making in the Department of Health and Social Security (DHSS). The Crossman and Castle diaries have enabled a more complete account of the dynamics of the policy process to be produced, and they have been drawn on freely in the subsequent chapters. Also, recent years have witnessed a burgeoning literature on the implementation of health policy, the processes of policy-making at the local level, and on the impact of services – a literature which was not available to Brown, but which in many ways confirms and adds to his perceptive insights. Again, this recent work has been used in this book to illustrate various aspects of the health policy process.

Like Brown, we will utilise concepts and theories from a range of disciplines in analysing health policy. Since the main focus is the politics of health care, political science and policy analysis have furnished a number of concepts which have proved valuable in examining decision-making, power and control. In addition, economics and sociology have been found helpful in making sense of questions of resource allocation and equity on the one hand, and concepts of health and illness on the other. In using these disciplines, this book seeks to go beyond Brown's study by attempting to make connections between different levels of analysis. To oversimplify only a little, there is a gulf between writers who concentrate on the detailed processes of decision-making in health care organisations, and those who direct their attention to the role of the state and its implications for health services. Very rarely are the two levels of analysis combined, and a key argument of this book is that there is a need to relate micro theories of the policy process to macro theories of the state. In the final chapter there is an attempt to do this, and to explore areas for further work.

The book has been written mainly for students of social policy and administration at the undergraduate level. Other students likely to use the book are those following courses of professional training, including health administrators, health visitors, social work students and community physicians. The contents should also be of relevance to those who provide health services, whether as members or officers of health authorities, as members of community health councils, or as civil servants in the DHSS. Many of the themes that are raised may also be of interest to the general reader seeking to appreciate the operation of the NHS and the processes of policy-making, and to an international audience concerned to understand the lessons of the NHS for other health care systems. At a time when the health services of countries such as Italy are moving in the direction of the United Kingdom, the NHS may increasingly be seen as an example for the rest of the world. Escalating health care costs constitute an international problem which the NHS has been relatively successful in tackling. There are many reasons for this success, including the strict budget limits imposed on the NHS by central government, the dependence on tax revenue as the main source of funds, and the existence of a system of regional planning with major hospital building schemes being subject to central approval (Abel-Smith, 1981).

The implications of rationing health care resources by budgets rather than markets are explored in the following chapters. Particularly important in the international context is the impact of a state-financed and organised health service on decision-making. Does 'socialised medicine' (Lindsey, 1962) lead to bureaucratic control of the medical profession, and to what extent are consumers able to influence what is decided? Within the budgetary limits imposed by government, how are priorities arrived at and resources allocated? What is the balance between central control of health services and local autonomy? And finally, does the removal of the price barrier to health services lead to equity in the use of services and the allocation of funds? These questions are especially pertinent in the light of moves to examine alternative methods of financing health services in the United Kingdom and to encourage the development of the private health care sector. An attempt is made to analyse and clarify these issues in this book. Recognising that an introductory textbook is likely to raise as many questions as provide answers, suggestions for further reading are included at the end of the book.

The structure of the analysis

The book is organised into seven chapters. Chapter 1 examines the way in which the state has increasingly become involved in providing health services in the United Kingdom. Starting with state involvement in public health in the nineteenth century, the chapter traces the development of health insurance measures in the first part of the twentieth century and the establishment of the NHS in 1948. Particular attention is given to events after 1948, including the reorganisation of the NHS in 1974 and its subsequent restructuring in 1982.

Chapter 2 provides an introduction to contemporary issues in health policy. The chapter examines health service financing and resource allocation in the NHS, and consideration is given to the geographical distribution of funds and to the allocation of resources to different services and client groups. Government policies for specific services are outlined, and attempts to establish priorities between these services are analysed. The relationship between health policy and other areas of social policy is also discussed.

Chapter 3 considers the meaning of policy and the nature of the policy process. After identifying the main features of policy and the relevance of a systems model of the policy process, the chapter examines the organisation of central government in Britain. The functions and powers of Parliament, the Cabinet, the Prime Minister, ministers, civil servants and outside interests are explored, in order to establish the political context of health policy-making.

Chapter 4 concentrates on the workings of the Department of Health and Social Security. The way in which the Deparment is organised is discussed, and this is followed by an examination of the various influences on health policy-making within central government. The role of pressure groups and other interests is considered, and the chapter concludes with a discussion of attempts within the DHSS to introduce a greater measure of analysis into the policy process.

Chapter 5 looks at the implementation of health policy, and the local influences on policy-making. A key issue here is the relationship between the DHSS and health authorities. Also significant is the position of the medical profession in the structure of administration and as major resource controllers at the local level. These issues are analysed, and the extent to which national policies are implemented is discussed. The chapter also considers the ability of health authorities to engage in independent policy-making.

Chapter 6 focuses on the impact of health services. Three aspects of inequality in health and the use of health services are examined: geographical, social class and client group. The chapter describes the nature of inequalities in each area, and discusses attempts by policy-makers to reduce inequalities. The scope for monitoring and evaluating health service provision is also considered.

Finally, Chapter 7 examines the distribution of power in the NHS. Through a discussion of different theories of power, the chapter asks whose interests are served by health services? The relevance of pluralist, Marxist and structuralist theories is assessed, and issues for further research are identified. The chapter seeks to stand back from the detailed discussion of health policy in earlier chapters in order to explore the variety of overarching approaches to understanding the development of health services and power relationships in health care.

Chapter 5 looks at implementation of health policy, and the local influences on policy-making. A key issue here is the relationship between the policies and health indicators, and the nature of the medical profession in the structure of administration in areas where central controllers at the local level.

The issues are analysed, and the extent to which interclass policies are implemented is discussed. The chapter also considers the status of health authorities, central in respect of policy-making.

Chapter 6 focuses on the impact of health services, and issues of inequality in health and the use of health services are examined, with particular social class and racial groups. The chapter discusses the nature of inequalities in health care, and the extent to which variations in the use of services for policy, monitoring and evaluating health service provision is also considered.

Finally, Chapter 7 examines the distribution of power in the NHS. Through a discussion of the way in which power in the chapter asks whose interests are served by health services. The relationship between Marxist and structuralist theories is explored, and some key issues for further research are identified. The analysis helps us to stand back from the detailed discussion of health policy in earlier chapters, in order to explore the history of developing a framework for understanding the development of health services and power relationships in health care.

1

The Development of Health Services and Health Policy

The National Health Service came into existence on 5 July 1948 with the aim of providing a comprehensive range of health services to all in need. One hundred years earlier the first Public Health Act was placed on the statute book, paving the way for improvements in environmental health which were to have a significant effect in reducing deaths from infectious diseases. The name of Aneurin Bevan is usually associated with the founding of the NHS, and that of Edwin Chadwick with the public health movement. However, legislation and policy are not made only or mainly by outstanding individuals. It has been said of Bevan that he was 'less of an innovator than often credited; he was at the end, albeit the important and conclusive end, of a series of earlier plans. He 'created' the National Health Service but his debts to what went before were enormous' (Willcocks, 1967, p. 104). Much the same applies to other health policy decisions. Individuals may have an impact, but under conditions not of their own making. What is more, most decisions in their final form result from bargaining and negotiation among a complex constellation of interests, and most changes do not go through unopposed. These points can be illustrated through the examples already cited.

Take the 1848 Public Health Act, for example. The main aim of the Act was to provide powers to enable the construction of water supply and sewerage systems as a means of controlling some of the conditions in which infectious diseases were able to thrive and spread. On the face of it, this was a laudable aim which might have been expected to win general public support. In fact, the Act was opposed by commercial interests who were able to make money out of insanitary conditions; and by anxious ratepayers, who were afraid of the public expense which would be involved. It was therefore only after a lengthy struggle that the Act was passed.

Again, consider the establishment of the NHS. The shape taken by the NHS was the outcome of discussions and compromise between ministers and civil servants on the one hand, and a range of pressure groups on the other. These groups included the medical profession, the organisations representing the hospital service, and the insurance committees with their responsibility for general practitioner services. Willcocks has shown how, among these groups, the medical profession was the most successful in achieving its objectives, while the organisations representing the hospital service were the least successful. A considerable part too was played by civil servants and ministers. In turn, all of these interests were influenced by what had gone before. They were not in a position to start with a blank sheet and proceed to design an ideal administrative structure. Thus history, as well as the strength of established interests, may be important in shaping decisions. Let us then consider the historical background to the NHS.

Public health services

The most important area of state involvement in the provision of health services during the nineteenth century, in terms of the impact on people's health, was the enactment of public health legislation. Infectious diseases like cholera and typhoid posed the main threat to health at the time. The precise causes of these diseases remained imperfectly understood for much of the century, and the medical profession was largely powerless to intervene. In any event, the main reason for the decline in infectious diseases was not to be advances in medical science, but developments in the system of public health. It was these developments which provided an effective counterweight to the sorts of urban living conditions created by the industrial revolution and within which infectious diseases could flourish.

As already mentioned, it was the 1848 Public Health Act that provided the basis for the provision of adequate water supplies and sewerage systems. Behind the Act lay several years of struggle by Edwin Chadwick and his supporters. As Secretary to the Poor Law Commission, Chadwick played a major part in preparing the

Commission's *Report of an Inquiry into the Sanitary Conditions of the Labouring Population of Great Britain*, published in 1842. The report, and the ever present threat of cholera, created the conditions for the Act, which led to the establishment of the General Board of Health. Subsequent progress was variable, with some local authorities keen to take action, while others held back. In practice, a great deal depended on the attitude of local interests, as the Act was permissive rather than mandatory, and the General Board of Health was only an advisory body.

Chadwick's campaign was taken forward by John Simon, first as Medical Officer to the General Board of Health, and later as Medical Officer to the Medical Department of the Privy Council, which succeeded the Board in 1858. Simon's work and the report of the Royal Sanitary Commission, which sat from 1869 to 1871, eventually bore fruit in the establishment of the Local Government Board in 1871, and the Public Health Acts of 1872 and 1875. The 1875 Act brought together existing legislation rather than providing new powers, while the 1872 Act created sanitary authorities who were obliged to provide public health services. One of the key provisions of the 1872 Act was that local sanitary authorities should appoint a medical officer of health. These officers – whose origins can be traced back to Liverpool in 1847 – were significant figures, both in the fight against infectious diseases, and in the campaign for better health. It was mainly as a result of their activities at the local level that more concerted action was pursued.

Mothers and young children

From the beginning of the twentieth century, the sphere of concern of medical officers of health extended into the area of personal health services as the result of increasing state concern with the health of mothers and young children. One of the immediate causes was the discovery of the poor standards of health and fitness of army recruits for the Boer War. This led to the establishment by government of an Interdepartmental Committee on Physical Deterioration, whose report, published in 1904, made a series of recommendations aimed at improving child health. Two of the outcomes were the 1906 Education (Provision of Meals) Act, which provided the basis for the school meals service, and the 1907 Education (Administrative Provision) Act, which led to the development of the school medical service. It has been argued that these Acts 'marked the beginning of the con-struction of the welfare state' (Gilbert, 1966, p. 102). Both pieces of legislation were promoted by the reforming Liberal government elected in 1906, and the government was also active in other areas of social policy reform, including the provision of old age pen-sions.

At the same time action was taken in relation to the midwifery and health visiting services. The 1902 Midwives Act made it necessary to certify midwives as fit to practise, and established a Central Midwives Board to oversee registration. The Act stemmed in part from the belief that one of the explanations for high rates of maternal and infant mortality lay in the lack of skills of women practising as midwives. Local supervision of registration was the responsibility of the medical officer of health, whose office was becoming increasingly powerful. This trend was reinforced by the 1907 Notification of Births Act, one of whose aims was to develop health visiting as a local authority service. The origins of health visiting are usually traced back to Manchester and Salford in the 1860s, when women began visiting mothers to encourage higher standards of child care. The state's interest in providing health visiting as a statutory service mirrored its concern to regulate midwives and provide medical inspection in schools, and the importance of health visiting was emphasised by the Interdepart-mental Committee on Physical Deterioration. The 1907 Act helped the development of health visiting by enabling local authorities to insist on the compulsory notification of births. An Act of 1915 placed a duty on local authorities to ensure compul-sory notification.

Arising out of these developments, and spurred on by the 1918 Maternity and Child Welfare Act, local authorities came to provide a further range of child welfare services. This involved not only the employment of health visitors and the registration of midwives, but also the provision of infant welfare centres and, in some areas, maternity homes for mothers who required institu-tional confinements. However, the Ministry of Health, which had been established in 1919, continued to be concerned at the high rate of maternal deaths, as the publication in 1930 and 1932 of the reports of the Departmental Committee on Maternal Mortality and Morbidity demonstrated. Particular importance was placed on the provision of adequate antenatal care. This led to an expansion of antenatal clinics, and, after the 1936 Midwives Act, to the development of a salaried midwifery service.

Health insurance

The 1911 National Insurance Act was concerned with the provision of general practitioner (GP) services. The Act was an important element in the Liberal government's programme of social policy reform, and it provided for free care from GPs for certain groups of working people earning under £160 per annum. Income during sickness and unemployment was also made available, and the scheme was based on contributions by the worker, the employer and the state.

Like other major pieces of social legislation, the Act was not introduced without a struggle. As Gilbert (1966, p. 290) has noted, 'The story of the growth of national health insurance is to a great extent the story of lobby influence and pressure groups'. Gilbert has shown how Lloyd George pushed through the Act to come into operation in 1913, but only after considerable opposition from the medical profession. The doctors were fearful of state control of their work, and of the possible financial consequences. They were persuaded into the scheme when the government agreed that payment should be based on the number of patients on a doctor's list, the capitation system, rather than on a salary, thereby preserving GPs' independence. Also, it was decided that the scheme should be administered not by local authorities, but by independent insurance committees or 'panels'. The insurance companies and friendly societies who had previously played a major part in providing cover against ill-health were given a central role on the panels. The professional freedom of doctors was further safeguarded by allowing them the choice of whether to join the scheme, and whether to accept patients. Finally, the financial fears of the profession were assuaged by the generous level of payments that were negotiated, and by the exclusion of higher income groups from the scheme. The exclusion of these groups created a valuable source of extra income for GPs. By the mid 1940s around 21 million people or about half the population of

Great Britain were insured under the Act. Also, about two-thirds of GPs were taking part. Nevertheless, the scheme had important limitations: it was only the insured workers who were covered, and not their families; and no hospital care was provided, only the services of GPs. Despite these drawbacks, the Act represented a major step forward in the involvement of the state in the provision of health services.

Hospital services

Public provision of hospitals developed out of the workhouses provided under the Poor Law. In parallel there grew up the voluntary hospital system, based at first on the monasteries and later on charitable contributions by the benevolent rich. Of the two types of institution, it was the voluntary hospitals that provided the higher standards of care. As the nineteenth century progressed, and as medicine developed as a science, the voluntary hospitals became increasingly selective in their choice of patients, paying more and more attention to the needs of the acutely ill to the exclusion of the chronic sick and people with infectious diseases. Consequently, it was left to the workhouses to care for the groups that the voluntary hospitals would not accept, and workhouse conditions were often overcrowded and unhygienic. Some of the vestiges of this dual system of hospital care can still be observed in the NHS today.

It was not perhaps surprising that workhouse standards should be so low, since one of the aims of the Poor Law was to act as a deterrent. The 'less eligibility' principle underpinning the 1834 Poor Law Amendment Act depended on the creation of work-house conditions so unattractive that they would discourage the working and sick poor from seeking relief. The Act was also intended to limit outdoor relief: that is, relief provided outside the workhouses. In the case of medical care, this was provided by district medical officers under contract to the Boards of Guardians who administered the Poor Law. Vaccination against smallpox was one of the services for which medical officers were responsible, beginning with the introduction of free vaccination for children in 1840.

There was some improvement in Poor Law hospital services in London after the passing of the 1867 Metropolitan Poor Act. The Act provided the stimulus for the development of infirmaries separate from workhouses, and the London example was subsequently followed in the rest of the country through powers granted by the 1868 Poor Law Amendment Act. However, the establishment of separate infirmaries coincided with a further campaign against outdoor relief. This was despite the fact that in some areas public dispensaries, equivalent to rudimentary health centres, were provided for the first time. Nevertheless, the legislation which encouraged the development of Poor Law infirmaries has been described as 'an important step in English social history. It was the first explicit acknowledgement that it was the duty of the state to provide hospitals for the poor. It therefore represented an important step towards the NHS Act which followed some eighty years later' (Abel-Smith, 1964, p. 82). And as Fraser has commented, 'through the medical officers and the workhouse infirmaries the Poor Law had become an embryo state medical authority providing in effect general practitioners and state hospitals for the poor' (Fraser, 1973, p. 87).

The 1929 Local Government Act marked the beginning of the end of the Poor Law, and was a further step on the road to the NHS. The importance of the Act was that it resulted in the transfer of workhouses and infirmaries to local authorities. County councils and county borough councils were required to set up public assistance committees to administer these institutions, and were empowered to appropriate from them accommodation for the care of the sick. The intention was that this accommodation should then be developed into a local authority hospital service. Although uneven progress in this direction was made before the outbreak of the Second World War, the 1929 Act was important in placing the Poor Law infirmaries in the same hands as the other public health services which were under the control of medical officers of health. These services included not only those already mentioned, but also the provision of specialised hospitals — for example, for infectious diseases and tuberculosis — which local authorities had developed rapidly from the last decades of the nineteenth century. In addition, local authorities had a duty to provide hospitals for the mentally ill and handicapped. Local magistrates had been given the power to erect asylums under the 1808 County Asylums Act, but fear of the cost meant that the power was not widely used. The legislation was made mandatory in 1845, leading to a rapid growth in asylums thereafter. By 1930 there were 98 public asylums in England and Wales accommodating about 120,000 patients (Jones, 1972, p. 357).

Accordingly, at the outbreak of the Second World War, local authorities were responsible for a wide range of hospitals. As part of the war effort, public hospitals joined the voluntary hospitals in the Emergency Medical Service (EMS), set up to cope with military and civilian casualties and to provide some co-ordination of a disparate range of institutions and services. The EMS, with its regional form of organisation, provided a framework for the administration of hospital services after the war. More important, it resulted in senior members of the medical profession seeing at first hand the poor state of local authority hospitals and the smaller voluntary hospitals. At the same time, regional hospital surveys were carried out by the Nuffield Provincial Hospitals Trust, a voluntary body concerned with the quality and organisation of hospital services, and with a particular interest in the regionalisation of hospitals. The surveys were conducted in conjunction with the Ministry of Health, and provided thorough documentation of the widely varying standards which existed (hospitals for the mentally ill and mentally handicapped were not included in the surveys). The summary report of the surveys, published in 1946 as the Domesday Book of the Hospital Services, pointed to considerable inequalities in the distribution of beds and staff between different parts of the country, as well as to the lack of organisation of the service as a whole (Nuffield Provincial Hospitals Trust, 1946). It was in this sense, then, that the experience of war may be said to have created pressure for change, although what form the change should take was very much an issue for debate.

The establishment of the National Health Service

We have seen how, in a variety of ways, responsibility for the provision of health care increasingly was taken over by the state. The key legislative developments were the 1808 County Asylums Act, the 1867 Metropolitan Poor Act and the 1929 Local Government Act, all emphasising the importance of public provision of hospital services; the Public Health Acts and the legislation relating to maternal and child welfare, placing on local authorities a duty to develop environmental and later some personal health services; and thirdly, the National Insurance Act, recognising the state's responsibility in relation to primary health care.

Given the *ad hoc* manner in which these developments occurred, it was not surprising that there should be calls for the co-ordination and consolidation of service provision. Thus the report of the Dawson Committee, set up in 1919 after the establishment of the Ministry of Health to make proposals for improving health services, recommended the provision of a comprehensive scheme of hospital and primary health care. Later reports from the Royal Commission on the National Health Insurance in 1926, the Sankey Commission on Voluntary Hospitals in 1937, and the British Medical Association (BMA) in 1930 and 1938, all pointed to shortcomings in the existing pattern of services, and made various suggestions for change. These included the need for greater co-ordination of hospitals, and for the extension of health insurance to other groups in the population. The Royal Commission's report also suggested that health service funding might eventually be derived from general taxation instead of being based on the insurance principle.

This view was not shared by the BMA, which, in an important report from its Medical Planning Commission published in 1942, advocated the extension of state involvement in the provision of health services. The BMA suggested that health insurance should be extended to cover most of the population and that the items covered by insurance should encompass the services of hospital specialists and examinations. The same year as the BMA's report appeared saw publication of an even more influential document, the Beveridge Report on Social Insurance and Allied Services. This made wide-ranging recommendations for the reform and extension of the social security system, together with proposals for a national health service. Coming a year after the government had announced its intention to develop a national hospital service at the end of the war, the Beveridge Report added impetus to the movement for change.

The movement gathered momentum in subsequent years, leading to a White Paper containing proposals for a national health service in 1944, the National Health Service Act in 1946, and the establishment of the Service itself in 1948. Prolonged negotiations accompanied the birth of the Service, and these negotiations at times seemed likely to prevent the birth taking place at all. Certainly, the medical profession, as in 1911, fought strongly for its own objectives, and was successful in winning many concessions: retention of the independent contractor system for GPs; the option of private practice and access to pay beds in NHS hospitals for hospital consultants; a system of distinction awards for consultants, carrying with it large increases in salary for those receiving awards; a major role in the administration of the Service at all levels; and success in resisting local government control. The concessions made to hospital doctors led Aneurin Bevan to say that he had 'stuffed their mouths with gold' (Abel-Smith, 1964, p. 480). In fact, Bevan cleverly divided the medical profession, winning the support of hospital consultants and specialists with generous financial payments, and thereby isolating and reducing the power of GPs, who were nevertheless successful in achieving many of their aims.

Far less successful were the local authorities, who lost control of their hospitals, despite the advocacy by Herbert Morrison in the Labour Cabinet of the local government point of view. The main reason for this, apart from the opposition of the doctors, was the unsuitability of local government areas for the administration of the hospital service. As a result, Bevan — and this was one of his personal contributions to the organisation of the NHS — decided to appropriate both the local authority hospitals and the voluntary hospitals and place them under a single system of administration. Another major personal contribution made by Bevan was to persuade the medical profession that the service should cover all of the population and not just 90 per cent as many doctors wished. Furthermore, the Service was to be funded mainly out of general taxation, with insurance contributions making up only a small part of the total finance.

This, then, is a very brief summary of the debate surrounding the organisation of the NHS. One point to note is the relative unimportance of Parliament in the debate. The policy in this case was more strongly influenced by extra-parliamentary forces, in particular by the major pressure groups with an interest in health services. As we shall argue later, these forces can be seen to comprise a policy community within which many issues are settled and agreed, either without or with only token reference to Parliament. In this sense, legislation is often little more than a record of the bargains struck in the health policy community. There are exceptions, and parliamentary influence can be important, but to recognise the importance of other factors is a useful corrective to conventional textbook views of British government and politics.

The structure of the National Health Service

The administrative structure of the NHS which came into being in 1948 was the product of the bargaining and negotiation which had taken place in the health policy community in the preceding years. It was therefore a representation of what was possible rather than what might have been desirable. The structure was also shaped by the historical antecedents which have been discussed, with the result that the Service was organised into three parts. First, representing the closest link with what had gone before, general practitioner services, along with the services of dentists, opticians and pharmacists, were administered by *executive councils*, which took over from the old insurance committees. Executive councils were appointed partly by local professionals, partly by local authorities and partly by the Ministry of Health, and they were funded directly by the Ministry. In no sense were executive councils management bodies. They simply administered the contracts of family practitioners (the generic term for GPs, dentists, opticians and pharmacists), maintained lists of local practitioners, and handled complaints by patients.

Second, and again closely linked with the previous system of administration, responsibility for a range of environmental and personal health services was vested in *local authorities*. These services included maternity and child welfare clinics, health visitors, midwives, health education, vaccination and immunisation, and ambulances. The key local officer continued to be the medical officer of health, and funding of the services was provided partly by central government grants and partly by local rates.

Third, hospitals were administered by completely new bodies — *Regional Hospital Boards (RHBs), Hospital Management Committees (HMCs), and boards of governors.* Special status was given to the teaching hospitals — the elite members of the old voluntary hospital system — which were organised under boards of governors in direct contact with the Ministry of Health. This was one of the concessions Aneurin Bevan made to the medical profession. The vast majority of hospitals, though, came under the Regional Hospital Boards, of which there were fourteen in England and Wales at first, and fifteen later, and Hospital Management Committees, numbering some 400 in total. RHBs were appointed by the Minister of Health, and they in turn appointed HMCs. Finance for the hospital service was passed down from the Ministry of Health through RHBs and on to HMCs. In the case of teaching hospitals, money was allocated straight from the Ministry to boards of governors. The tripartite structure of the NHS is illustrated in Figure 1.1.

FIGURE 1.1   *The structure of the NHS, 1948–74*

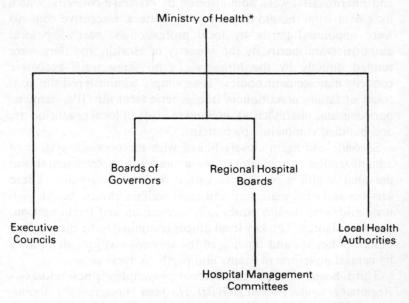

Ministry of Health*

Boards of Governors

Regional Hospital Boards

Executive Councils

Local Health Authorities

Hospital Management Committees

* Superseded by the Department of Health and Social Security in 1968.

The NHS between 1948 and 1974

One of the assumptions that lay behind the NHS, and which had been made in the Beveridge Report, was that there was a fixed quantity of illness in the community which the introduction of a health service, free at the point of consumption, would gradually reduce. It was therefore expected that expenditure would soon level off and even decline as people became healthier. In fact, the reverse happened. Health service spending in the years immediately after 1948 was much greater than had been allowed for in parliamentary estimates, and supplementary funding was necessary. Concern at the cost of the Service was reflected in the appointment of the Guillebaud Committee of Enquiry in 1953:

> to review the present and prospective cost of the National Health Service; to suggest means, whether by modifications in organisation or otherwise, of ensuring the most effective control and efficient use of such Exchequer funds as may be made available; to advise how, in view of the burdens on the Exchequer, a rising charge upon it can be avoided while providing for the maintenance of an adequate Service; and to make recommendations. (Guillebaud Committee, 1956)

The Committee's report, published in 1956, concluded that there was no evidence of extravagance or inefficiency in the NHS. Indeed, using research carried out by Richard Titmuss and Brian Abel-Smith, the Committee showed that, expressed as a proportion of the gross national product, the cost of the service had actually fallen from 3.75 per cent in 1949–50 to 3.25 per cent in 1953–54. If anything, the Committee felt that more money, not less, should be allocated to the NHS, particularly to make up for the backlog of capital building works needing to be undertaken. The Committee also considered that more could be done to strengthen the links between the three branches of the Service, although it was not prepared to recommend any major organisational change.

The call for extra resources was echoed by a number of individuals and organisations, and it is not difficult to see why. The 1950s have been characterised aptly as the years of 'make do and mend' in the hospital service, with capital expenditure during the decade amounting to only £100 million. Within this budget, no new hospitals could be built, and critics maintained that doctors were having to practise twentieth-century medicine in nineteenth-century buildings. This was the argument of two hospital consultants, Abel and Lewin, who in a study commissioned by the BMA and published in 1959, argued for greatly increased expenditure (Abel and Lewin, 1959). The response came in the form of the 1962 Hospital Plan, providing for an expenditure of £500 million in England and Wales in the ten years up to 1971. The key concept behind the plan was the District General Hospital (DGH), a hospital of between 600 and 800 beds providing specialist facilities for all but the rarest illnesses for a population of 100,000 to 150,000. Several completely new DGHs were to be built during the decade, while many more existing hospitals were to be upgraded to DGH standard. Thus, after a number of years of restraint, the hospital building programme witnessed a significant expansion.

The 1950s were not, however, wasted years in the hospital service. The amalgamation of local authority and voluntary hospitals soon brought results in terms of a better use of resources. The grouping of hospitals on a district basis under the control of a Hospital Management Committee, and the introduction of a system of regional planning, helped to eliminate some of the shortages and overlaps that had existed before 1948. A good example was the rationalisation of infectious diseases hospitals and the release of beds for alternative uses. Also, there was an increase in the number of medical staff employed, and the services of hospital consultants became much more widely available. Before the establishment of the NHS, most consultants worked in urban areas where there were plentiful opportunities for private practice. After 1948, the introduction of a salaried service for hospital doctors with national salary scales and conditions of service, assisted in bringing about a more even distribution of staff. At the same time, the hospital out-patient service was further developed. These were some of the advantages to accrue from a national hospital service (see Ham, 1981).

As far as general practitioners were concerned, it has been argued that 'it was general practice, sustained for 37 years by National Health Insurance and gaining substantial additional support from the new system, which really carried the National

Health Service at its inception' (Godber, 1975, p. 5). A cause of concern, though, was the increasing gulf that developed between GPs and their consultant colleagues. Contact was maintained between the two branches of medical practice through a variety of mechanisms, including part-time hospital appointments for GPs and allowing GPs direct access to hospital diagnostic facilities. But on the whole, the gulf between general practice and specialist practice widened, despite recommendations from bodies like the Guillebaud Committee that bridges should be built between the two branches of the NHS.

The most significant developments in general practice did not occur until almost twenty years after the creation of the NHS. These were the growth of health centres, and the emergence of the primary health care team. Equally important was the distribution of GPs between different parts of the country, which was overseen by the Medical Practices Committee, set up under the 1946 NHS Act. The Committee could not direct doctors to work in particular places, but it could designate areas so that well-provided areas did not improve their position at the expense of less-well-provided areas. A study carried out in 1971 concluded that:

> the broad pattern of staffing needs have not changed dramatically over the last twenty to thirty years. Areas which are currently facing the most serious shortages seem to have a fairly long history of manpower difficulties, whilst those which are today relatively well supplied with family doctors have generally had no difficulty in past years in attracting and keeping an adequate number of practitioners. (Butler, Bevan and Taylor, 1973, p. 42)

In 1966 a financial inducement – a designated area allowance – was introduced to try to attract doctors to less-well-provided areas, and more recent figures indicate that the average list size of doctors practising in designated areas has steadily fallen and the proportion of the population living in designated areas has also fallen significantly (Office of Health Economics, 1984). There are, however, a number of outstanding problems in relation to the quality and coverage of general practitioner services, and these are discussed further in Chapter 2.

The third branch of the Service, that provided by local authorities, developed slowly after 1948, with ambulances comprising the main element of expenditure. Care of mothers and young children, home helps and home nurses were the other major items in the local authority health budget. At the opposite end of the scale came vaccination and immunisation, and, until the second half of the 1960s, health centres, which local authorities were responsible for building. It is relevant to note that under the 1948 National Assistance Act and other legislation, local authorities also provided a range of welfare services, including old people's homes and social workers. The division of responsibility for these services and health services became a matter of increasing concern, particularly as long-term plans for both sets of services were developed in the 1960s.

The significance of the 1962 Hospital Plan has already been mentioned. A year later, the Ministry of Health published a parallel document, *Health and Welfare: The Development of Community Care*, setting out proposals for the development of local authority health and welfare services. This was much less of a national plan than the Hospital Plan. It was essentially the bringing together in one place of the ideas of local authorities for the growth of their health and welfare services. The difference between the two documents was a reflection of the greater measure of autonomy enjoyed by local authorities as compared with Regional Hospital Boards and Hospital Management Committees. Nevertheless, the Health and Welfare Plan was important in displaying publicly the directions in which local authority services were intended to develop. One point to emerge was the considerable variation in the plans of authorities, and it was hoped that comparisons would lead to the revision of plans and greater uniformity between areas. This happened to some extent, but the second revision of the Health and Welfare Plan, published in 1966, illustrated that wide differences still existed.

Both Health and Welfare Plans outlined developments in relation to four main client groups: mothers and young children, the elderly, the physically handicapped, and the mentally ill and handicapped. As far as the mentally ill and handicapped were concerned, a greater onus was placed on local authorities by the 1959 Mental Health Act, which, among other provisions, heralded a shift from hospital care to community care. The intention was that a range of community services should be developed, including homes and hostels, social clubs, sheltered workshops and social work support. The Health and Welfare Plans indicated what authorities were proposing to provide, and demonstrated that the commitment in central government to the community care policy was not always shared at the local level. Indeed, in a policy document published in 1975, the government noted that 'By and large the non-hospital community resources are still minimal... The failure...to develop anything approaching adequate social services is perhaps the greatest disappointment of the last 15 years' (DHSS, 1975a, p. 14).

A further set of ten-year plans for local authority services was prepared in 1972. In this case, the plans covered the newly established social services departments, which were created in 1971 following the report of the Seebohm Committee. The main effect of the Seebohm reforms was to divorce those local authority health services deemed to involve mainly medical skills – such as vaccination and immunisation, and health education – from those services deemed to involve mainly social work skills – such as home helps and residential care. The former were retained by the health departments of local authorities under the control of the medical officer of health, while the latter were transferred to the new social services departments under the director of social services. The new departments comprised a range of services previously provided by the local authority welfare and children's departments, as well as some of those previously administered by the health departments. The main aims of the reforms were to integrate services which had been administered separately in the past, and to provide for the development of a comprehensive family service through the new departments.

One of the points to emerge from the Health and Welfare Plans was the commitment of local authorities to the building of health centres. For a variety of reasons, including the shortage of money and hesitancy among the medical profession, health centres did not develop in the 1950s in the way that had been envisaged by the architects of the NHS. However, local interest in health centres revived in the early 1960s, and was matched by central government attaching greater priority to health centre building. The consequence was that whereas in 1965 in England and Wales there were only 28 health centres from which 215 GPs worked, by 1983 there were 1190 in operation, with 6,659 GPS. As a result, 29 per cent of all GPs work in health centres, and many more work in group practices.

Simultaneously there has been a greater emphasis placed on the primary health care team, rather than on the GP working in isolation. This development was very much in line with the thinking behind the Gillie Report on *The Field of Work of the Family Doctor*, published in 1963. Although much less ambitious than either the Hospital Plan or the Health and Welfare Plan, the Gillie Report can to some extent be seen as the GPs' counterpart to these documents. The report argued for more ancillary help to be made available to GPs, and for a closer integration between GPs and other health services, particularly hospitals.

The theme of integration was taken up in a number of reports as the problem of securing co-ordination between the three different parts of the NHS gained increasing importance in the 1960s. The nature of the problem could be seen clearly with elderly people, who might need a short hospital stay followed by a period of convalescence and care in a local authority old people's home, and subsequent assistance at home from the GP, home help and meals on wheels service. In a case such as this, there was a need not only to secure close collaboration between the different professional staff involved, but also to ensure the appropriate joint planning of services. The development of long-term plans for the respective services in the early 1960s heightened this, and again pointed to the difficulty of providing a comprehensive and co-ordinated range of facilities within the existing system of administration, despite exhortations from central government that hospital authorities, local authorities and executive councils should plan and work together.

A second problem which had become apparent by the late 1960s was the poor quality of care provided to certain patient groups. Public attention was drawn to this issue in 1967 with publication of allegations of low standards of service provision and even the ill-treatment of elderly patients at a number of hospitals in different parts of the country (Robb, 1967). This was followed two years later by the report of the official committee which enquired into conditions at Ely Hospital, Cardiff. Ely was a mental handicap hospital, and the committee of enquiry found there had been staff cruelty to patients at the hospital. The committee made a series of recommendations for improving conditions at Ely and for preventing a similar situation arising elsewhere. Subsequently, the Department of Health and Social Security, which had been created in 1968 through the amalgamation of the Ministry of Health and the Ministry of Social Security, set aside special money to be spent on mental handicap hospitals, and this was later extended to hospitals for the mentally ill and the elderly. In addition, the Hospital Advisory Service (HAS) (in 1976 made the Health Advisory Service) was established to visit and report on conditions at these hospitals. A review of policies was also put in hand, leading to the publication of White Papers on services for the mentally handicapped in 1971, and the mentally ill in 1975. Despite these initiatives, the Ely Hospital 'scandal' was followed by further reports on conditions at other long-stay hospitals, including Whittingham, South Ockenden, Farleigh, Napsbury, St Augustine's and Normansfield, demonstrating that the process of change in what came to be known as the 'Cinderella' services was often slow, and that significant improvements were difficult to achieve (Martin, 1984).

A third problem, related to the first two, concerned the system of administrative control in the NHS. The neglect of long-stay services was not new, and had been recognised by successive Ministers of Health from the early 1950s onwards. Equally, the need for authorities to work in collaboration had been endorsed and advocated by the Ministry since the establishment of the NHS. The difficulty was in achieving and implementing these policy intentions at the local level. A variety of means of control were available to the Ministry, including circulars, earmarking funds for particular purposes, and setting up special agencies like the Hospital Advisory Service. At the same time, the bodies that were responsible locally for the administration of health services were not just ciphers through which national policies were implemented. They had their own aims and objectives, and, equally significant, they were responsible for providing services where professional involvement was strong. Doctors constitute the key professional group in the NHS, and within the medical profession some interests are stronger than others. In the hospital service it is the consultants in the acute specialities such as surgery and general medicine who have traditionally been most influential. In contrast, consultant psychiatrists and geriatricians have wielded less influence. This helps to explain why it has been difficult to shift resources in favour of services for groups like the elderly and mentally ill.

The reorganisation of the NHS

These were some of the problems which had emerged in the NHS some twenty years after its establishment. Suggestions on the best way of tackling the problems varied, but increasingly a change in the tripartite structure of the Service came to be seen as a significant part of the solution. This was the view of the Porritt Committee, a high status body representing the medical profession, which in a report published in 1962 suggested that health services should be unified and placed under the control of area boards. The first statement of government intentions came in 1968, when the Labour government published a Green Paper which echoed the Porritt Committee's suggestion, and asked for comments on the proposal that forty to fifty area health boards should be responsible for administering the health services in England and Wales.

One possibility was that a reorganised NHS would be administered by local government, which was itself undergoing reform at the same time. However, this was discounted in the second Green Paper, published by the Labour government in 1970. The second Green Paper put forward the idea that there should be around ninety area health authorities as the main units of local administration, together with regional health councils carrying out planning functions, and some 200 district committees as a means of local participation. These proposals were developed further in the following year by the Conservative government in the Consultative Document, which strengthened the role of the regional tier of administration and provided a separate channel for local participation in the form of community health councils. The Consultative Document, and the subsequent White Paper, also emphasised the importance of improving management efficiency in the NHS. These proposals were enshrined in the 1973 National Health Service Act and came into operation on 1 April 1974. The reorganised structure in England is illustrated in Figure 1.2.

FIGURE 1.2   *The structure of the NHS, 1974–82*

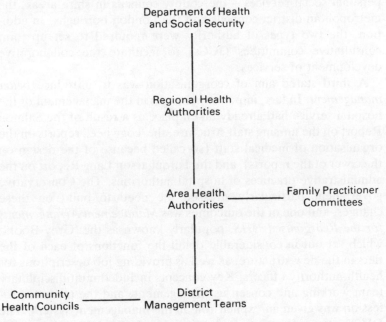

Department of Health
and Social Security

Regional Health
Authorities

Area Health _____ Family Practitioner
Authorities   Committees

Community _____ District
Health Councils   Management Teams

NOTE: This structure applied only in England. The position in the rest of the United
Kingdom is explained in the text.

Reorganisation had three main aims. First, it was intended to
unify health services by bringing under one authority all of the
services previously administered by Regional Hospital Boards,
Hospital Management Committees, boards of governors, executive councils and local health authorities. Unification was not,
however, achieved in full because general practitioners remained
independent contractors, with the functions of executive councils
being taken over by family practitioner committees. Also, a small
number of postgraduate teaching hospitals retained separate
boards of governors.

Second, reorganisation was intended to lead to better *co-
ordination* between health authorities and related local government services. To achieve this, the boundaries of the new Area
Health Authorities were, in most parts of the country, made the

same as those of one or more of the local authorities providing personal social services – the county councils in shire areas, the metropolitan district councils and the London boroughs. In addition, the two types of authority were required to set up joint consultative committees (JCCs) to facilitate the collaborative development of services.

A third stated aim of reorganisation was to introduce *better management*. In fact, important changes in the management of the hospital service had already taken place as a result of the Salmon Report on the nursing staff structure, the 'cogwheel' reports on the organisation of medical staff (so called because of the design on the cover of the reports), and the Farquharson Lang Report on the administrative practices of hospital authorities. The Conservative government particularly stressed the need to build on these changes, and one of the outcomes was *Management Arrangements for the Reorganised NHS*, popularly known as the 'Grey Book', which set out in considerable detail the functions of each of the tiers in the new structure, as well as providing job descriptions for health authority officers. Key concepts included multidisciplinary team working and consensus management, and the medical profession was given an explicit role in the management system. The DHSS also referred to the principle of 'maximum delegation downwards, matched by accountability upwards' to illustrate the spirit behind the new structure. Another significant aspect of the concern to improve management efficiency was the introduction of a corporate planning system in 1976, two years after the structural reforms. All of these measures were part of a wider interest within government to borrow ideas from the private sector in the hope of improving performance. It was therefore no coincidence that the new arrangements were devised with the assistance of the management consultants, McKinsey & Co. Ltd. But the changes also reflected the particular concern in the NHS, discussed earlier, to find a more effective means of pursuing national priorities at the local level, and of shifting resources in favour of neglected groups.

The reorganised National Health Service

Thus, after almost twenty-six years, the NHS underwent a major organisational change. Within the new structure, Regional Health

Authorities (RHAs) took over from Regional Hospital Boards, with somewhat wider responsibilities and slightly modified boundaries. The members of RHAs were appointed by the Secretary of State for Social Services, and their main function was the planning of health services. Beneath RHAs there were ninety Area Health Authorities (AHAs) in England, and their members were appointed partly by RHAs, partly by local authorities, and partly by members of the non-medical and nursing staff. The AHA chairman was appointed by the Secretary of State. Some AHAs contained a university medical school and teaching hospital facilities, and were designated as teaching areas. AHAs had planning and management duties, but one of their most important functions was to develop services jointly with their matching local authorities. Both RHAs and AHAs were supported by multidisciplinary teams of officers. Alongside each AHA was a Family Practitioner Committee (FPC) which administered the contracts of GPs, dentists, pharmacists and opticians. FPC members were appointed by the AHA, local professionals and local authorities. Finance for health authorities and FPCs was provided by the Department of Health and Social Security. Most areas were themselves split into health districts, each of which was administered by a district management team (DMT), which in practice became the lowest tier of the Service. At district level were located Community Health Councils (CHCs), introduced as part of the reorganised structure to represent the views of the public to health authorities. There were around 200 Community Health Councils in England.

It is pertinent to note that somewhat different arrangements were made in Wales, Scotland and Northern Ireland, which until reorganisation had had similar structures to those existing in England. The Welsh reorganisation bore the closest resemblance to that of England, the main exception being the absence of RHAs in Wales, where the Welsh Office combined the functions of a central government department and a regional authority. The differences were rather greater in Scotland, where again there was no regional tier of administration. Instead, the Scottish Office dealt directly with fifteen health boards, a majority of which were divided into districts. There was no separate system of administration for family practitioner services, and the Scottish equivalent of CHCs were called Local Health Councils. In Northern Ireland, there were four health and social services boards, in direct contact with the DHSS (Northern Ireland), and each of the boards was split into a number of districts. As their name indicated, these boards were responsible for personal social services as well as health services. What is more, as in Scotland, there was no separate system of administration for family practitioner services. District Committees performed the function of CHCs.

These, then, were the administrative changes brought into being in 1974. However, almost before the new system had had the chance to settle down, the reorganised structure became the subject of attack from a number of quarters. Criticism centred on delays in taking decisions, the difficulty of establishing good relationships between administrative tiers, and the widespread feeling that there were too many tiers and too many administrators. In fact, the DHSS acknowledged in evidence to the House of Commons Public Accounts Committee that there had been an increase of 16,400 administrative and clerical staff as a result of reorganisation, although some of these staff had previously worked in local authority health services, while others were recruited to the new Community Health Councils (Public Accounts Committee, 1977, p. xvii).

Research on the operation of the new structure pointed to other problems, including the unexpectedly high cost of reorganisation, both in terms of finance and, more particularly, of the impact on staff morale (Brown, 1979). These issues were the subject of analysis and review by the Merrison Royal Commission on the NHS, which was established in 1976 at a time of considerable unrest in the NHS. The unrest stemmed from industrial action by various groups of health service workers, and discontent in the medical profession with the government's policy of phasing out private beds in NHS hospitals. The Commission was asked 'To consider in the interests both of the patients and of those who work in the National Health Service the best use and management of the financial and manpower resources of the National Health Service' (Royal Commission on the NHS, 1979), and it reported in 1979. In its report,the Commission endorsed the view that there was one tier of administration too many, and recommended that there should be only one level of authority beneath the region. A flexible approach to change was advocated, and the Commission pointed out that structural reform was no panacea for all of the administrative problems facing the NHS. Other conclusions in a wide-ranging survey were that Family Practitioner Committees should be abolished, and Community Health Councils should be strengthened.

It fell to the Conservative government which took office in May 1979 to respond to the report. In *Patients First*, a consultative paper published at the end of 1979, the government announced its agreement with the proposal that one tier of administration should be removed, and suggested that District Health Authorities should be established to combine the functions of the existing areas and districts. *Patients First* also stated that Family Practitioner Committees would be retained, and that views would be welcomed on whether Community Health Councils would still be needed when the new District Health Authorities were set up (DHSS, 1979a).

The Government's final decisions on the main aspects of reorganisation were published in July 1980 (DHSS, 1980a). In large part, they endorsed the *Patients First* proposals, and in addition announced that Community Health Councils would remain in existence, though their functions would be reviewed. The result was the creation of 192 District Health Authorities (DHAs) in England. The DHAs came into operation on 1 April 1982, and within districts emphasis was placed on the delegation of power to units of management. Detailed management arrangements varied considerably, with some units covering services in districts as a whole, such as psychiatric services, while others were limited to a single large hospital. Health authorities were expected to establish management structures within overall cost limits set by the DHSS, and in 1983 it was estimated that the amount spent on management in the NHS had fallen from 5.12 per cent of the total budget in 1979–80 to 4.44 per cent in 1982–3, representing a saving of £64 million. Apart from the reduction in administration, the main change wrought by the reorganisation was the loss in many parts of the country of the principle of coterminosity between health authorities and local authorities. Equally significant was the announcement in November 1981 that Family Practitioner Committees (FPCs) were to be further separated from the mainstream of NHS administration and given the status of employing authorities in their own right. This change was brought into effect by the Health and Social Security Act 1984 and FPCs achieved their independent status on 1 April 1985. The structure of the NHS in England after 1982 is shown in Figure 1.3.

FIGURE 1.3   *The structure of the NHS after 1982*

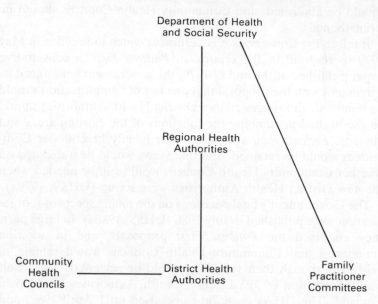

Department of Health
and Social Security

Regional Health
Authorities

Community
Health
Councils

District Health
Authorities

Family
Practitioner
Committees

NOTE The structure applies only in England. The position in the rest of the
United Kingdom is explained in the text.

In the rest of the United Kingdom different changes were made, reflecting the different administrative structures existing in Scotland, Wales and Northern Ireland. In Wales the main change was the abolition of the district level of management, and the establishment in its place of a system of unit management on a similar basis to that developed in England. In Scotland, a varied approach was pursued initially, some health boards deciding to abolish the district tier, others opting to retain it. However, in 1983 the Secretary of State for Scotland announced that all districts would be abolished and that they would be replaced by a system of unit management from 1 April 1984. As in England and Wales, the importance of delegating power to the local level was stressed. The same principle of delegation applied in Northern Ireland, where the basic structure of health and social services boards was retained. Within boards, district teams were superseded by unit management arrangements.

The Griffiths Inquiry into NHS management

Shortly after the 1982 reorganisation in England, the Secretary of State for Social Services appointed a small team, under the leadership of Roy Griffiths, the Deputy Chairman and Managing Director of Sainsbury's, to give advice on the effective use of management and manpower and related resources in the NHS. The team reported in October 1983 and made a series of proposals for overcoming what it identified as significant weaknesses in the management of the Service. The main thrust of the critique offered in the Griffiths Report was that the NHS lacked a clearly defined general management function. As the Report argued:

> Absence of this general management support means that there is no driving force seeking and accepting direct and personal responsibility for developing management plans, securing their implementation and monitoring actual achievement. It means that the process of devolution of responsibility, including discharging responsibility to the Units, is far too slow. (Griffiths Report, 1983, p. 12)

Accordingly, the Report recommended that general managers should be appointed at all levels in the NHS to provide leadership, introduce a continual search for change and cost improvement, motivate staff and develop a more dynamic management approach. At the same time, the Report stated that doctors 'must accept the management responsibility which goes with clinical freedom' (p. 18) and should be closely involved in management. Another key proposal was that the management of the NHS at the centre should be streamlined and strengthened through the establishment of a Health Services Supervisory Board and an NHS Management Board within the DHSS, with the Chairman of the Management Board being drawn from outside the NHS and the Civil Service. This proposal was designed to change the stance and style of management at the centre involving a greater concern with the strategic direction of the Service and less involvement in detailed management issues. The Griffiths Report did not attempt to offer a comprehensive analysis of management arrangements in the NHS but rather a series of recommendations for immediate action. As the Inquiry team concluded, 'action is now badly needed and the Health Service can ill afford to indulge in any lengthy self-imposed Hamlet-like soliloquy as a precursor or alternative to the required action' (p. 24).

This advice was heeded by the Secretary of State for Social Services, who, in welcoming the Report, announced that he accepted the general thrust of what the team had to say. The Health Services Supervisory Board was to be established immediately, and urgent consultation would take place with professional and staff interests and health authorities on the introduction of the general management function. The Secretary of State also stressed that implementation of the Report did not involve any further structural reorganisation. All the recommendations were designed to occur within existing legislative arrangements and without affecting the constitutional position of Parliament, Ministers and health authorities.

In the ensuing debate, attention centred on the proposal that general managers should be appointed as a way of strengthening the management process. Professional and staff interests expressed concern that this might lead to autocratic decision-making and might undermine the contribution made by groups such as nurses to management. Doubts were also expressed about the validity of the Griffiths critique of consensus management. It was argued that in an organisation like the NHS involving a large number of different occupations management had to operate with the agreement of those affected by decisions and could not function independently. In its analysis, the House of Commons Social Services Committee accepted the general critique offered by Griffiths but felt that there should be some flexibility in implementation. Specifically, the Committee argued that the general management function could be developed either through strengthening the system of multi-disciplinary team management or by the identification of a separate general manager (Social Services Committee, 1984a).

In the event, in June 1984 the Government asked health authorities to appoint general managers at all levels in the Service by the end of 1985 (DHSS, 1984b). A phased programme of implementation was planned, beginning with the identification of regional general managers followed by general managers at district and unit levels. The Government also endorsed the Report's view that doctors should be encouraged to play a more active role in management and that management budgets for doctors should be developed. Although the Report did not cover Scotland, Wales or Northern Ireland, similar changes were planned in both Scotland and Wales although over a longer time-scale. In Northern Ireland, it was decided to strengthen the management of the health service at the centre along the lines proposed by Griffiths in England, and in a consultative letter issued in April 1984 views were sought on whether general managers should be appointed within the health and social services boards. Firm decisions were expected to be made at the end of 1984.

Conclusion

This chapter has provided a general overview of the development of state involvement in the provision of health services in the United Kingdom. It has set out the historical and organisational context for discussions in the rest of the book on the dynamics of health policy formation. Already, however, some key questions about health policy have been raised, if not answered. These can be summarised as follows: first, the importance of focusing on negotiation and bargaining in the policy community in seeking to understand and explain the detailed processes of health policy-making. In particular, our preliminary analysis has highlighted the significance of identifying the key interest groups and of examining their interaction with the official decision-makers. This issue is discussed further in Chapter 4.

Second, we have noted that there may sometimes be a gap between the intentions of policy-makers and what happens in practice. This was considered in relation to the continued neglect of 'Cinderella' services, and the failure to develop adequate community-based services for the mentally ill. These examples draw attention to the importance of policy implementation, which is examined further in Chapter 5.

A third question concerns the relationship between policy-makers and service providers. A factor of major significance in the NHS is the position occupied by doctors as service providers and their concern to retain control over their own work. We have seen how the medical profession has fought strenuously to keep its independence, most especially in the campaign by GPs to be independent contractors rather than salaried employees. Hospital doctors have been equally concerned to maintain their autonomy even though they are in a salaried service. As the DHSS acknowledged in evidence to the House of Commons Expenditure Committee, 'the existence of clinical freedom undoubtedly reduces the ability of the central authorities to determine objectives and priorities and to control individual facets of expenditure' (Expenditure Committee, 1971). The concept of clinical freedom therefore poses peculiar difficulties for policy-makers seeking to change patterns of resource allocation. It also raises central questions about the power structure in the NHS, questions to which we return in later chapters.

Related to this, a fourth issue not addressed directly so far but of crucial importance, concerns the relationship between health services and society. In other words, what purposes are served by health services, and what is the significance of the dominant position occupied by the medical profession? These issues are rarely discussed explicitly in books on health services and health policy. Instead, implicit assumptions are often made about the benevolent motives underlying state involvement in the provision of health services. Thus, the NHS is viewed as a great social experiment, and as a concrete expression of the development of more humane attitudes to disadvantaged groups in society. In short, the Service is seen as one of the main planks in the welfare state.

In contrast to this interpretation, recent writings from Marxist and political economy perspectives have questioned the benevolence of the NHS, and have pointed to the way in which health services help to reproduce labour power and maintain a healthy workforce. Marxists also emphasise the crucial role played by doctors in individualising problems which may have social causes. According to this line of analysis, health services and their operation cannot be understood in isolation from the class structure of society. These are key issues which are considered in the final chapter of the book.

2
Contemporary Issues in Health Policy

In its report published in 1979, the Royal Commission on the National Health Service noted that 'the demand for health care is always likely to outstrip supply and ... the capacity of health services to absorb resources is almost unlimited. Choices have therefore to be made about the use of available funds and priorities have to be set' (Royal Commission on the NHS, 1979, p. 51). It follows that issues of resource allocation and priority setting are of key importance in the NHS, and it is to a consideration of these issues that most of this chapter is devoted. The chapter begins with a discussion of the financing of health services, noting the growth of the NHS budget and examining the proposal that greater reliance might be placed on health insurance rather than taxation as a source of health service funds. Consideration is then given to the growth of the private health care sector and policy initiatives designed to increase the efficiency with which NHS resources are used. This is followed by an analysis of resource allocation within the NHS, with particular attention being paid to the geographical distribution of funds, and the allocation of resources to different types of services, age groups and client groups. Attention then shifts to a description of government policy in the NHS under a number of headings: primary care, community health and preventive medicine; hospital services and the development of policy on district general hospitals and community hospitals; services for elderly people, mentally handicapped people and mental illness; and maternity and child-care services. Attempts to establish priorities between the services are discussed, and the role of the NHS Planning System in translating national priorities into local action is outlined. The chapter concludes by focusing on joint planning and collaboration between health authorities and local authorities.

Health services financing

One of the assumptions made in the Beveridge Report was that expenditure on health services would decline once the backlog of ill health which was thought to exist in the community had been eradicated by the introduction of a health service free at the point of consumption. This assumption turned out to be false, and far from declining, expenditure increased steadily in the years after the establishment of the NHS. Whereas in its first full year of operation the service cost £437 million to run, by 1984 expenditure in the United Kingdom had risen to an estimated £16,985 million. Over the same period, the real cost of the Service has increased threefold, and the NHS share of total public expenditure has risen from 11.8 per cent in 1950 to 12.6 per cent in 1982.

As Figure 2.1 shows, the proportion of the gross national product consumed by the NHS has increased from 3.9 per cent in 1949 to 6.2 per cent in 1984 (Office of Health Economics, 1984). Thus, on all indicators, it can be seen that the NHS has consumed more resources and not less, although it should be noted that spending on health care in the United Kingdom is still lower than in most other advanced industrialised societies.

FIGURE 2.1   *Cost of the NHS as % of GNP*

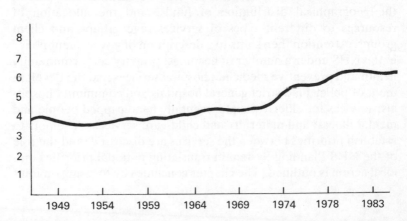

Why has the NHS budget continued to expand? One of the main reasons is that it is now recognised that the demand for health care is potentially limitless. Health policy-makers acknowledge that there is not a fixed quantity of disease, as the idea of a 'backlog of ill health' implies, but rather that there is an infinity of demand. Part of the explanation of this is that more medical interventions are now possible. Expanding medical technology has opened up new areas of work, including heart surgery, kidney transplants and hip replacements, which simply were not feasible at the inception of the NHS. The development of new techniques therefore tends to create demand, as does the greater availability of services which the NHS has brought about. At the same time, there is evidence of unmet need in the community. Examples include the long waiting times for certain operations, and the problems sometimes experienced in finding hospital accommodation for elderly people. And, despite increasing expenditure and the employment of additional staff, some vulnerable groups in the population do not use services. There are a variety of reasons for this, including difficulties of access, the money and time costs involved, and unfriendly attitudes among staff. It is clear, then, that more resources could be spent on health services without all demands and needs being met.

Currently, health service funds come from three sources. As Figure 2.2 shows, by far the largest of these is general taxation, followed by national insurance contributions and charges. The scope for increasing the amount of money made available to the NHS through general taxation and national insurance contributions is limited, particularly at a time when economic goals have been given priority over social goals. In any case, in respect of taxation the NHS has to compete with other public services for its share of available funds, and this tends to restrict the potential for major changes in the historic pattern of financing. Charges offer an alternative means of increasing NHS funds, but at no time have they contributed more than 5.6 per cent of the NHS budget, and the revenue to accrue from the imposition of new charges has to be balanced against the cost of collection. Nevertheless the idea has been sufficiently attractive to win the support of influential groups like the British Medical Association. Charges, like proposals for private health insurance, carry the attraction for some of shifting the burden of paying for health care from the state to the individual.

FIGURE 2.2   *Sources of NHS finance, 1983–4–Great Britain*

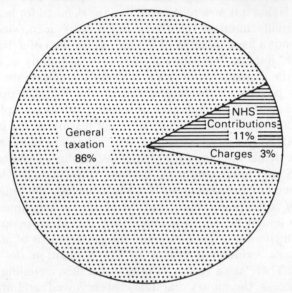

The Conservative government elected in 1979 has sought to encourage the development of private health care, and to this end the government set up a working party to examine alternative financing methods. The working party was composed of representatives from the DHSS, the Treasury, and the Health Departments of Wales, Scotland and Northern Ireland, together with two specialist advisers with experience of the private health sector. The working party's report was submitted to Ministers at the beginning of 1982. Although the report was not published, the Secretary of State for Social Services announced in July 1982 that the government had no plans to change the system of financing the NHS largely from taxation. This was understood to mean that there would be no attempt to finance the NHS on an insurance basis. However, after the re-election of the Conservative government in 1983 the Chancellor of the Exchequer called for a review of spending on the welfare state, and published a Green Paper on public expenditure and taxation in the 1990s. Coming after the leak of a confidential report from the Central Policy Review Staff, which set out various options for reducing government spending, the Chancellor's review prompted speculation that alternative methods of financing the NHS might again be under serious consideration. In fact, the Green Paper did not put forward specific proposals for particular expenditure programmes, but the government did argue that it was necessary to decide what could be afforded in terms of public expenditure and then set expenditure plans consistent with that decision. One analyst has argued that a system of health insurance could reduce the NHS budget by £6,000 million by 1990 (Minford, 1984), and it seems likely that the debate about the public–private mix for health (McLachlan and Maynard, 1982) will continue. It is therefore important to consider the arguments for and against moving away from a health service based on taxation to an insurance-based system.

Private health care

The claimed advantages of private insurance are that it will reduce the burden on public expenditure, allow a cut in taxation, restore freedom of choice to consumers, and encourage more responsible behaviour by patients and doctors who would be made aware of the costs of their actions. Whether all of these advantages would be realised in practice would depend on the particular insurance proposals under consideration. A wide variety of possibilities exist, including insurance through commercial companies, non-profit making friendly societies, employers and trades unions; insurance for a basic level of cover or for all risks; and insurance which covers all of the cost of treatment or only a proportion of the costs. Many of the proponents of private insurance argue the need to re-establish the link between the provision of a service and payment, which implies a fee-for-service system, in which the patient pays the doctor or hospital and is reimbursed in whole or in part by the insurance organisation. Systems like this operate in a number of Western European countries, and the experience of these countries has been studied by the working party on alternative financing.

The anticipated drawbacks of private insurance are that some groups are high risks, for example people needing long-term care and the elderly, and would not be able to purchase insurance. There would therefore still be a need for a taxation-based service for these groups. Provision would also have to be made for poor people who would not be able to afford the cost of insurance. A particular difficulty in considering the position of less advantaged groups in the population is that introducing a fee-for-service system might deter these groups from using services. This would further worsen the health position of these groups in relation to other sections of society. But there are additional difficulties with private insurance. First, it may generate higher health care costs by encouraging doctors to provide more services and more expensive services. Fee-for-service arrangements in particular stimulate cost-generating behaviour. Second, administration and bureaucracy would be increased as insurers employed staff to collect premiums, process claims and check fees.

Reviewing these arguments, the Royal Commission on the NHS concluded: 'We do not think that the NHS should be funded by health insurance. The advantages of the market place could well be real but there would certainly be significant disadvantages' (Royal Commission on the NHS, 1979, p. 338). Other writers have reached a similar conclusion, arguing that there is no guarantee that private insurance will lead to a more efficient use of health care resources (Maynard, 1979). As Abel-Smith has stated, 'A major move towards health insurance, so far from solving our present problems, would be counter-productive. The long-term damage could be enormous' (Abel-Smith, 1981, p. 376). Whether this view continues to prevail remains to be seen.

Apart from the debate about funding the NHS through insurance, there has been a considerable growth in subscriptions to private health insurance schemes in recent years. By the end of 1982, the number of people with private insurance, including dependants, totalled 4.2 million, nearly 8 per cent of the population (Central Statistical Office, 1983). Most insurance policies are carried by the provident associations such as BUPA, Private Patients Plan and the Western Provident Association. In the main, private insurance provides finance for a limited number of services, in particular 'cold surgery' (i.e. non-emergency surgery) for conditions such as hernias and varicose veins. The biggest increase in subscriptions has been through group schemes, especially those provided by companies as fringe benefits. As Figure 2.3 shows, after a period of rapid growth in the five years to 1981, the rate of increase in subscriptions has declined. At the same time, premiums have been increased because of the growing number and size of claims. Indeed, the pressure of claims was such that BUPA

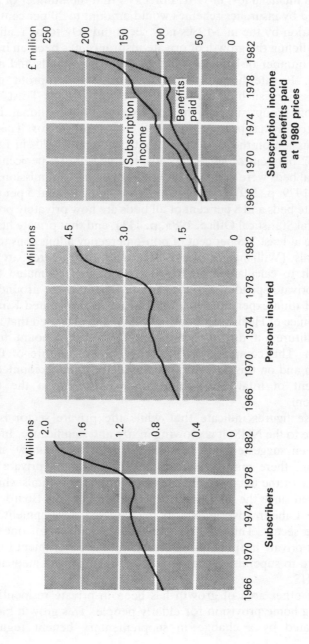

FIGURE 2.3 _Private medical insurance in the United Kingdom_

SOURCE: Central Statistical Office (1983).

made a financial loss in 1981. Forecasts that the number of people covered by insurance schemes would amount to 20 per cent of the population by the mid-1980s now seem unlikely to be realised.

Paralleling the growth of private insurance has been an increase in the number of beds provided in private hospitals and nursing homes. Private hospitals are run both by non-profit making organisations such as the Nuffield Nursing Homes Trust and by for-profit groups such as American Medical International. Expansion recently has been greatest in the for-profit sector. The Royal Commission on the NHS noted that in the mid-1970s in England about 2 per cent of all 'acute' hospital beds and 6 per cent of all hospital beds were in the private sector (Royal Commission on the NHS, 1979, p. 289). More recent figures indicate that 5 per cent of all acute beds and 8 per cent of all beds are now privately provided (Central Statistical Office, 1983, p. 111), and that private hospitals receive at least 7–8 per cent of non-emergency admissions to acute hospitals (Williams *et al.*, 1984). Spending figures are more difficult to calculate. The Royal Commission estimated that in 1976 private spending on health care amounted to around 3 per cent of total expenditure on health care in the United Kingdom. The Office of Health Economics (1984) has calculated that in 1982 expenditure on private health care expenses amount to £435 million. This compared with total NHS expenditure of £14,444 million and on this basis the private sector again accounted for 3 per cent of total expenditure on health care in the United Kingdom.

These figures indicate that while the private sector is small relative to the NHS, it is growing in size and significance. Indeed it has been suggested that in some parts of the country, notably London, there may be a surplus of beds in the private sector because of the uncontrolled growth of private hospitals which has occurred since the abolition of the Health Services Board, set up by the Labour government to regulate the development of the private sector. This has led the general manager of one of the largest private hospital groups to call on the government to create a board to supervise a partnership between private medicine and the NHS.

One other area of growth has been in private residential and nursing home provision for elderly people. This growth has been stimulated by a change in supplementary benefit regulations whereby the payments available to people being cared for in private and voluntary homes are much higher than before. This financial incentive has led to a considerable increase in the number of places available in the private sector, and it has been estimated that the payments involved total around £100 million a year.

Health and efficiency

Table 2.1 shows that the rate of increase in resources allocated to the NHS has slowed considerably in recent years. The high growth rates experienced in the 1960s and 1970s have given way to much more modest increases in the 1980s. The reason for this is that since the election of a Conservative government in 1979 there has been an attempt to restore economic growth by restraining public expenditure. Priority has been given to achieving economic prosperity and this has meant that spending in the social policy field has been subject to much closer scrutiny than in the past. In the face of changed priorities, the NHS has fared rather better than a number of other public services. At a time when spending on housing has fallen significantly, and when education programmes have also been reduced, there has been continuing growth in the NHS budget, albeit on a small scale.

Detailed figures for the NHS in England are displayed in Table 2.2. The figures show that current spending on hospital and community health services, leaving aside efficiency saving which we shall discuss later, increased by 4 per cent in volume terms (that is, after allowing for inflation) over the period 1979–80 to 1983–4. Over the same period, current spending on family practitioner services increased by 9 per cent, current spending on centrally financed services by 28.5 per cent and NHS capital spending by 23 per cent. The real volume growth allocated to the NHS as a whole in this period amounted to 7 per cent, again omitting efficiency savings. In terms of future plans, long-term resource assumptions issued to health authorities in 1983 indicated that authorities should assume that resources for hospital and community health services in England would grow at 0.5 per cent per annum over the next ten years.

Since 1976 health authority budgets have been subject to a system of cash limits. The way this system works is that each year

46

TABLE 2.1 *NHS expenditure UK 1949–84*

Year	Total £m	Total NHS cost at 1949 prices £m
1949	437	437
1950	477	463
1951	503	448
1952	526	429
1953	546	432
1954	564	439
1955	608	452
1956	664	470
1957	720	492
1958	764	506
1959	826	545
1960	902	588
1961	981	619
1962	1,025	621
1963	1,092	648
1964	1,191	685
1965	1,306	716
1966	1,432	756
1967	1,556	802
1968	1,710	841
1969	1,797	839
1970	2,046	898
1971	2,323	932
1972	2,681	1,003
1973	3,038	1,042
1974	3,948	1,167
1975	5,242	1,248
1976	6,200	1,267
1977	6,906	1,218
1978	7,872	1,281
1979	9,077	1,303
1980	11,779	1,433
1981	13,452	1,463
1982	14,444	1,446
1983	15,575	1,459
1984	16,985	1,490

SOURCE: OHE (1984)

TABLE 2.2 Trends in NHS expenditure 1979–80 to 1983–4, England

	Years	Gross expenditure £m	Cash increase	Inflation etc.	Change in volume	Efficiency saving	Change from 1979–80 to 1983–4*
					as %		
Hospital and community health services (current expenditure)	1979–80	5,333	20.6	20.5	0.1	—	—
	1980–1	6,886	29.1	28.0	0.9	—	—
	1981–2	7,631	10.8	8.1	2.5	0.2	—
	1982–3	8,142	6.7	6.5	0.2	0.3	—
	1983–4	8,580	5.4	5.1	0.3	0.5	4.0
Family practitioner services (current expenditure)	1979–80	1,684	17.4	17.0	0.3	—	—
	1980–1	2,114	25.6	25.5	0.1	—	—
	1981–2	2,440	15.4	13.1	2.1	—	—
	1982–3	2,827	15.8	11.7	3.7	—	—
	1983–4	3,053	8.0	5.1	2.8	—	9.0
Centrally financed health services (current expenditure)	1979–80	288	22.4	16.8	4.8	—	—
	1980–1	364	26.3	20.0	5.2	—	—
	1981–2	413	13.4	9.6	3.4	—	—
	1982–3	465	12.6	7.3	4.9	—	—
	1983–4	539	15.8	5.1	10.2	—	28.5
NHS capital	1979–80	407	11.6	20.7	-7.5	—	—
	1980–1	552	35.6	25.7	7.8	—	—
	1981–2	673	21.9	3.6	17.7	—	—
	1982–3	699	3.9	1.6	2.2	—	—
	1983–4	746	6.6	3.7	2.8	—	23.0
NHS total expenditure	1979–80	7,712	19.5	19.6	-0.1	—	—
	1980–1	9,917	28.6	27.0	1.2	—	—
	1981–2	11,158	12.5	9.0	3.3	0.1	—
	1982–3	12,134	8.7	7.5	1.2	0.2	—
	1983–4	12,919	6.5	5.0	1.4	0.3	7.0

SOURCE: Derived from Social Services Committee (1984b)

* omitting efficiency savings

the budget is increased by an amount which reflects the government's forecast of inflation. To this is added any growth money made available to the NHS. The total allocation resulting from this calculation represents the cash limit for the year. Health authorities have a statutory duty to keep within their cash limits although there is provision to carry forward over- and under-spending of up to 1 per cent from one financial year to another and to switch funds between capital and revenue allocations. The significance of cash limits is that if the government's forecast of inflation is too low, health authorities have to make up the difference from their own allocation. Equally, if the inflation forecast is too high, health authorities will have additional resources available. In reality, the former is more likely, as in 1984–5 when health authorities were required to find part of the cost of paying the salary increases agreed for staff from their budgets. It should be noted that the budgets of Family Practitioner Committees are not cash-limited. Expenditure on family practitioner services is determined by demand and the cost of these services is met in full.

Another point to bear in mind in interpreting the figures in Table 2.2 is that the NHS needs an estimated 1.2 per cent per annum to meet the demands of an ageing population and to fund advances in medical technology. With many health authorities not receiving increases on this scale, the government has called for greater efficiency as the way to finance new developments. Accordingly, a stream of initiatives has emanated from the DHSS, including efficiency savings, Rayner scrutinies, the publication of performance indicators and competitive tendering. Efficiency savings are the savings the government expects health authorities to make while maintaining the same level of service provision. Health authorities were required to make efficiency savings of 0.2 per cent in 1981–2, 0.3 per cent in 1982–3 and 0.5 per cent in 1983–4. In 1982 the House of Commons Social Services Committee expressed doubts as to whether health authorities could make efficiency savings on the scale required, and stated, 'There is some suspicion that "efficiency savings" are becoming a regular euphemism for "expenditure cuts"' (Social Services Committee, 1982, p. xiii). In 1984–5 efficiency savings were replaced by cost-improvement programmes under which authorities were asked to demonstrate how they intended to improve the efficiency of their services and release resources for improvements.

Rayner scrutinies involve short, intensive studies of areas affecting the efficiency of the NHS along the lines of those carried out in the civil service by Sir Derek Rayner and his staff. Rayner, a joint managing director of Marks and Spencer, was brought in to advise the government in 1979, and the approach which bears his name was first applied to the NHS in 1982. The scrutinies are carried out by NHS officers and areas examined include transport services, recruitment advertising and the collection of payments due to health authorities under the provisions of the Road Traffic Act. One of the most controversial studies concerned the use of residential accommodation for NHS staff where it was suggested that up to £750 million could be saved through the sale of property. In 1984 health authorities were asked to take action on a number of the scrutinies and to report to the DHSS on the savings achieved.

Performance indicators were developed during the course of 1982 and were published in 1983 (DHSS, 1983a). The indicators cover clinical services, finance, manpower, and estate management. In essence, performance indicators represent a set of statistical information which enables health authorities to compare their performance with what is being achieved elsewhere. The information uses readily available statistics and includes variables such as costs per case, length of stay and waiting lists. The DHSS has emphasised that the indicators are a starting point for a district's assessment of performance and not its conclusion. The published statistics are not intended to be league tables and it has been stressed that local knowledge is important in interpreting the figures. Nevertheless, health authorities whose performance is apparently exceptional are expected to investigate the reasons for this and to take remedial action where appropriate.

Policy on competitive tendering was set out in a circular issued to health authorities in 1983. Authorities were asked to test the cost-effectiveness of catering, domestic and laundry services by inviting tenders for the provision of these services from their own staff and from outside contractors. DHAs were requested to submit a timetable for competitive tendering to enable tenders for all services to be submitted by September 1986. The existing level of contracting out is low. In 1982–3 the value of outside contracts in England amounted to 0.23 per cent in catering, 11.5 per cent in laundry, and 2 per cent in cleaning. According to one estimate,

£300 million a year could be saved through contracting out (Forsyth, 1982) although the advantages and pitfalls of commercial service contracts remain unclear.

In addition to these initiatives, there have been a number of other attempts to increase efficiency and cut costs in the NHS. These include reductions in manpower; a review of arrangements for audit; and an enquiry into land and property. Taken together, these initiatives mark a significant change in emphasis from the 1970s when the health policy agenda was dominated by issues such as the need to give greater priority to the Cinderella services, to switch resources to community care, and to place more emphasis on prevention of illness. While these issues remain important, and are discussed more fully later, the basic objectives of the NHS – promoting health, ensuring equal access to services and providing comprehensive coverage – have taken a back seat while Ministers seek to root out waste and inefficiency.

Resource allocation in the NHS

There are four main ways of examining the distribution of the health services budget. First, there is the allocation of resources between different geographical areas. What this demonstrates is the considerable variation in spending per capita between the different regions of England. The most favoured regions are the four Thames regions covering London and south-east England. The least favoured regions are currently Wessex, Trent and East Anglia. Government policy is to bring about a fairer allocation of funds over a period of years. The policy has been developed following the report of the Resource Allocation Working Party (RAWP), published in 1976 (DHSS, 1976a) which is discussed more fully in Chapter 6. Similar policies are being pursued in Scotland, Wales and Northern Ireland.

Second, there is the distribution of the health services budget between different types of service. Figures for the United Kingdom for 1983 show that hospital services accounted for 62 per cent of the budget, community health services for 6.5 per cent, the drugs bill for 10.5 per cent, general medical services for 7 per cent, general dental services for 4 per cent, general opthalmic services for 1 per cent, and other items the remaining 9 per cent (Office of

Health Economics, 1984). Government policy since 1976 has sought to shift the balance of expenditure away from hospitals and towards general medical and community health services. The aim is to avoid the need for hospital admission by enabling people to remain in the community with appropriate help from general practitioners, home nurses, health visitors and other community-based staff. This implies a reversal of policies pursued since 1948 which have benefited hospitals more than any other branch of the Service.

A third way of analysing resource allocation is to examine expenditure on different age groups. Table 2.3 shows that expenditure on health care is greatest around the time of birth and in old

TABLE 2.3 *Estimated gross current expenditure per head, England, 1981–2 in £s*

	Total popu-lation	Births	0–4	5–15	16–64	65–74	75+
Hospital and community health services	160	915	150	70	85	325	770
Family prac-titioner services	50	60	50	40	45	65	115
Total	210	975	200	110	130	390	885

SOURCE: HM Treasury (1984).

age. The effect is most marked in the hospital and community health services. It follows that increases in the birth rate and in the proportion of people aged 65 and over will put pressure on health services. It has been estimated that the demographic factor requires additional spending of around 0.7 per cent per annum on the NHS if standards are to be maintained.

A fourth way of analysing resource allocation is to examine expenditure on different client or patient groups. As Table 2.4 shows, general and acute hospital and maternity services take the lion's share of funds, followed by primary care. The smallest proportion of the budget is spent on services for the mentally handicapped, children and the mentally ill. Government policy is

TABLE 2.4   *Spending on health and personal social services, 1981–82*

	% of current and capital expenditure
General and acute hospital and maternity services	38.1
Primary care	19.7
Elderly and physically handicapped	15.1
Mentally handicapped	4.4
Mentally ill	7.5
Children	5.7
Other	9.5

again trying to shift the balance away from acute and maternity services and in favour of comparatively neglected groups such as the mentally handicapped.

The principal mechanism through which these policies are being pursued is the NHS Planning System. The System was a key element in the 1974 reorganisation of the NHS, and was seen by the DHSS as 'the main means of giving practical effect to the requirements and intentions of the NHS Reorganisation Act 1973' (DHSS, 1976e). The System was launched with publication of the consultative document *Priorities for Health and Personal Social Services in England* in 1976 (DHSS, 1976b). The consultative document did not enunciate any new policies. What it did do was to bring together in one place existing policies, and to make a clear statement of government priorities on which services should be developed and which held back. The intention was that in the light of these priorities, health authorities should prepare plans for the local development of services.

The Planning System was very much an attempt to tackle some of the problems experienced before 1974, in particular in implementing national policies at local level and in shifting resources in favour of disadvantaged groups. Not surprisingly, the government's priorities included services for the mentally ill, the mentally handicapped, the elderly, the physically handicapped and children. Also, community health services, primary care and prevention were to receive priority. And at least in the initial stages of the Planning System, general and acute hospital and maternity services were to be held back while these other services developed. Let us now consider in more detail the policies being pursued in each area of service provision, and then return to examine how the Planning System attempts to relate one area to another.

Primary care, community health and prevention

For most patients, primary care is the first point of contact with the NHS. In 1982 there were 22,800 GPs working in England, and the average number of patients on each GP's list was 2,150. In the course of the development of the NHS, GPs have come to work increasingly as part of a primary health care team. Membership of these teams varies, but usually includes health visitors and nurses, and occasionally social workers. At the same time, an increasing proportion of GPs have operated from health centres, which have grown in number since the late 1960s. A range of services is provided in health centres, including vaccination and immunisation, ante-natal and post-natal care, and advice on the prevention of ill health. Although successive governments have given priority to primary care services, the latest statement of policy indicates that in future purpose-built health centres may not develop as rapidly as in recent years. Instead, the development of group practices and primary care teams in premises owned by doctors themselves will be encouraged.

A significant aspect of general practice is the position of GPs as independent contractors rather than salaried employees. This places some limits on the extent to which primary care services can be planned. As we saw in Chapter 1, the Medical Practices Committee (MPC) does exercise control over the distribution of GPs between different parts of the country, seeking to help under-doctored areas at the expense of well provided areas. However, the MPC has no power of direction, and cannot force GPs to work in areas not of their own choosing. Its powers are mainly negative, enabling the Committee to prevent GPs moving into areas already well served by family doctors.

One of the difficulties which arises from the independent position of GPs is the high cost of the drugs bill in general practice. GPs have complete freedom to prescribe the drugs they consider appropriate for their patients, making it difficult to control expenditure in this area. It is the independent professional decision of the doctor which determines how much is spent and on whom. DHSS policy in recent years has attempted to contain the drugs bill and this is done mainly through the provision of information, and exhortation by ministers and civil servants. There is a system of monitoring the prescribing habits and costs of GPs, and of penalising those doctors whose costs are higher than the average, but in practice this system is of limited effectiveness.

The Royal Commission on the NHS pointed to the poor quality of primary care in certain declining inner-city areas as one of the most significant problems facing the NHS. In the large conurbations such as London, Birmingham and Manchester, the elderly, single-handed general practitioner working from run-down, lock-up premises is a familiar figure. Many doctors in these areas deliberately limit the number of patients they accept, creating an anomalous situation in which the area as a whole is designated as adequately served even though people have difficulty in finding a GP. The Royal Commission recommended as a matter of urgency that steps should be taken to provide health centres in these areas and that experiments should be made with salaried appointments and reduced list sizes as a way of attracting doctors. A subsequent report from the Acheson Committee on primary care in London reiterated these points, and made a series of recommendations for bringing about improvements (DHSS, 1981f). In the event, the more radical proposals contained in the Acheson report were not accepted, and instead the government announced in 1983 a £9 million programme spread over four years involving the payment of higher grants for the improvement of general practice premises in inner city areas, additional funds to meet the cost of training health visitors and district nurses, and allocations for the development of primary health care projects.

A third issue of concern has been the increasing reliance by GPs on deputising services. The traditional practice of a single GP or group of doctors providing a personal 24-hour service has been eroded, and around one-third of all GPs currently make use of commercial deputising services. There have been complaints about these services, and in 1984 guidance was issued to Family Practitioner Committees on arrangements for consenting to the use of deputising services and monitoring their operation. Certainly from the profession's point of view, deputising services often provide a valuable respite, although among patients they may be seen as a serious inroad into the established pattern of general practice.

It is important to note that primary care services cover not just the work of GPs, but also the work of other health professionals such as health visitors and home nurses. In this respect, they overlap with and are often indistinguishable from community health services and prevention. In contrast with GPs, though, these latter services are provided directly by health authorities, who took over responsibility for them from local authorities at the time of health service reorganisation in 1974. A range of activities are included under the general umbrella of community health services and prevention, including family planning clinics, vaccination and immunisation, health education, clinics for mothers and children, and fluoridation.

In 1976 the DHSS published a separate consultative document entitled *Prevention and Health: Everybody's Business* (DHSS, 1976d), which noted that improvements in health in the previous century had resulted largely from the public health movement rather than from specific medical intervention, and argued that further gains were very much dependent on people taking care of themselves by changing their life-style. Individuals were urged to stop smoking, take more exercise and adopt an appropriate diet in order to reduce the risk of ill health and death. The consultative document stressed personal rather than governmental action as the means by which advances were to be achieved. These views were reiterated in a White Paper on *Prevention and Health*, published a year later (DHSS, 1977a), and a series of other publications have given advice on issues such as safety during pregnancy, eating for health and avoiding heart attacks.

The significance of prevention has been emphasised in other reports on specific areas of service provision, such as the Court Report on child health services (discussed later) and in particular campaigns. The Health Education Council, operating on a small but increasing budget, has allocated a large proportion of its resources to campaigns on the risks of cigarette smoking and the importance of adopting a healthy life-style. In 1983 the Council published a report on nutrition and health, prepared for the National Advisory Committee on Nutrition Education. The report offered nutritional guidelines for health education in Britain, including proposals for reducing the consumption of fat, sugar and salt. In a related field, government action has been proposed to draw attention to the increasing prevalence of alcohol-related diseases, and to phase out lead in petrol. Undoubtedly the renewed importance attached to prevention is a reflection of concern at escalating service costs, as well as deriving from a conviction that a strategy of preventive medicine may bring better results in terms of health outcomes.

Hospital services

Policy on hospital services since the Hospital Plan of 1962 has centred on the provision of District General Hospitals (DGHs) catering for all but the most specialised needs. The intention as set out in the Plan was to provide each district of 100,000 to 150,000 people with a general hospital of between 600 and 800 beds. A DGH would contain beds and services for all needs except those of the long-term mentally ill, the mentally handicapped and certain regional specialities, for example neurosurgery. The programme of hospital building which occurred after the Plan resulted in the building of many completely new DGHs, and the upgrading of several existing hospitals to DGH standard, often on more than one site. The Bonham Carter Report of 1969 (Central Health Services Council, 1969) proposed that even larger DGHs should be built to serve bigger populations, but these proposals were not accepted. Instead, government policy swung back in favour of a continuing role for small hospitals, known as Community Hospitals, providing services mainly for elderly patients.

Recent developments on hospitals policy have included the idea of the nucleus hospital as a way of constructing new general hospitals. Initially nucleus hospitals provide 300 beds, but are capable of expansion to 600 and 900 beds. They offer a quick and cheaper means of building hospitals than the methods previously used. However, government policy has moved against large general hospitals, and a consultative paper issued by the DHSS in 1980 suggested that in future provision should centre on smaller DGHs supported by local hospitals containing both acute and long-stay services (DHSS, 1980b). The paper indicated that this might be achieved through a reduction in the target of geriatric beds to be provided in the DGH from 50 per cent to 30 per cent, and the provision of smaller psychiatric units. The result would be a minimum size of 450 beds, with 600 beds being the normal maximum for a main DGH serving a population of around 200,000. Alongside these hospitals would be developed small local units providing casualty services, some acute services, out-patient clinics, geriatric services and some mental illness provision.

Overall, general and acute hospital services have not fared well from recent reductions in public expenditure and developments in health policy. After experiencing a period of unprecedented growth in the decade after the Hospital Plan, cuts in the amount of money available for new building beginning in 1973 meant the delay and sometimes the abandonment of many long planned schemes. On top of this, the 1976 consultative document on *Priorities* argued for a slowing down in the growth of revenue spending on general and acute hospital services in order to enable other services to develop. An analysis carried out by the DHSS in 1983 pointed out that over half of hospital expenditure occurs in general acute hospitals and the use of resources in such hospitals is therefore of considerable significance (DHSS, 1983a). Figures for the decade to 1981 illustrate that average case costs in the acute sector as a whole rose in the first half of the 1970s and declined thereafter. The DHSS has attributed this reduction in unit costs to falling lengths of stay and an increase in the number of cases treated. More detailed analysis of the acute sector (DHSS, 1981f) reveals variations between specialties in activity levels. Thus, there is evidence to indicate that the number of cases treated in medical specialties has increased more rapidly than in surgical specialties. There are also variations between regions in the efficiency with which resources are used. Regions with a greater number of beds tend to use beds less intensively than regions with a smaller number of beds.

One point to note is that during the 1970s the increase in the number of medical staff employed in hospitals was greater than the increase in activity rates. The reasons for this are not entirely clear. One significant change has been the increase in the number of elderly people using acute services. Patients aged 65 and over occupy 40 per cent of acute hospital beds and their treatment needs are often more complex than those of other age groups. Another explanation is that new techniques have been developed requiring more intensive staffing levels. The pressures resulting from medical innovations are estimated to add 0.5 per cent per annum to expenditure on hospital and community health services, although some commentators have suggested that this figure is on the low side. What is not in question is that advances such as diagnostic ultrasound, bone marrow transplants and new methods of treating haemophilia patients place increasing demands on health authority budgets, particularly in respect of drugs and equipment.

With growth money limited, hospital doctors have been exhorted to examine more closely the use of resources to see if savings can be made and applied elsewhere. It has been estimated that the average consultant controls resources to the value of £530,000, and there have been a number of attempts to make hospital doctors more aware of the costs of their decisions, including experiments in specialty costing and clinical budgeting. Clinical budgeting involves agreeing service and expenditure plans for a particular specialty with the doctors involved. The doctors are then responsible for keeping within the agreed budget and may be able to redeploy any resources saved. Evidence from clinical budgeting suggests that improvements in efficiency can be achieved (Wickings *et al.*, 1983) and work is in hand to develop a system of management budgeting as recommended by the Griffiths NHS Management Inquiry (Griffiths Report, 1983). The need for such an approach has been endorsed by the *British Medical Journal* which has argued that at a time of resource constraints:

clinicians may have to accept that they can no longer claim total freedom to order investigations and prescribe treatments as they think best. Even in the affluent United States doctors are being forced to conform to overall cost limits, and some form of clinical budgeting seems inevitable for the NHS. Doctors should be seen to be willing to co-operate in efforts to improve their cost effectiveness. (BMJ, 1983)

Despite this endorsement, the clinical freedom of hospital doctors means that it is ultimately doctors alone who decide the appropriate form of treatment for their patients.

Services for elderly people

People aged 65 and over are heavy users of all health services. This applies particularly to the very old – that is, people over 75 years of age. With the proportion of elderly people in the population growing annually, there has been increased pressure on the geriatric hospital and district nursing services. The number of elderly people attending hospital as day-patients has risen, and in general DHSS policy is to help elderly people to remain in the community as long as possible. This means increasing the availability of services such as day centres, home helps and meals-on-wheels. These services are the responsibility of local authority social services departments rather than health authorities. The joint planning of the health and personal social services is of particular importance in relation to elderly people, and this is discussed later in the chapter. Here we may note that expenditure controls on local authorities have constrained the growth of services for elderly people in recent years.

As far as hospitals are concerned, DHSS policy has been to move towards a situation in which around 30 per cent of each district's designated geriatric beds are provided in the District General Hospital. Spending targets set out in the 1976 consultative document on *Priorities* proposed that revenue expenditure on services used mainly by the elderly should grow by 3 per cent per annum, and it noted that the elderly would also benefit from capital developments. A further consultative document, *A Happier Old Age* (DHSS, 1978a), was concerned specifically with the needs of elderly people, and invited comments on ways in which services should be developed. Subsequently a White Paper, *Growing Older*, was published in 1981. The White Paper provided a summary of existing policies for elderly people, and stressed the need for statutory services to support the care provided by families, friends and neighbours. In the words of the White Paper, 'Care in the community must increasingly mean care by the community' (DHSS, 1981b, p. 3). There was therefore a need to mobilise individuals and to provide support through informal caring networks, and this was also emphasised in a DHSS review of community care published in 1981 (DHSS, 1981a). As far as health services were concerned, the White Paper noted the important role played by hospital, community health and family practitioner services in assisting elderly people, and it indicated that an experiment would take place with nursing home provision within the NHS, as an alternative to hospital accommodation for long-term patients.

In 1982, the Health Advisory Service published a report on mental illness in old age, *The Rising Tide* (Health Advisory Service, 1982), drawing attention in particular to the increasing incidence of dementia in the elderly population. *The Rising Tide* offered a checklist of questions for use by health authorities and local authorities in deciding how to develop specialised services in this field. Partly in response to the report, the Government launched a £6 million programme in 1983 to stimulate the development of comprehensive local services for the elderly mentally ill.

An important recent development which affects statutory services for elderly people has been the growth of private old people's homes. Changes in supplementary benefit regulations have stimulated the development of these homes which provide an increasing number of places for elderly people. There has been concern that standards in some parts of the private sector may be inadequate and doubts about whether health authorities and local authorities have sufficient powers and resources to inspect homes and monitor performance.

Mentally handicapped people

Policies for mentally handicapped people underwent a major change following the Report of the Committee of Enquiry into Ely Hospital, Cardiff (Ely Report, 1969). The new policies were set out in the White Paper, *Better Services for the Mentally Handicapped*, published in June 1971 (DHSS, 1971). The main objective of the White Paper was to bring about a reduction of about one-half in the number of hospital beds provided for the mentally handicapped. This was to be accompanied by an expansion of local authority services in the community, including an increase in the number of places in residential homes and training centres and the provision of foster homes and lodgings. Standards in hospitals were also to be improved in order to overcome the kind of deficiencies noted in the Ely Report. These deficiencies included low nursing and medical standards, inadequate facilities, and custodial attitudes towards patient care. To assist in the process of change, two significant innovations were made: money was earmarked by central government to be used only on the development of mental handicap hospitals; and the Hospital Advisory Service was established with the remit of visiting these and other long-stay hospitals and advising on how services might be improved.

A review conducted by the DHSS and published in 1980 indicated progress made in meeting these objectives (DHSS, 1980c). As far as mentally handicapped adults were concerned, the review showed that the number of adults in hospital had fallen, although at a slower rate than envisaged. At the same time, places in local authority training centres and residential homes had increased. Updated figures for the *Better Services* White Paper demonstrated that 38,700 adult training centre places were provided in 1977 in England, compared with 23,200 in 1969 and an estimated need of 74,900 in 1991. Similarly, 11,700 residential home places were provided in 1977 in England, compared with 4,200 in 1969 and an estimated need of 30,000 in 1991.

As far as mentally handicapped children were concerned, the increase in local authority residential provision was much slower. Only 1,600 places were available in local authority homes in England in 1977 compared with 1,200 in 1969. This was combined with a greater than expected reduction in the number of children in hospitals, so that overall fewer residential services were provided for children. The DHSS review acknowledged that the White Paper's estimates of bed needs for children and adults were too high. A new objective was therefore set of providing fewer beds in smaller units. The review went on to re-emphasise the need to develop local authority services, and stated that joint planning between health authorities and local authorities was essential, particularly at a time of expenditure constraints.

These aims have also been stressed in the reports of the National Development Group for the Mentally Handicapped. The Group was set up in 1975 under the chairmanship of Professor Peter Mittler to advise the Secretary of State for Social Services on mental handicap policy and its implementation. In a series of pamphlets and reports the Group has provided guidance on various aspects of mental handicap policy, including helping mentally handicapped people in hospital, day services for adults, joint planning, and helping handicapped school-leavers. In 1980, at the time of its dissolution, the Group published an important check-list of standards, aimed at improving the quality of services for mentally handicapped people; and in its final report, which was highly critical of DHSS thinking, the Group reiterated the need to move towards a locally based service. Since 1976 a Development Team has been working, first alongside the Group but now alone, visiting hospitals, homes and centres operated by health authorities and local authorities in order to provide assistance in the development of local services. The Team has taken over the work on mental handicap formerly carried out by the Hospital Advisory Service in England, and it continues to provide a valuable, though sometimes controversial, service.

As much of this comment suggests, the focus of attention in NHS provision has often been on residential services, to the relative neglect, until recently, of the range of supportive services required by the large number of mentally handicapped people living at home with their families. Following the suggestion of both the National Development Group and the Development Team, one aspect of current attempts to rectify this imbalance can be seen in the creation of multi-professional community mental handicap teams. These teams are adding a significant specialist element to existing community services, particularly through the work of community nurses and field social workers. In addition, both statutory agencies and voluntary organisations have developed a range of innovative services in the community, and these have been fully documented by Ward (1982).

One of the issues which remains unresolved in relation to mentally handicapped people is the balance to be struck between hospital and community services. Although there has been a significant move away from hospital services since 1971, the bulk of services continue to be provided in a hospital setting. It has been suggested that eventually no hospital beds will be required, and that all services should be provided in small local units. This was the view of the Jay Committee on Mental Handicap Nursing and Care, which, in its report published in 1979, recommended a model of care based outside hospitals (Jay Report, 1979). The report emphasised the importance of enabling mentally handicapped people to live a normal life within the community. However, the Committee was not unanimous in making this recommendation, and there is a continuing debate on whether certain groups of handicapped people, particularly adults with severe handicaps, require hospital care. Whatever the strength of the different viewpoints, current restraints on the money available to health authorities and local authorities make a rapid movement towards the Jay model unlikely, even if government policies were to support such a move.

In 1981 it was estimated that 15,000 mentally handicapped people living in hospitals, about one third of the total, could be discharged immediately if services were available (DHSS, 1981d). Developments in the policy on joint finance (discussed later) have helped to stimulate an increase in the provision of community services and in 1983 the DHSS allocated special funds to assist in getting mentally handicapped children out of hospital. A further central initiative aiming to improve support for mentally handicapped, mentally ill and elderly people living in the community by providing assistance to families, friends and volunteers was announced in 1984. This initiative was important in its acknowledgement that unless support was provided to people living in the community the beds vacated by patients moving out of hospital might soon be filled by new admissions.

Mental illness

Most in-patient services for people who are mentally ill are provided in large old hospitals. These are the former asylums typically built during the Victorian period and usually located outside the main centres of population. Despite their size, these hospitals are considerably smaller than in the past, their population having reached a peak of 150,000 in 1955. After that date patient numbers declined, spurred on by advances in treatment and a shift in policy in favour of care in the community. The policy shift was reflected in the 1959 Mental Health Act and was confirmed by the 1962 Hospital Plan. The Minister of Health at the time of the Plan, Enoch Powell, had told the annual conference of the National Association for Mental Health in 1961 that mental illness hospitals would be run down, and the Plan itself forecast that the number of beds allocated to mental illness would be almost halved by 1975, falling from 3.3. beds per 1,000 population to 1.8. In parallel with the reduction in beds in the large old hospitals, it was the intention to develop acute psychiatric units in District General Hospitals, as well as out-patient services and day care facilities. At the same time, local authorities were urged to develop their services, including the provision of hostels, group homes, social work support and day centres. Most of these developments were facilitated by the discovery of new drugs for the treatment of mental illness. Although these drugs did not provide a cure for mental illness, they did allow the symptoms to be controlled and relieved, and together with changes in public and staff attitudes and other therapeutic advances, they provided the conditions in which a movement towards community care could be started.

This movement was reflected in the publication of a circular on hospital services for the mentally ill in 1971, and, more significantly, in the publication of the White Paper, *Better Services for the Mentally Ill*, in 1975 (DHSS, 1975a). These documents, which form the basis of current policies, recommended the provision of district-based psychiatric services in which all mental illness beds, and not just those for the acutely ill, could be provided in a general hospital unit. It was estimated that 0.5 beds per 1,000 population were required, together with 0.65 day patient places per 1,000 population, and out-patient services. These were to be supported and supplemented by various community services provided by local authorities, including day centres (estimated to require 0.6 places per 1,000 population), hostels (requiring between four and six beds per 1,000 population) and long-stay accommodation (estimated to require between fifteen and twenty-four beds per 1,000 population).

The 1975 *Better Services* White Paper was presented as a general statement of objectives rather than a specific programme of action, and it was acknowledged that achievement of the White Paper's goals would take many years. Restrictions on public expenditure have prevented a rapid movement towards the kinds of service envisaged in the White Paper, and the development of local authority services has been particularly slow. This is explained as much by central government's reluctance to give local authorities approval to carry out new building as by local authorities' unwillingness to provide services for the mentally ill. The result has been a considerable shortfall in residential and day centre places provided by local authorities.

In the hospital service, the bed reduction envisaged in the Hospital Plan has been achieved, and in 1977, 1.8 beds per 1,000 population were available. Again, however, restrictions on capital spending have meant that only limited progress has been made in providing comprehensive psychiatric services in general hospitals. Consequently, the large old hospitals remain. Indeed, the Royal Commission on the NHS, reporting in 1979, argued that there was a continuing need for these hospitals and that they should close only in exceptional circumstances. The consultative paper on hospital services published in 1980 confirmed this view, and noted that districts with a well sited mental illness hospital, some seventy in total, would continue to be served by these hospitals. This would enable districts served by a distant or unsuitable institution to develop their own services, permitting the closure of perhaps thirty hospitals.

Within mental illness hospitals, the visiting teams from the Health Advisory Service (HAS), created in 1976 out of the Hospital Advisory Service, have stimulated improvements in the quality of care. Often under-staffed and under-resourced, these hospitals have frequently benefited from the reports prepared by the HAS teams. Not least, the reports have provided ammunition for those seeking improvements to the physical fabric and facilities of these hospitals, and to the amenities available to patients. Longer term changes in staff attitudes and in working relationships have proved more difficult to achieve, and the continuing series of enquiries into mental illness hospitals indicates the gap between aspiration and achievement. Nevertheless, the HAS has provided a useful service, not least in opening up what were previously often closed and insular institutions, thereby exposing staff to a wider set of practices and ideas than would otherwise be available.

The problem of organising and managing mental illness services was examined in the Nodder Report, published in 1980 (DHSS, 1980d). The report was the outcome of the deliberations of a working group set up by the DHSS to examine some of the difficulties in mental illness hospitals highlighted in HAS and Committee of Enquiry reports. The working group recommended a clearer management structure for psychiatric services, involving the establishment of district psychiatric services management teams and hospital management teams to provide leadership in the development of local services and facilities. The Nodder Report emphasised also the need for each psychiatric hospital and unit to have objectives, standards and targets against which to measure its progress, and recommended that an annual progress report should be produced. The significance of joint planning with local authorities and of community involvement through community health councils and voluntary organisations was also emphasised.

Apart from specialist hospital in-patient services, the needs of people who are mentally ill have been met by a steady increase in day hospital provision, a growth in homes and hostels provided by local authorities and voluntary organisations, and the development of day centres. Help is also available through social workers, community psychiatric nurses and general practitioners. However, the lack of specialist skills among some of these professionals, and the pressures on their time, limit the assistance that can be given to individual patients. This applies in particular to GPs, and there is increasing concern at the extent to which psychotropic drugs are being prescribed. In some cases voluntary organisations have developed innovative approaches to the care of people with psychiatric problems, but by no means all needs are met in this way.

The law relating to mental illness changed in 1983 with the passage of the Mental Health Act. The provisions of the Act affect in particular those patients who are compulsorily detained, about 10 per cent of all patients admitted to mental illness hospitals. The Act resulted in the establishment of the Mental Health Act Commission which has a general responsibility to protect the rights of detained patients and to keep under review the exercise of the compulsory powers and duties conferred by the Act. The Secretary of State for Social Services has the power to extend the jurisdiction of the Commission to informal patients.

Maternity and child health services

These services became the focus of attention in 1976 following publication of the Report of the Committee on Child Health Services, *Fit for the Future*, under the chairmanship of Sir Donald

Court (Court Report, 1976). The Committee noted that despite improvements in child health, the United Kingdom had not performed as well as a number of other developed countries. In addition, striking differences in infant and childhood mortality rates remained between different parts of the country, and between social classes. Indeed, the Court Report argued that 'In contemporary terms infant mortality is a holocaust' (Court Report, 1976, p. 6), and accordingly it made recommendations for an integrated child health service. These recommendations have been accepted in principle, although many of the report's specific proposals, such as the employment of specialised health professionals to work with children, have been rejected. Consequently, government policies have concentrated on extending existing services rather than developing new ones.

In the community health services, priority has been given to the employment of additional health visitors, and to reaching out to vulnerable groups who do not use the services. The consultative document on *Priorities*, published in 1976, suggested a 6 per cent increase in annual expenditure on health visiting, and subsequently emphasis has been given to providing antenatal and child health services to sections of the population known to be most at risk. Various initiatives, including the provision of more accessible clinics, the employment of health workers with specialist skills, and the greater use of out-reach approaches in which services are taken to vulnerable groups, have been undertaken in some areas.

In the hospital services, the movement towards all births taking place in hospitals has continued. This policy has been pursued following a report from the Cranbrook Committee in 1959 which recommended that 70 per cent of births should occur in hospital (Cranbrook Report, 1959), and the Peel Committee Report in 1970 which advocated 100 per cent hospital confinements (Peel Report, 1970). At the same time the provision of regional units for low birth-weight babies and others needing special care and attention has been encouraged. Currently, around 98 per cent of births take place in hospital, and special units are provided or are being developed in each health region. To achieve these goals, expenditure on maternity services has been increased in real terms. This is a reversal of the policy set out in the consultative document on *Priorities* of reducing spending as a result of the falling birth rate. The renewed concern with poor standards of infant and child health, coupled with an upward movement in the birth rate beginning in 1978, helped to cause this policy shift.

Two reports published in 1980 reaffirmed the importance of tackling ill health and handicap among babies and children. The Short Report (1980) on perinatal and neonatal mortality, which resulted from an investigation by the House of Commons Social Services Committee, drew attention to the potential for improvements in the period around birth, and suggested an investment of resources in health services, particularly in hospital-based medical services. In contrast, the Black Report (1980) on inequalities in health stressed the significance of broader social, economic and environmental influences on health. Focusing in particular on social class differences in mortality and morbidity rates, the Black Report argued that attention needed to be paid to factors such as housing, income support and nutrition, if class differences were to be reduced. In the view of the Black working group, improvements in these services had to go hand in hand with the development of community-based health services in any long-term strategy to improve child health. In practice, central government was critical of both reports, in particular of their claim for extra resources.

However, the government did accept the Short Report's recommendation that a maternity services advisory committee should be established, and the new committee published a guide to good practice and a plan for action on antenatal care in 1982. A further report, on care during childbirth, was issued in 1984. Also in 1984, the Social Services Committee published a follow-up to its 1980 report on perinatal and neonatal mortality, noting the reduction in mortality rates which had occurred, but calling for action to bring about further improvements.

Planning and priorities

The NHS Planning System, introduced in 1976, is one of the main means by which the policies for the various client groups just discussed are intended to be implemented. The System was introduced following health service reorganisation in an attempt to ensure greater compliance among health authorities with central government's priorities. The instruments for achieving this objective are guidelines and plans. The guidelines flow down from the DHSS and are amended and elaborated by Regional Health Authorities to take account of local circumstances. In the reverse direction plans flow up the System starting at district level. The arrangements introduced in 1976 involved the production of strategic plans by regional and area authorities, covering developments over a ten to fifteen-year period. These provided the context for annual operational plans prepared by areas and districts, setting out changes to occur over a three-year period (DHSS, 1976e).

A key feature of the guidelines issued by the DHSS has been the attempt to identify priorities for service development. The 1976 *Priorities* document was the first manifestation of this. Underpinning the document was the annual programme budget prepared by the DHSS. The programme budget is a tool for allocating expenditure between programmes or client groups. There are seven of these groups, broadly similar to the headings used earlier in the chapter to discuss specific policies: general and acute hospital and maternity services; primary care; services mainly for the elderly and physically handicapped; services for the mentally handicapped; services for the mentally ill; services mainly for children; and other services, for example social work. The programme budget enables comparisons to be made of past trends in expenditure on these groups, and it provides a basis for projecting future spending patterns, including the setting of priorities. The *Priorities* document of March 1976 established central government's priorities as the development of services for all client groups except the largest single category, general and acute hospital and maternity services. Health authorities were particularly encouraged to develop provision for comparatively neglected groups like the mentally ill and handicapped, and to build up primary care and community health services.

In practice, the Planning System did not operate in quite the way intended. In the first place, not all health authorities prepared plans. The absence of relevant skills, coupled with constraints on spending, sometimes resulted in a lack of commitment to planning among health authorities. Expectations of the System were also set very high, and the complexities involved in the comprehensively rational planning framework set out by the DHSS soon became apparent. As the Permanent Secretary of the DHSS acknowledged in 1981, 'the National Health Service planning system ... we have felt has produced more paper than effective results so far' (Public Accounts Committee, 1981, p. 55). Consequently, as part of the restructuring of the NHS in 1982, the Planning System was simplified, with District Health Authorities having a key role in the new System.

The second way in which the System departed from original aspirations was in the nature of the guidelines issued by central government. The *Priorities* document contained relatively specific guidelines, often expressed in quantitative terms. The suggestion that expenditure on health visiting should increase at 6 per cent annually was an example. The document also proposed percentage growth rates for the major client groups. Subsequently, *The Way Forward*, published in 1977 as the successor to the *Priorities* document, embodied a rather different approach, containing fewer quantitative guidelines and indicating in broad terms, as illustrative projections only, the kinds of developments which might occur (DHSS, 1977b). This trend was continued in subsequent annual planning guidelines published by the DHSS, and it was taken further in 1981 with the publication of *Care in Action* (DHSS, 1981c). This handbook of policies and priorities did not attempt to set out in detail how priority services should develop. Instead, *Care in Action* gave a general account of government policies for different services and client groups, and stated that priority setting was a matter for local decision and local action.

The third, and arguably the most important, area where the System deviated from the initial intention concerned the substance of the priorities which were established. *The Way Forward*, in summarising comments on the *Priorities* document, noted that there was concern at the restraint imposed on general and acute hospital services, and on maternity services. It went on to suggest that more money might have to be spent on the rationalisation of acute services to permit other desired developments, for example in geriatric hospital provision, to take place. In 1978, the annual planning guidelines went much further and announced that the policy of cutting spending on maternity services was to be changed in favour of maintaining expenditure in real terms (DHSS, 1978b). While guidelines have been changing in this way, in practice the designated priority services have not always received the increased share of resources intended. For example, the proportion of current and capital expenditure on health and personal social services allocated to mental illness actually declined from 7.6 per cent to 7.5 per cent between 1975–6 and 1981–2.

The reasons behind these developments are complex, but a significant factor is undoubtedly the power of certain key interests within the medical profession, and their ability to maintain the existing distribution of benefits. As Brown noted shortly after the introduction of the Planning System, 'the year 1976–77 has been spent in learning not only what was unattainable because it was unrealistic, but also what was unattainable because it was not acceptable to the health authorities and their advisors' (Brown, 1977, p. B12). This observation draws attention to the inherently political nature of health planning. In design, the NHS Planning System appeared to be an attempt to challenge the power structure within the NHS: to provide a means of countervailing the entrenched interests of hospital doctors, particularly those working in the acute services. In practice, the System was challenged by these interests, with the consequent shift in priorities noted above. As a result, the System was itself changed, in recognition that 'Health planning is *necessarily* the subject of adaptation, compromise, bargaining and reconciliation of conflicting interests' (Barnard *et al.*, 1980, p. 263).

The simplified Planning System introduced in 1982 identified the DHA as the basic planning unit. Comprehensive operational annual plans were replaced by short-term programmes setting out the action proposed over a two-year period to carry forward the district strategy. Consistent with the policy shift noted at the beginning of the chapter, short-term programmes must include a cost-improvement programme. Strategic plans are prepared every five years and cover a forward period of ten years. The most important change concerns the new arrangements for accountability that have been introduced, involving annual regional review and district review meetings. These arrangements, which were in part a response to criticisms by the House of Commons Public Accounts Committee about the lack of control exercised by the DHSS over the NHS, involve Ministers and senior DHSS officials holding a meeting in each region with the regional chairman and regional officers. After the regional review the RHA holds similar performance review meetings with each of its district health authorities. The reviews provide an opportunity to examine plans, problems and objectives for the ensuing year in the light of the government's strategic policies. They also enable performance indicators to be discussed. The accountability review process is considered in more detail in Chapter 5. The point to note here is that the reviews have introduced a greater element of central involvement in planning. The reviews are also significant in signalling a shift away from planning by circular and consultative document, the method which has predominated since the introduction of the Planning System in 1976, to planning by dialogue. It remains to be seen whether the dialogue will result in changes to government policies or action to ensure local compliance with those policies.

Joint planning

One of the recurring themes of this chapter has been the importance of joint planning between local authorities and health authorities. This is a reminder that health services cannot be considered in isolation from the range of services which are concerned in different ways with contributing to people's welfare. As we saw in Chapter 1, from an historical perspective improvements in health were due more to the development of sewerage systems and water supplies and improvements in nutrition than to specific medical interventions. Equally, contemporary health problems have multiple causes, and their solution is as much dependent on action outside the NHS as on the development of health services. A number of writers have drawn attention to the so-called diseases of affluence, that is diseases associated with industrialisation and its effects. These diseases result from the processes of production, distribution and consumption, and include stress-related illnesses such as heart disease; illnesses which result from the uneven distribution of resources, like malnutrition and hypothermia; and illnesses which have their roots in the consumption of goods known to be damaging to health, such as tobacco and alcohol (Draper *et al.*, 1977). Future improvements in health therefore require attention being paid to the social and economic conditions which give rise to illness and disease. While action by individuals to prevent ill health clearly has a role and has been emphasised by the government, action on these conditions would seem to be equally significant.

These arguments highlight the need for a concerted approach to health problems. Not only does this apply to the prevention of ill health, but also to the provision of services to people who become ill or who are born with disabilities. Within central government the case for a joint approach to social policy has been articulated by the Central Policy Review Staff, while at the local level collaboration between health authorities and local authorities was one of the key objectives of the 1974 reorganisation. It is in relation to groups like the mentally ill, the mentally handicapped and the elderly that collaboration is particularly important. The development of a policy of community care for these groups at a time when the majority of existing statutory services are hospital-based is dependent for its success on effective collaboration. In recognition of this, various administrative arrangements have been made to encourage collaboration, including overlapping membership between authorities, the establishment of joint consultative committees and planning teams, and, at least until 1982, coterminous boundaries between health authorities and the local authorities responsible for personal social services. The initial failure of these arrangements to promote joint planning prompted the introduction of a special financing arrangement, known as joint finance, in 1976.

Joint finance entails the allocation of money to health authorities to be spent mainly on personal social services projects after discussion between the two types of authority. Eight million pounds was allocated in the first year of operation in England, and this increased to £100 million in 1984–5. The money has been spent mainly on services for the elderly and the mentally handicapped. Schemes receiving funds have included old people's homes, adult training centres and group homes. Support has also been given to the employment of additional staff such as social workers and home helps. Although the introduction of joint finance has forced health authorities and local authorities together to discuss how to spend the money, doubts remain as to whether it has encouraged joint planning. Organisational and political differences between health authorities and local authorities, including different member and officer structures, budgeting cycles and planning systems, work against the collaborative development of services, and the restructuring of the NHS in 1982 – with the loss in many areas of coterminosity – has made joint planning more difficult in some parts of the country.

A consultative document published in 1981 put forward a number of proposals for transferring patients and resources from hospitals to the community (DHSS, 1981d). The document discussed the potential for achieving such a transfer in relation to elderly people, mentally handicapped people and the mentally ill. The proposals included an extension of joint finance and the sale of hospital buildings and land, with the proceeds being used to develop community services. The definitive statement of policy, issued in 1983 (DHSS, 1983b), was a classic example of incremental policy development. The government announced that the more radical options set out in the consultative document would not be pursued. Rather, there was to be a modest increase in the amount of money made available for joint finance, a relaxation of the rules on the use of joint finance to allow support to be provided over a longer period of time, and a change in the law to allow joint finance to be used on education for disabled people and housing. The change came into effect on 1 April 1984 under the provisions of the Health and Social Services and Social Security Adjudication Act 1983. The DHSS emphasised that despite the change it was expected that joint health and personal social services activities would remain at the centre of joint planning and joint finance, a concession to the social services lobby which was concerned at the possible loss of joint finance support to housing and education. In addition, a programme of pilot projects was launched, aiming to explore and evaluate different approaches to moving people and resources into community care. Twelve projects involving 600 people were supported in the first phase of funding. The government also suggested that independently of joint finance health authorities might find money from their main programmes to make lump sum payments or continuing grants to local authorities to care for people moved from hospital to the community.

While these developments have provided further encouragement to joint planning, attempts by central government to control local government expenditure have made many local authorities reluctant to take on future spending commitments. The imposition of grant penalties on local authorities deemed to be spending above the level necessary in relation to the population served, and the proposal to introduce ratecapping against high spending councils, militate against the use of joint finance at the local level. A small concession was granted in 1984–5 when the Treasury agreed that increases in joint finance commitments over 1983–4 would be exempted from grant penalties. Despite this, considerable concern exists about the impact of central government policies on the joint finance initiative. Indeed, there is a certain irony in the fact that while health authorities and local authorities are being encouraged to collaborate, central government departments seem to be pursuing inconsistent policies.

Conclusion

In this chapter we have noted that increasing demands on health services, coupled with limited resources, have created the need to make choices on which services should be developed and which held back. Essentially, this entails the rationing of scarce resources between different geographical areas, types of service and client groups. The Resource Allocation Working Party (RAWP) and the Planning System are the principal mechanisms for resource allocation and priority setting in the NHS, and experience of operating both mechanisms has highlighted the political environment within which health care is delivered. For example, opposition to RAWP from areas standing to lose resources has led to the very gradual implementation of the policy. The RAWP policy has involved cuts in real expenditure in areas designated as above target, and as a consequence there have been strong objections from those affected most adversely. Objections have also arisen in the NHS Planning System from those groups not identified as priorities for development. Indeed, the System has served to demonstrate the comparative strength of the groups threatened by the policies set out in the consultative document on *Priorities*, and the weakness of the groups likely to benefit from those policies. Although there is evidence to indicate that the proportion of expenditure allocated to general and acute hospital and maternity services has fallen, it is equally clear that priority services such as mental illness and mental handicap have failed to improve their relative position (see

Chapter 4). The operation of health planning since 1976 indicates that planning is inherently political, and changes to the Planning System suggest that this lesson has been learned.

This chapter has sought to provide a general introduction to the substance of contemporary issues in health policy. No attempt has yet been made to provide a definition of policy, but implicit in the chapter has been the assumption that policy emanates largely from central government. It is for this reason that attention has focused on the content of White Papers, consultative documents and the like. An alternative view, however, is that policy is not what comes out of central government, but what happens at the local level in health authorities. From what has already been said it will be clear that the two are not always the same, and it is to a consideration of these different views of policy that we now turn.

3

The Policy-Making Process in Central Government

What is policy?

Although many writers have attempted to define policy, there is little agreement on the meaning of the word. It is therefore tempting to follow Cunningham and argue that 'policy is rather like the elephant – you recognise it when you see it but cannot easily define it' (quoted in Smith, 1976, p. 12). Attractive as this interpretation is, it may be worth spending a little time clarifying the meaning of policy, and the different ways in which it has been used.

A useful starting point is the work of David Easton, who has argued that political activity can be distinguished by its concern with 'the authoritative allocation of values' within society (Easton, 1953, p. 136). Easton uses values in a broad sense to encompass the whole range of rewards and sanctions that those in positions of authority are able to distribute. Values are allocated by means of policies, and for Easton 'A policy ... consists of a web of decisions and actions that allocate ... values' (Easton, 1953, p. 130). A number of points can be made about this definition.

First, Easton argues that the study of policy examines both formal decisions and actions. He points out that a decisioin by itself is not an action, but merely the selection among alternatives. What happens in practice may be different from what was intended by decision-makers, and it is important to focus on the processes that follow from a decision. Put another way, we need to consider how policy is implemented as well as how it is made.

A second point about Easton's definition is that it suggests that policy may involve a web of decisions rather than one decision.

There are two aspects to this. First, the actors who make decisions are rarely the same people as those responsible for implementation. A decision network, often of considerable complexity, may therefore be involved in producing action, and a web of decisions may form part of the network. The second aspect is that even at the policy-making level, policy is not usually expressed in a single decision. It tends to be defined in terms of a series of decisions which, taken together, comprise a more or less common understanding of what policy is.

Third, policies invariably change over time. Yesterday's statements of intent may not be the same as today's, either because of incremental adjustments to earlier decisions, or because of major changes of direction. Also, experience of implementing a decision may feed back into the decision-making process, thereby leading to changes in the allocation of values. This is not to say that policies are always changing, but simply that the policy process is dynamic rather than static and that we need to be aware of shifting definitions of issues.

Fourth, the corollary of the last point is the need to recognise that the study of policy has as one of its main concerns the examination of non-decisions and inaction. Although not encompassed in Easton's definition, the concept of non-decision-making has become increasingly important in recent years, and a focus on decision-making has been criticised for ignoring more routine activities leading to policy maintenance and even inertia. Indeed, it has been argued that much political activity is concerned with maintaining the *status quo* and resisting challenges to the existing allocation of values. Analysis of this activity is a necessary part of the examination of the dynamics of the policy process (Bachrach and Baratz, 1970).

Fifth and finally, Easton's definition raises the question of whether policy can be seen as action without decisions. While Easton wishes to stress that policy is more than a formal, legal decision, it is also appropriate to consider the view that there may be policies in the absence of decisions. Can it be said that a pattern of actions over a period of time constitutes a policy, even if these actions have not been formally sanctioned by a decision? In practice it would seem that a good deal of what happens in public agencies occurs because 'it has always been done this way', and cannot be attributed to any official pronouncement. Further, writers on policy have increasingly turned their attention to the actions of lower level actors, sometimes called street-level bureaucrats, in order to gain a better understanding of policy-making and implementation. It would seem important to balance a decisional 'top-down' perspective on policy with an action-oriented, 'bottom-up' perspective (Barrett and Fudge, 1981). Actions as well as decisions may therefore be said to be the proper focus of policy analysis. Accordingly, in this and the subsequent chapter the main focus of attention is on the policy-making process in central government, while Chapter 5 examines the implementation of centrally determined policies and the local influences on health policy-making.

The policy process

The discussion may be taken a stage further by considering a framework for analysing the policy process. Easton's work again provides a valuable point of reference, and his analysis of political activity in terms of systems theory may help to clarify the complex range of phenomena under investigation. Later on we shall note some criticisms of Easton's approach, but to begin with let us examine the central elements of his analysis.

Easton, unlike many other political scientists, does not take as his starting point the analysis of power in political systems. This, he feels, is of secondary importance compared with the question of how it is that political systems persist and change over time. Power analysis presupposes the existence of relatively stable political activity and does not consider the conditions under which this activity is able to continue. It is the latter question which interests Easton, who seeks to develop a general theory of political life (Easton, 1953; 1965a; 1965b).

Underpinning Easton's theory is the assumption that political activity can be analysed in terms of a system containing a number of processes which must remain in balance if the activity is to survive. The paradigm that he employs is the biological system whose life processes interact with each other and with the environment to produce a changing but nonetheless stable bodily state. Political systems are like biological systems, argues Easton, and exist in an environment which contains a variety of other systems, including social systems and ecological systems.

One of the key processes of political systems is inputs, which take the form of demands and supports. Demands involve actions by individuals and groups seeking authoritative allocations of values from the authorities. Supports comprise actions such as voting, obedience to the law, and the payment of taxes. These feed into the black box of decision-making, also known as the conversion process, to produce outputs. Outputs are essentially the decisions and the policies of the authorities. Outputs may be distinguished from outcomes, which are the effects that policies have on citizens. Easton's analysis does not end here, for within the systems framework there is allowance for feedback, through which the outputs of the political system influence future inputs into the system. The whole process is represented in Figure 3.1.

FIGURE 3.1   *A simplified model of a political system*

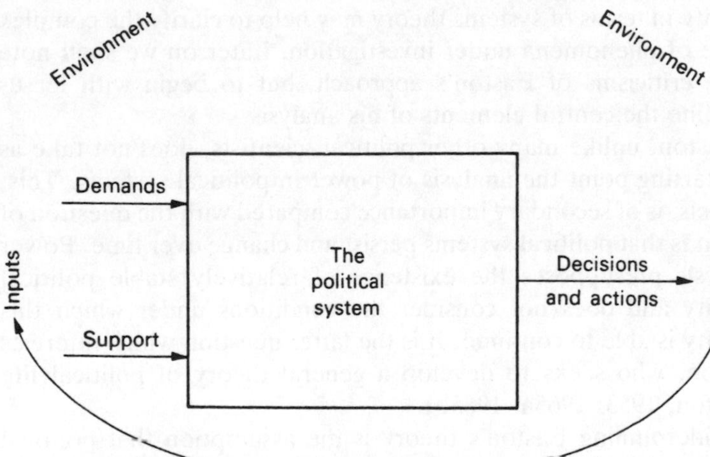

SOURCE: Easton (1965a).

The objects of support in political systems are threefold. First, there are the authorities, that is those who hold office at a particular point in time. Second, there is the regime, or the set of constitutional arrangements within which political activity takes place. Third, there is the political community, by which Easton means the readiness of the members of the political system to co-operate in solving political problems.

Easton notes that stress may result from a decline in support or from the pressure of demands. Demand stress may be produced by the sheer volume of demands being placed on the political system or by the content of demands. That is, the authorities may be faced with more demands than they are able to cope with, as well as demands which are unacceptable in terms of the prevailing system of values. Demand stress can occur even though processes of demand regulation are at work serving to reduce pressures on the authorities. Support stress may result from neglect of demands by the authorities, or by the failure of outputs to satisfy demands. In Easton's analysis, one of the characteristics of political systems is their ability to respond and adapt to stress. Responses may take the form of authoritative allocations of values, changes in the authorities, or adaptations to the regime. Put another way, there may be changes in policies, movements in the personnel in authority, or fundamental alterations to the constitutional order, including the creation of new political structures. Political systems are able to develop in these ways without threatening the political community. Systems are therefore responsive and dynamic, and open to influences from a wider environment.

A number of writers have found Easton's framework to be a useful tool in analysing the policy process. Certainly the systems approach has merit in offering a way of conceptualising what are often complex political phenomena. Systems theory is also valuable in emphasising the interdependence of the various processes which comprise political activity, and in showing how these processes fit together to form a whole. A particular strength of the approach is Easton's detailed analysis of demands and the process of demand regulation through gatekeepers and cultural exclusion. Furthermore, although it is the persistence and stability of political systems which most interest Easton, he is able to demonstrate how stability is maintained through change. It is for these reasons that the systems approach is of value. However, the approach is not without its drawbacks, and our understanding of the policy process may be developed further by examining various points of criticism.

First, it would be wrong to accept Easton's conceptualisation of the political system as an accurate description of the way systems work in practice. While Easton's identification of processes is valuable, the neat, logical ordering of those processes in terms of demand initiation, through the conversion process to outputs, rarely occurs so simply in the practical world of policy-making. For example, the authorities themselves may be the source of demands, and although Easton recognises the significance of what he terms 'withinputs', consideration needs to be given to the manner in which individual and group behaviour may be shaped by political leaders. A growing body of work suggests that, far from arising autonomously in the community, political demands may be manufactured by leaders, who thereby create the conditions for their own action (Edelman, 1971). Through the manipulation of language and the creation of crises, the authorities may impose their own definitions of problems and help to frame the political agenda. Recognition of these processes is an important corrective to the naive assumptions found in some applications of systems theory.

Second, the systems approach does not raise the question of who benefits from the persistence of systems. This is because Easton started from a critique of what he saw as the partial theories of writers who focused solely on the allocation of power in politics. Easton set himself the goal of developing general theories which sought to explain the stability of systems over time. Nevertheless, it is necessary to complement general systems theory with an analysis of who gains and who loses from the authoritative allocation of values, a question which is explored in Chapters 6 and 7.

A third criticism is that the systems framework highlights the central importance of the conversion process, the black box of decision-making, but gives it relatively little attention when compared with the detailed analysis of demands and supports. Of course, for some researchers the conversion process remains a black box because of the difficulties of penetrating the decision-making activities of governmental agencies. Traditionally, accounts of the organisation of central government in Britain have been limited to formal descriptions of the major institutions such as the Cabinet and Parliament. In the last decade, however, recollections by former Cabinet Ministers of their experiences in office have provided new inside views of the black box, views which we will now discuss in exploring the central policy-making machinery in the British political system.

British central government

The organisation of British central government can be described simply. General elections, which must be held at least every five years, result in the election to the House of Commons of some 650 Members of Parliament (the precise number varies as constituency boundaries are redrawn). The leader of the largest single party in the Commons is asked by the monarch to form a government and the leader becomes the Prime Minister. The Prime Minister appoints from among his or her supporters around 100 people to take up ministerial appointments. The most senior of these, usually numbering twenty, comprise the Cabinet. The government is thus made up of Cabinet and non-Cabinet ministers, the majority of whom will be MPs. The remaining members of the government come from the House of Lords. Occasionally people from outside Parliament are appointed to the government, but they must become MPs or be made life peers.

Ministers are responsible for the day-to-day running of the government's business through the major departments of state. These departments include the Treasury, which is responsible for all matters to do with finance, and the Department of Health and Social Security. Most of the work of the departments is in practice carried out by civil servants. Ministers are, however, individually responsible for the work done by civil servants in their name, and are held accountable by Parliament. Parliament also monitors the work of government departments through a system of select committees. Although not part of the formal machinery of government, pressure groups have a key role in the central policy-making system. Pressure groups are one of the main sources of demands and supports within the system, and provide an important means of direct representation of specific interests.

Much has been written about the relative power of the various institutions within central government. To summarise this literature briefly, the historical decline in the power of the monarchy and the House of Lords gave rise to the thesis that Britain had a system of 'Cabinet government'. In his book, *The English Constitution*, published in 1867, Walter Bagehot argued that the monarchy and the Lords had become 'dignified' elements in the constitution, compared with the Commons, the Cabinet and the Prime Minister which he described as the 'efficient' elements (Bagehot, 1963). Of these latter institutions, Bagehot saw the Cabinet as pre-eminent. Almost 100 years later, Richard Crossman, writing an introduction to a new edition of Bagehot's book, contended that Prime Ministerial government had replaced Cabinet government. In Crossman's view, the extension of the suffrage to all adults, the creation of mass political parties and the emergence of the civil service administering a large welfare state all contributed to the Prime Minister's power (Crossman, 1963). This interpretation was confirmed by Crossman's experience as a Cabinet Minister, although initially he felt the Cabinet might be more influential than he had thought. His more considered view, however, was that the Prime Minister was in a dominant position. In addition, he noted the important part played by official committees in Whitehall, a facet of government he had not observed while in opposition; and he encountered the power of civil servants to challenge and frustrate the wishes of ministers. These observations have been broadly confirmed by the accounts of other former Cabinet Ministers, and there is a growing consensus that the House of Commons has joined the Lords and the monarchy as a dignified element in the constitution. Indeed, a recent textbook on British government carried the subtitle 'the policy process in a post-parliamentary democracy' (Richardson and Jordan, 1979). It may be as well to begin, then, by examining the role of Parliament – specifically the House of Commons – in the organisation of central government today.

Parliament

It is important to distinguish the formal power of Parliament from its effective role. Although formally Parliament passes legislation, examines public expenditure and controls the government, effectively it carries out these functions within strictly defined limits. As long as there is a House of Commons majority to support the government (a condition which has not always been met in recent years), then Parliament has few significant powers within the system of central government. In Mackintosh's words, 'Parliament is one of the agencies through which the government operates and it is the place where the struggle for power continues in a restricted form between elections' (Mackintosh, 1974, p. 125).

The task of securing the government's majority in the House of Commons falls to the party whips. They ensure that MPs are present to vote, and that the government's legislative programme is passed safely. Most legislation originates from the government, and bills have to go through a number of stages before becoming law. Parliamentary debates on legislation provide an opportunity for party views to be reiterated, and occasionally the government will accept amendments put forward by opposition parties. On occasions, important legislation may be defeated or withdrawn. But the existence of a parliamentary majority coupled with strong party discipline ensures that these occasions will be rare.

Parliament provides opportunities for individual MPs to propose legislation in the form of private members' bills. The most important method of promoting a private member's bill is through the ballot of members which takes place every session. Usually, around twenty names are drawn in the ballot, but because of the pressure on parliamentary time only one-third to one-half of the MPs who are successful in the ballot stand a chance of having their bills enacted. Even in these cases, though, the MPs concerned are dependent on the government not being opposed to the legislation they propose. The Abortion Act of 1967, promoted by the Liberal MP, David Steel, is an example of a private member's bill which became law.

Individual MPs are able to use Parliament in two other main ways. First, they can put down parliamentary questions, asking ministers about aspects of the work for which they are responsible. Some of these questions receive written replies, while others are answered orally, in which case there is an opportunity to ask a supplementary question. Second, MPs can raise adjournment debates, which are often on local or constituency issues. These debates provide a chance to air matters of concern to MPs and their constituents, and force ministers and departments to make a response. Also, although most of the parliamentary timetable is controlled by the government, certain days are available to the opposition to debate subjects of their choosing.

One of the key developments in Parliament in recent years has been the use of select committees. These are committees of MPs which investigate particular topics and publish reports on their findings. The aim of the committees is to provide MPs with a more effective means of controlling the executive, and to extract information about the government's policies. The establishment of the committees was in part a response to the perceived decline in the power of the Commons to control the government.

Although select committees have existed in a variety of forms ever since the establishment of the Public Accounts Committee in 1861 and the Estimates Committee in 1912, they have developed most recently in the period since 1966 when Richard Crossman, as Leader of the House of Commons, began an experiment with the setting up of select committees on agriculture and on science and technology. The experiment was taken a stage further in 1971 when the Expenditure Committee was established in place of the Estimates Committee and a number of the select committees. The Expenditure Committee worked through a range of sub-committees, including one on employment and social services. The latest development has been the replacement of the Expenditure Committee by fourteen new committees, organised along the lines of government departments. The committees' main function is to enable MPs to question civil servants and ministers about government policies.

The Social Services Committee, which covers the work of the DHSS, has undertaken a number of major inquiries, including investigations into perinatal and neonatal mortality, the Griffiths Inquiry into NHS Management, and community care. Also, every year the Committee reviews the expenditure plans and priorities of the DHSS. The reports from the Committee in this area and the replies by the DHSS provide a continuing dialogue on the issues involved in planning and monitoring the expenditure programmes within the control of the DHSS. A third type of inquiry concerns topical issues or problems which require a speedy response. An example was the Committee's investigation of the effect of cuts in university spending on medical services. The MPs on the Committee are supported by a House of Commons clerk and his staff, and by specialist advisers (Nixon and Nixon, 1983). As well as taking evidence from civil servants and ministers, the Committee has called witnesses from outside the DHSS, including the officers and chairmen of a number of health authorities. This practice has also been followed by the Public Accounts Committee, which continues to examine the way in which government money has been spent, including spending on health services. The Public Accounts Committee has published a number of reports which have been critical of the management of the NHS, including analyses of manpower control, building defects and arrangements for premature retirement of staff.

The actual impact of select committees on policy is largely determined by the government's willingness to accept their recommendations. Although it is expected that departments will respond to committee reports, this does not mean that the committees' findings will have an immediate influence on policy. Indeed, the call by the Social Services Committee for additional resources to be spent on maternity and child health services was rejected by the DHSS in its response to the Committee's report on perinatal and neonatal mortality. Nevertheless, it can be suggested that committees create a more informed House of Commons, force departments to account for their actions, submit ministers to a level of questioning not possible on the floor of the House, and help to put issues on the agenda for discussion. Furthermore, at a time when the role and influence of individual MPs have come into question, the committees have given MPs useful and often satisfying work to do. Finally, they enable outsiders to gain a better understanding of what is going on in Whitehall, and the information they extract provides ammunition for pressure groups to use in particular campaigns.

The establishment of the new select committee system in 1979 is one of the factors which has led some writers to argue that the House of Commons is more powerful than often assumed. This is the view held by Norton (1981), who has drawn on evidence of a decline in the cohesion of political parties within Parliament and an increase in government defeats in division lobbies to suggest that the Commons can effectively scrutinise and influence government. As Norton points out, the key to government control of Parliament historically has been the existence of a single majority party with strong discipline being exercised by the whips, and any moves away from this system, such as the formation of minority or coalition governments, would further strengthen the position of those who wish to reassert the influence of the House of Commons.

The Prime Minister and Cabinet

The pre-eminence of the Prime Minister in the British system of government can be explained in a number of ways. First there is the Prime Minister's patronage. He or she has sole responsibility for appointing members of the government, and in addition has considerable discretion over the conferment of honours. Of course, the Prime Minister's power of patronage is not total, and is usually exercised with regard to the influence of other actors in the system. In appointing the Cabinet, for example, the Prime Minister will want to include people drawn from different parts of the majority party, possibly including former opponents. Nevertheless, it is ultimately the Prime Minister alone who decides, and who accepts responsibility for the appointments made.

Second, there is the Prime Minister's position as chairman of the Cabinet. This gives the Prime Minister control over the Cabinet agenda, and the power to appoint the members and chairmen of Cabinet committees. Much of the Cabinet's work is now done by committees, although relatively little is known about their organisation and work because of official secrecy. However, the Prime Minister will usually chair the key committees such as those on defence and economic strategy, and appoint his or her supporters to chair the other committees. The Crossman and Castle diaries indicate that the Social Services Committee of the Cabinet handles any important business which is the concern of the DHSS (Crossman, 1977; Castle, 1980).

Third, the Prime Minister may establish informal groupings of senior ministers to act as an inner Cabinet. The inner Cabinet may serve as a sounding board for the Prime Minister, and may help to incorporate potential rivals into the centre of government decision-making. The Prime Minister will also negotiate with individual ministers in order to gain influence over specific policies. Fourth, the Prime Minister's position is strengthened by the support of the Cabinet Office. Within the Cabinet Office the Cabinet Secretary is the key person, and the Secretary acts as the personal adviser to the Prime Minister. The Cabinet secretariat controls the distribution of minutes and papers in the Cabinet system, and enables the Prime Minister to keep a close eye on what is taking place in Cabinet committees. In addition to these sources of strength within the Cabinet system, the Prime Minister's powers are enhanced by his or her position as leader of the majority party and head of the Civil Service.

All of these factors give the Prime Minister a more powerful role than the traditional description, *primus inter pares*, suggests. Crossman's *Diaries* indicate that there were occasions when the Cabinet did engage in collective decision-making, but these tended to be when the Prime Minister had no definite view and was prepared to let the Cabinet decide. What seems clear is that the Prime Minister is rarely defeated in Cabinet, and an alliance between the Prime Minister and the Chancellor of the Exchequer, or the Prime Minister and the Foreign Secretary, is virtually unstoppable. Yet there may be occasions when even this kind of alliance is unsuccessful. For example, during the course of 1981 informed newspaper reports indicated that proposals for cuts in public expenditure put forward by the Chancellor of the Exchequer with support from the Prime Minister were defeated by the so-called 'wets' in the Conservative Cabinet. Here, then, is an indication of the limits of prime ministerial power. However, it should be remembered that on questions of government strategy or on broad economic policy the Prime Minister is usually in an advantageous position because of the reluctance of ministers to step outside their own areas of concern. Crossman bemoaned the absence of an overall strategy in the 1964–70 Labour government, and he explained it in terms of the entrenched departmentalism within Whitehall (Crossman, 1975, 1976, 1977). The Prime Minister, unencumbered by specific departmental responsibilities, is able to take the wider view, and so can set the direction of government policy as a whole. Only when the Prime Minister's leadership poses a threat to the government and its future electoral chances is the Prime Minister's dominance likely to be seriously challenged by Cabinet colleagues.

Ministers and civil servants

The view that ministers decide policy and civil servants carry it out is no longer widely held. The memoirs of Crossman, Castle and other former ministers (RIPA, 1980) indicate that civil servants have considerably more influence over policy-making than allowed for in conventional textbook accounts. In the first volume of the

Crossman diaries (1975) the struggle between ministers and civil servants became personalised in terms of the battle between Crossman and his permanent secretary at the Ministry of Housing, Dame Evelyn Sharp. Later volumes of the diaries suggested that it was not simply the personality of Crossman or Dame Evelyn that was important, but the very nature of civil service power. At the DHSS, for example, Crossman had to overcome the reluctance of civil servants before he succeeded in establishing the Hospital Advisory Service in 1969 after the Report of the Committee of Enquiry into Ely Mental Handicap Hospital, Cardiff (Crossman, 1977). What the Ely example demonstrates is that a minister with clear views and a strong commitment can achieve his goals. On other issues, though, ministers may have to bargain, cajole and compromise before they get their way.

The Crossman diaries show that a proposal included in an election manifesto carries considerable weight with civil servants. This draws attention to the role of political parties as sources of inputs into the policy process. A newly elected government is likely to use its election manifesto as a basis for formulating a programme of legislation to put before Parliament. What is more, a government will seek to claim a mandate to implement any proposals contained in a manifesto. Manifesto proposals therefore constitute an influence on policy-making, particularly in the early years of a government. Yet with few exceptions, the ideas articulated by political parties are often very general and may be modified, sometimes in significant ways, as they are developed in detail by civil servants. It is therefore important not to overemphasise the influence of political parties on policy-making within central government. As Klein (1984) has demonstrated in the case of health policy, party ideology does not always predict policy, and the areas about which politicians are most concerned are often those of least significance in terms of their actual impact on the services provided to the public.

Civil servants influence policy-making in various ways. Their familiarity with the Whitehall machine, coupled with access to information and a repository of knowledge developed over a period of years, creates an expertise which is not easily challenged. Often, it is the strength of the departmental view on an issue, rather than any ideological antipathy, which politicians have to overcome (Young and Sloman, 1982). In many cases, ministers are not well placed to challenge this view, if only because parties in opposition devote relatively little time to developing the policies they intend to carry out when in office. In addition, ministers may not always have the intelligence or skill to counter the weight of advice offered by civil servants. The debate about the relative influence of ministers and civil servants may therefore be more to do with weak ministers than conspiratorial civil servants. Ministers are not always appointed for their administrative ability or their analytical skills, and it is perhaps not surprising that they do not always carry through significant changes in policy.

Apart from personal factors – and these should not be under-rated – there are organisational reasons why ministers sometimes do not make a major impact. One of the most important is the key role played by interdepartmental committees of civil servants, which prepare the ground for ministers and for Cabinet commit-tees. Interdepartmental committees have been seen by Richard Crossman and Tony Benn, among others, as a key source of civil service power within Whitehall. As Crossman noted:

> in addition to the Cabinet committees which only ministers normally attend, there is a full network of official committees ... This means that very often the whole job is pre-cooked in the official committee to a point from which it is extremely difficult to reach any other conclusion than that already determined by the officials in advance; and if agreement is reached at the lower level of a Cabinet committee, only formal approval is needed from the full Cabinet. This is the way in which Whitehall ensures that the Cabinet system is relatively harmless. (Crossman, 1975, p. 198)

Unfortunately it is not possible to discover a great deal about the work of official committees because of the secrecy which sur-rounds their operation. However, commentators from both inside and outside the system of central government have increasingly pointed to the importance of their work.

Another reason why ministers may be less than fully effective is the variety of different jobs they are expected to do: run their department; participate in Cabinet and Cabinet committee discus-sions; take care of their constituents as MPs; and take part in the work of the House of Commons. With so many competing demands on their time, it may be easier for ministers to accept the advice they are given and to rely on their departmental briefs than to attempt to exercise an independent policy-making role. It is worth noting, though, that there have been attempts to bolster the position of ministers through the appointment of specialist political advisers. These advisers were first appointed on a large scale in the 1960s by Labour ministers as a source of outside information and to provide an alternative form of briefing to that supplied by civil servants. Harold Wilson has identified seven functions for advisers:

as a sieve, examining papers for politically sensitive or other important problems; as a deviller, chasing ministers' requests or instructions; as a thinker on medium and long term planning; as a policy contributor to departmental planning groups; as a party contact man, keeping in touch especially with the party's own research department; as a pressure group contact man; and as a speech writer. (quoted in Blackstone, 1979)

Advisers have been used by both Labour and Conservative governments, and they come and go with governments. Professor Brian Abel-Smith of the London School of Economics was used as a political adviser in the DHSS by Richard Crossman in the late 1960s, and by Barbara Castle and David Ennals in the mid–1970s. The more astute advisers are able to enhance their position by building up relationships directly with civil servants, senior and junior, rather than always working with or through ministers (Young and Sloman, 1982). In this way they seek to extend their influence over policy-making. A number of former ministers, including Shirley Williams, Barbara Castle and William Rodgers, have argued that political advisers perform a useful function (RIPA, 1980; Castle, 1980) and they are likely to become increasingly significant as they are used on a more regular basis.

Relationships between departments

In discussing the role of the Cabinet we noted that attempts to develop overall government strategies were frustrated by the strength of individual departments. The importance of 'departmental pluralism' (Richardson and Jordan, 1979, p. 26) is nowhere more apparent than in the annual budgeting process of central government, the so-called PESC cycle. PESC is the acronym for the Public Expenditure Survey Committee, the committee of officials which co-ordinates the preparation of the government's expenditure plans. PESC is one example of the interdepartmental committees of civil servants which organise much of the government's business. The Public Expenditure Survey Committee is especially important because of the impact of overall spending levels on the policies which it is possible to pursue. Ministers will not be able to launch new policy initiatives unless the expenditure involved has first been approved during the PESC process. In this process, a great deal of time is taken up with bilateral negotiations between the Treasury and individual spending departments on the departments' estimates of their expenditure plans.

The Public Expenditure Survey Committee prepares a report for ministers on the basis of these negotiations, pointing out where agreements cannot be reached. Cabinet and ministerial deliberations then follow until final decisions are made. The outcome of the process is the annual public expenditure White Paper, which projects spending over future years. This provides the basis for expenditure on individual services such as the NHS. *The Castle Diaries 1974–76* provide fascinating insights into the PESC negotiations, particularly as they affect health services. During the later months of 1975 and early 1976 – a time of increasing control over public expenditure – Castle and her officials were in the position of defending the NHS budget against attempts by the Chancellor of the Exchequer and the Treasury to achieve significant reductions in planned spending levels. As Castle records in her diaries, the public expenditure White Paper 'demonstrated vividly how much more successful I have been than some of my colleagues in defending my programmes' (Castle, 1980, p. 641). And as she explained to a meeting of Regional Health Authority chairmen, the outcome was

> no absolute cut; overall growth rate for health of 1½ per cent per annum; expansion of health centre programme; yearly growth of family practitioner services of 3½ per cent; no need to cut back services; capital programme levelling out at £250 million a year; joint financing to the tune of £20 million by

1978–79; enough elbow room to move towards the better system of regional allocation under the Resource Allocation Working Party criteria, based on deprivation; the greater flexibility in switching between revenue and capital which Dick Bourton (a Deputy Secretary in the DHSS) has won from the Treasury (I paid him a public tribute on this); last, but not least, greater flexibility in carrying over spending from one year to the next (1 per cent instead of the ¼ per cent we had won from them this year). Tough, but not catastrophic. (Castle, 1980, p. 654)

The PESC negotiations are important not least in influencing the reputation of a minister. In particular, a minister who is successful in the negotiations will earn the respect of his or her civil servants and achieve a reputation for toughness.

Since the period referred to in the Castle diaries, constraints on public spending have become even tighter, especially following the election of a Conservative government in May 1979. As a result, while traditionally the vast bulk of inherited expenditure has been left unquestioned, and most of the detailed negotiations within the PESC process have occurred at the margins, increasingly all spending has come under scrutiny. At the same time, PESC itself has become more an instrument for controlling public expenditure than a means of planning future spending patterns (Heclo and Wildavsky, 1981). One of the key difficulties has been the development of a corporate approach to public expenditure planning through PESC. The strength of departmentalism means that individual departments seek to defend their own budgets and are reluctant to attack those of other departments. In theory, the Treasury and Cabinet are in a position to provide a wider view of priorities, but the Treasury is mainly concerned with the overall scale of public expenditure, while attempts within the Cabinet system to transcend departmentalism, such as the establishment of a Committee of Non-Spending Ministers in the early 1960s under the Conservatives and again in the late 1960s under Labour, have not proved effective.

The need to develop joint approaches between departments has been emphasised many times. The Central Policy Review Staff (CPRS), the government think-tank which started work in 1971 and was disbanded in 1983, had as one of its functions the

examination of issues with implications for more than one department, but its resources were small compared with those of the
departments. The CPRS, which worked for ministers as a whole
under the supervision of the Prime Minister, carried out strategy
reviews of government policy, prepared major studies on specific
issues, and provided collective briefs for ministers. In a report
published in 1975 the CPRS argued the case for a joint approach to
social policies, stressing the importance of greater co-ordination
between the various central government departments concerned
with social policies. From time to time government departments
do publish joint circulars or joint White Papers, but most of their
activity is concerned with single programmes or services, and the
CPRS argued that 'a new and more coherent framework is
required for the making and execution of social policies' (Central
Policy Review Staff, 1975, p. 1). As at the local level, collaborative
planning and policy-making is beset by such difficulties as different
organisational and professional structures, a mismatch between
planning systems and cycles, and competing definitions of social
problems. Although the CPRS report resulted in the establishment of a co-ordinating committee of ministers, this had a short
life and the initiative slowly fizzled out. The demise of the CPRS
itself is a further indication of the difficulty of developing cross-
departmental approaches within Whitehall.

Outside interests

So far we have discussed the black box of decision-making itself. It
is now necessary to examine inputs into the system from outside
interests, in particular from pressure groups. In examining this
issue, Richardson and Jordan suggest that the central policy-
making machinery is divided into sub-systems organised around
central departments. They designate these sub-systems as 'policy
communities' (Richardson and Jordan, 1979, p. 44) and point to
the close relationships which exist in these communities between
departments and pressure groups. Indeed, the relationships may
be so close that shared priorities develop between the inside and
outside interests, amounting to 'clientelism' (Richardson and
Jordan, 1979, p. 55). The boundaries between groups and govern-

ment thereby become indistinct, with in some cases a high degree of interpenetration taking place.

The significant place occupied by pressure groups in the British political system exemplifies the growth of what Beer has called 'the collectivist theory of representation' (Beer, 1969, p. 70). This legitimises a much greater role for groups than earlier theories of representation. As Beer notes, as government sought to manage the economy it was led to bargain with organised groups of producers, in particular worker and employer associations. Governments of both parties sought the consent and co-operation of these associations, and needed their advice, acquiescence and approval. Similarly, the evolution of the welfare state provoked action by organised groups of consumers of services, such as tenants, parents and patients. The desire by governments to retain office led them to consult and bargain with these consumer groups, in an attempt to win support and votes.

Relationships between groups and governments vary, but it is the producer groups which tend to have the closest contacts and the greatest degree of influence. The extent to which some of these groups have been incorporated into the political system has been illustrated by moves towards tripartism, that is the three-sided talks between government, employers' organisations and trade unions which have occupied a central place in the development of economic policy in recent years. Likewise, a close, almost symbiotic relationship exists between the National Farmers Union and the Ministry of Agriculture, Fisheries and Food, the teachers' unions and the Department of Education and Science, and the British Medical Association (BMA) and the DHSS. As Beer points out, producer groups and governments are brought together by the desire of groups to influence the authoritative allocation of values, and by the need of government departments for the information which groups are able to offer, the co-operation they provide in the implementation of policy, and the importance which group endorsement of policy brings.

Consumer groups tend to have somewhat less influence, partly because their co-operation is usually not as significant for policy-makers. It is mainly information and expertise they have to offer, and consumer groups have to operate through influence rather than through the use of sanctions. Traditionally, the consumers of services have been less well organised than the producers. However, a variety of consumer groups are active in the central policy-making system, including generalist organisations like the National Council of Voluntary Organisations, and specialist associations such as Shelter, representing homeless people, Age Concern, campaigning on behalf of elderly people, and MIND, concerned with mental health. Many of these organisations are consulted on a regular basis by government, and indeed public money is spent supporting their activities. These groups also participate in the extensive network of advisory bodies which assist government departments in the development of their policies. It is important to add, though, that while some groups have close connections and good relationships with government, others have to attempt to exert pressure from a distance. Not all organisations are as well integrated into the decision-making system as the BMA, and attempts to influence policy indirectly through Parliament and the mass media are still an important part of pressure group behaviour. Examples in the health policy community of groups yet to achieve the status of insiders would include the organisations concerned with the reform of the abortion laws such as LIFE, the Society for the Protection of the Unborn Child and the Abortion Law Reform Association.

Pluralism or corporatism?

The growth of pressure groups has been paralleled by work which has attempted to redefine democracy in a way which accommodates the part played by groups in the political system. Beer's (1969) analysis of the collectivist theory of representation was one of the first efforts in this direction, and Dahl's (1961) elaboration of pluralist theory was another. Pluralist theory argues that power in western industrialised societies is widely distributed among different groups. No group is without power to influence decision-making, and equally no group is dominant. Any group can ensure that its political preferences are adopted if it is sufficiently determined. The pluralist explanation of this is that the sources of power – like money, information, expertise and so on – are distributed non-cumulatively and no one source is dominant. Essentially, then, in a pluralist political system power is fragmented and diffused, and the basic picture presented by the pluralists is of a political market-place where what a group achieves depends on its resources and its 'decibel rating'.

The importance of pluralist theory is demonstrated by the fact that, implicitly if not always explicitly, its assumptions and arguments now dominate much writing and research on politics and government in Britain. An example is Richardson and Jordan's analysis (1979) of post-parliamentary democracy, a study very much in the pluralist tradition. Yet despite its influence, pluralism has come under increasing challenge in recent years from writers who have questioned whether the British political system is as open to group influence as the pluralists maintain. In particular, it has been suggested that pluralism has given way to a system of corporatism in which some groups are much stronger than others and are in a good position to influence the decisions of government agencies.

The political history of corporatism in Britain has been outlined most fully by Middlemas (1979). Middlemas argues that a process of corporate bias originated in British politics in the period 1916 to 1926 when trade unions and employer associations were brought into a close relationship with government for the first time. As a consequence, these groups came to share government power, and changed from mere interest groups to become part of the extended state. Effectively, argues Middlemas, unions and employers' groups became 'governing institutions' (Middlemas, 1979, p. 372) so closely were they incorporated into the governmental system. By incorporation, Middlemas means the inclusion of major interest groups into the governing process and not their subordination to that process. The effect of incorporation is to maintain harmony and avoid conflict by allowing these groups to share power. Middlemas' thesis finds echoes in Cawson's (1982) discussion of corporatism and welfare. Cawson argues that 'The pressure-group world is not fluid and competitive, but hierarchical, stratified and inegalitarian' (Cawson, 1982, p. 37). He maintains that groups are not all of the same kind, and that organisations such as the BMA are well-placed to bargain for favourable policy outcomes by virtue of their strategic location in society. According to this argument, corporatism is not confined to the field of economic policy-making but extends into the sphere of social policy. Indeed, for Cawson, the NHS provides one of the best examples of corporatist policy making because government intervention in the provision of health services has necessitated close co-operation between the medical profession as the key producer group and government agencies. While some writers argue that corporatism has replaced pluralism, in Cawson's analysis corporatist policy-making coexists with pluralist or competitive policy-making. In the latter, consumer groups like MIND and Age Concern bargain with government agencies but lack the leverage available to producer groups. We shall return to discuss these issues at greater length in Chapter 7. The important point to note here is that pressure groups differ markedly in their ability to influence decisions in the health policy community, and use of the terminology developed by writers in the pluralist tradition does not entail acceptance of the pluralist analysis of power.

Conclusion

It was stated earlier that it is possible to describe the organisation of the British political system in simple terms. It is more difficult to locate precisely the key points of power and decision-making within the system. In Easton's terminology, the conversion process involves a complex range of actors and activities, and the boundaries of the process, as we saw in the discussion of pressure groups, are by no means clear cut. So what conclusions can be drawn about the system?

In general terms, the main centres of decision-making are to be found in Whitehall rather than Westminster. Although Parliament retains formal, and in a few cases effective, powers over legislation, expenditure and administration, in Bagehot's language it is more of a dignified than an efficient element of the constitution. The efficient elements are government departments, the Cabinet and the Prime Minister, with an increasingly important part being played by outside interests. Within departments power is shared between ministers and civil servants, the exact balance depending to a considerable extent on the strength and personality of the minister. It is naive to assume that civil servants exercise no influence, and it is equally erroneous to argue that they have absolute control. Much depends on the weight of the departmental view on issues, the quality of the advice rendered by political advisers, and the commitment of the minister to a particular course of action.

Civil service influence extends beyond departments into the Cabinet system. The network of official committees which support Cabinet committees is the main means by which this influence is secured. Cabinet committees occupy a key place within the central decision-making system, and, through the Prime Minister's power of appointment, assist in strengthening the Prime Minister's position. Indeed, the powers available to the Prime Minister suggest that Prime Ministerial government is a more accurate description of the British political system than Cabinet government.

We have noted that the strength of individual departments is a feature of central government. Yet departmentalism, although a barrier to the development of corporate approaches, facilitates the establishment of informal policy communities between departments and their client pressure groups. And it is in these policy communities that a great deal of the more routine and less controversial aspects of government policy are worked out.

Finally, what are the implications of this discussion for the student of health policy? It should be clear that the starting point for gaining an understanding of the dynamics of health policy-making is to focus on the operation of the DHSS. An analysis of the workings of the Department, including its relationships with outside interests and its connections with other parts of Whitehall and Westminster, would seem to offer valuable insights into how health policies are made within central government. In turn, this analysis will form the basis of a discussion of the processes of policy-making and implementation in the NHS.

4
Making and Changing Health Policy

The Department of Health and Social Security (DHSS) was formed in 1968 as a result of the merger of the Ministry of Health and the Ministry of Social Security. The Department is responsible for three groups of services: social security, including pensions, housing benefit and supplementary benefit; personal social services, including social work and residential care; and the National Health Service. The political head of the DHSS is the Secretary of State for Social Services, who is a member of the Cabinet. He or she is supported by a number of junior ministers, including on the health side a Minister of State and one or more Parliamentary Under Secretaries of State. Health services outside England are the responsibility of the Health and Social Work Department in the Welsh Office, the Scottish Home and Health Department in the Scottish Office, and the Department of Health and Social Services in the Northern Ireland Office.

The DHSS is one of the largest government departments and is responsible for around 40 per cent of all public expenditure. Despite the amalgamation of the two ministries in 1968, within the DHSS health and personal social services are still administered separately from social security. In 1972 the health and personal social services side of the Department underwent an administrative change which resulted in the formation of four main organisational groups for carrying out this aspect of the Department's work. These were the NHS Personnel Group, which dealt with pay and conditions of service, and the recruitment and training of staff; the Finance Group, which handled all issues to do with finance, including negotiations with the Treasury and overseeing the income and expenditure of the DHSS and NHS; the Regional

Group, which maintained contact with health authorities and gave support in the running of the Service; and the Services Development Group, which was concerned with the development of appropriate policies and supported field authorities and the Regional Group in implementing these policies. In addition, the Administration and Social Security Operations Group provided help across the Department on such matters as research, computers and management services, and the Top of the Office helped the Secretary of State provide central leadership and advised him on choices and priorities. Apart from some adjustments within groups, the basic structure of the Department remained the same until 1984 when the Griffiths Report resulted in a number of changes in the management of the health service at the centre. Before discussing these changes, let us consider in a little detail some of the key characteristics of the DHSS.

The generalist administrators in the DHSS are organised in a hierarchy headed by the Permanent Secretary. Each main group within the Department is led by a Deputy Secretary, and divisions within groups are organised around Under-Secretaries. An important feature of the DHSS is the strong professional input to decision-making. Parallel to the administrative hierarchy are a number of professional hierarchies. The most significant of these is the one involving medical staff, which is headed by the Chief Medical Officer – a civil servant equivalent in rank to a permanent secretary and who has equal access to ministers. The Chief Medical Officer publishes an annual report, *On the State of the Public Health*, providing a commentary on medical and related developments. Other key professional groups within the Department are nurses, dentists, pharmacists and social workers. Each group is organised in its own division and contributes in various ways to the work of the Department. In contrast, the *Works Group*, which provides guidance to health authorities on the design and construction of buildings and monitors the progress of major capital building schemes, is not organised separately but is an integrated administrative and professional organisation. In 1984, 5,500 civil servants worked in DHSS headquarters, and of this number around 2,200 were employed mainly in the field of health and personal social services.

The prominent position occupied by the generalist administrator in British central government is a familiar theme. In the case of the

DHSS, however, this is tempered by the involvement of professionals at all stages in decision-making. The existence of separate hierarchies has prevented the complete integration of the Department's work, but professionals do not just give advice to administrators. As Brown has written, 'The DHSS tradition is of multi-disciplinary working in which questions are settled by agreement between the administrators and members of the appropriate professional hierarchy' (Brown, 1975, p. 58). An example would be the teams responsible for liaising with the health authorities in a particular region which include a doctor, a nurse, an administrator and a social worker. Again, policy development for particular client groups is likely to be a multi-disciplinary exercise: policy on services for elderly people, for example, is organised around an assistant secretary working with a team consisting of a senior medical officer, a nursing officer, and a principal social work services officer (Kaye, 1977).

It is apparent, then, that the DHSS is not a monolith. Just as government departments as a whole differ in that they have distinctive characteristics and working styles, so too groups and divisions within departments vary. In the case of the DHSS, this is partly a reflection of the variety of professions which make up the Department's staff, but it also results from the different functions of the main organisational groups. For example, the divisions and branches of the Services Development Group come to be identified to a certain extent with the particular client groups or services for which they have responsibility, such as the elderly or the mentally ill, and act as a lobby for those groups or services. Again, the Regional Group, as well as communicating DHSS policies to health authorities, at times acts as a pressure group for the NHS within the Department. The status of the groups which make up the Department varies according to the kinds of issues on the health policy agenda. In the 1970s when attention was focused on planning and priorities, the Services Development Group was prominently placed. In the 1980s, with resources for growth constrained, and with the emphasis placed on efficiency and accountability, the Finance Group and Regional Group became more significant. The divisions which exist within the DHSS mean that health policy-making tends to be fragmented. In general, it is only at the apex of groups, at Deputy Secretary level, that a capability exists for formulating priorities across the board, and only at Permanent Secretary level is there overall responsibility for policy, finance, implementation and monitoring.

The fragmentation which exists at the centre was highlighted in an enquiry into the working of the DHSS carried out by three regional health authority chairmen in 1976. The chairmen argued that many tasks performed by the Department should be devolved to health authorities, and they called for a sharper management focus for the NHS within the Department. These points were reiterated in the Griffiths Inquiry into NHS Management. Brian Bailey, former chairman of the South Western RHA, was a member of both inquiries. The Griffiths Report pointed out that ministers and senior officials have demanding responsibilities other than the management of the NHS, with the result that the Department's capacity for overseeing the operation of the Service is underdeveloped. To overcome this weakness, the Report proposed the establishment of a Health Services Supervisory Board and an NHS Management Board within the DHSS. This proposal was accepted by the Secretary of State and the Supervisory Board was established in 1983 under the chairmanship of the Secretary of State. Other members include Health Ministers, the Permanent Secretary, the Chief Medical Officer, the Chief Nursing Officer and Roy Griffiths. The functions identified for the Supervisory Board in the Griffiths Report were: determination of purpose, objectives and direction for the NHS; appraisal of the overall budget and resource allocation; strategic decisions; and receiving reports on performance and other evaluations from within the NHS.

The NHS Management Board will be set up as soon as the chairman of the Board has been appointed. It is intended to appoint a chairman from outside the NHS and the civil service. The chairman will also be a member of the Supervisory Board. The Management Board will work under the direction of ministers, and will be responsible for planning the implementation of policies approved by the Supervisory Board, giving leadership in the management of the NHS, controlling performance, and achieving consistency and drive over the long term. The Griffiths Report suggested that other members of the Management Board should include individuals with responsibility for personnel, finance, procurement, property, scientific and high technology management and service planning.

As an interim step towards the creation of the Management Board, a Management Group was formed within the DHSS in February 1984. The Group brought together those divisions with an interest in the management of health authorities under a single Deputy Secretary. The Services Development Group continued to carry responsibility for policy development, and there was a refocusing of responsibilities in relation to family practitioner services leading to the formation of a new group concerned with family practitioner services and the pharmaceutical industries. Other changes are likely to follow from the call in the Griffiths Report for a significant shift in the stance and style of management at the centre. In essence, the Report argued that the centre should set broad strategic objectives for the Service and ensure through appropriate planning and monitoring mechanisms that these objectives were achieved. The development of a coherent management process would, the Report argued, enable the Department to 'vigorously prune many of its existing activities' (Griffiths Report, 1983, p. 15). To assist in this process, a regional administrator and a regional treasurer were seconded into the DHSS in 1984 to review communications between the NHS and DHSS with a view to reducing contact to essential matters.

One other issue raised by analysis of the Griffiths Report is whether the functions of the DHSS might be separated into a Ministry of Health and Personal Social Services and a Ministry of Social Security. Sir Patrick Nairne, a former Permanent Secretary in the DHSS, has suggested that a self-contained Ministry of Health and Personal Social Services would be large enough for any Minister and Permanent Secretary, adding that 'it would be wrong to suggest that it would bring no advantages' (Nairne, 1983, p. 250). On balance, though, Nairne argues that there are benefits in terms of collaboration between services in having a single department, and these outweigh the costs. While the possibility of separation cannot be ruled out, the various attempts to develop a coherent approach to policy-making in the DHSS discussed at the end of this chapter suggest that the pressure to link policy-making between services is at least as strong as the concern to provide a clearer management focus for the NHS. In any case, as Nairne has noted, the ethos in central government in the 1980s is to accept departments as they are, and to seek to improve management efficiency within existing structures.

The policy community

In the previous chapter we introduced Richardson and Jordan's idea of the policy community to denote the extent to which policies are increasingly developed in consultation between government departments and outside interests. Consultation may take place through a variety of channels: through standing advisory committees or groups; through *ad hoc* enquiries or working groups set up to advise on particular issues; and through the more or less regular pattern of negotiation and discussion in which the DHSS engages with pressure groups of various kinds.

Four standing committees on medical services, nursing and midwifery, dentistry and pharmaceuticals advise the Secretary of State on the development of health services. These were formerly committees of the Central Health Services Council, a body containing members drawn from the main health professions and the lay public. The Council was charged with making recommendations on any aspect of the health services, but was dissolved by the Health Services Act 1980. However, its committees remain as a source of advice, and a series of reports have emanated from the Council and its committees on such matters as the welfare of children in hospital, and domiciliary midwifery and maternity bed needs. Although the Secretary of State has often commended the Council's advice to health authorities, he is not obliged to accept its recommendations. Indeed, a report published in 1969 on the size and functions of District General Hospitals received a very cool response from the government of the day.

The Health Advisory Service (HAS) is another example of a standing advisory group under the aegis of the DHSS. Originally set up as the Hospital Advisory Service in 1969 after the Ely Report, HAS visits health authorities and local authorities to examine services for the mentally ill, the elderly and for children receiving long-term hospital care. As well as providing advice on the local development of services, HAS acts as the Secretary of State's 'eyes and ears' and makes suggestions as to any national action which could improve standards for the groups for which it is concerned. HAS is staffed by doctors, nurses and administrators, and these multi-disciplinary teams work alongside social workers drawn from the Social Work Service of the DHSS. From 1 January 1985, reports on HAS visits will be published.

It is worth noting that since the election of a Conservative government in 1979 there has been a reduction in the number of standing advisory committees in Whitehall. As far as the DHSS is concerned, this has meant the abolition of several groups, including the National Development Group for the Mentally Handicapped, the Children's Committee, the Personal Social Services Council, and the Central Health Services Council. Nevertheless, there are other channels through which advice is provided, one of which is the *ad hoc* enquiry or working group.

The Merrison Royal Commission on the National Health Service, which sat between 1976 and 1979, is an example. The Royal Commission made a series of recommendations concerned with the organisation, financing and policies of the NHS. Again, the Working Group on Inequalities in Health, which reported in 1980, was established by the Secretary of State for Social Services to review the evidence on social class differences in health and the use of health services, to suggest areas for further research, and to make proposals for changes in policy. A third example of an *ad hoc* enquiry is the Jay Report on mental handicap nursing and care, published in 1979. The report resulted from the work of a committee of enquiry set up by the Secretary of State to make proposals for the development of mental handicap services. One of the most influential inquiries in recent years, as we have noted, was that carried out into NHS Management by the team under the leadership of Roy Griffiths. The team, which reported in October 1983, made a series of proposals for developing a general management function within the NHS. The team's report was endorsed by the Secretary of State and a start was made in implementing the proposals in the NHS in 1984. There are many similar examples of commissions, committees and working parties established by the DHSS to provide advice on specific subjects.

A third means by which the Department obtains the views and ideas of outside interests is through the informal links which exist between the DHSS and the organisations concerned with its work. Sometimes these links are extremely close, as in the contact enjoyed by the medical profession through its representative groups, the British Medical Association (BMA) and the Royal Colleges. The profession expects to be consulted on any matters which affect its members. These matters include not only pay and conditions of service, but also the organisation of the NHS, the financing of health services, and policies for health care. Eckstein (1960) has shown how it is negotiation rather than consultation which characterises the profession's relationship with the central department, and which ensures that medical interests are well placed to influence decision-making. Occasionally relationships become strained, as in the disputes over pay beds and a new contract for hospital consultants in the mid 1970s, but for the most part there is a partnership between the medical profession and the DHSS equivalent to those which exist in the educational and agricultural policy communities between the relevant departments and their client groups.

Strong informal links also exist between health authorities and the DHSS. The Regional Group in the Department provides a two-way channel of communication between the DHSS and the NHS, and its activities are augmented through regular meetings between ministers and Regional Health Authority chairmen, and between civil servants and chief officers of Regional Health Authorities. Increasing reliance has been placed on chairmen in recent years, to the extent that the Secretary of State for Social Services has said that regional chairmen 'operate as a health cabinet as far as I am concerned' (Social Services Committee, 1984d, p. 165). Meetings with regional chairmen enable ministers to explain and test their policies and to advise chairmen on the direction in which they would like to see the Service develop. In turn, regional chairmen meet with district chairmen to ensure that central policies are fully explained and discussed at the local level.

A further source of advice at the national level is the National Association of Health Authorities (NAHA). In her diary, Barbara Castle notes that, as Secretary of State for Social Services, she attended the first annual conference of the Association and encouraged NAHA 'to become a pressure group for the NHS' (Castle, 1980, p. 459). By 1984, NAHA was operating on a budget of £150,000, employed nine staff and performed a number of functions including expressing NHS views to ministers and civil servants, investigating specific issues and problems, and maintaining relationships with the press and Parliament.

The position of consumer groups within the health policy community is somewhat weaker. Consumer groups may be able to exert influence on some issues, and the formation of Community Health Councils (CHCs) in 1974 helped to strengthen the consumer voice in policy-making at the local level. Nationally, the Association of CHCs in England and Wales acts as a forum for expressing CHC views. Organisations like MIND (The National Association for Mental Health) and Age Concern are consulted by the DHSS, but their position is much less secure than that of producer groups (Ham, 1977). Consumer groups are heavily dependent on the advice, information and expertise they have to offer, and cannot threaten sanctions in the same way as producer groups. Because their co-operation is usually not vital to the implementation of policy, consumer groups are dependent on the quality of their arguments and the willingness of ministers and civil servants to listen to what they have to say. In most cases, too, they have to supplement the pressure they exert on the DHSS by operating through Parliament and the mass media. Yet despite their weak position, some consumer groups are able to exercise influence. An example was the circular issued by the DHSS in 1980 recommending that health authorities should engage in raising funds from the general public. The circular was amended after protests from voluntary organisations concerned at the effect this would have on their fund-raising activities. Discussions between the DHSS and the National Council of Voluntary Organisations led to the publication of supplementary guidance stressing the importance of collaboration between the NHS and voluntary bodies on fund-raising.

These are some examples of the informal channels through which advice is given to the DHSS. Many other instances could be cited, but the key point to note is that outside interests play an important part in the development of health policies. In Richardson and Jordan's terms it may be misleading to use the word 'outside' to describe these interests. Richardson and Jordan's analysis emphasises the high degree of interpenetration which exists between pressure groups and government, and they point to the similarities which develop between departments and their client groups (Richardson and Jordan, 1979). Valuable as this analysis is, it is necessary to recognise that not all groups are equally well integrated into the national health policy community. We have noted the relatively weak position occupied by consumer groups, and Brown, commenting on this, notes that 'the machinery on the health and welfare side of DHSS tends to be dominated by those who provide services rather than those for whom the

services are intended' (Brown, 1975, p. 193). Thus, although the
health policy-making system appears to be pluralistic in that a wide
range of interests is involved in the policy process, in practice this
system may be skewed in favour of the well organised groups who
have a key role in the provision of health services.

Producer groups are well able to promote and defend their
interests, and this puts the DHSS in the position of appeasing
these groups and resolving conflicts whenever they occur. As we
argued in Chapter 3, corporatism may be a more accurate description than pluralism of a policy-making system in which producer
groups are dominant.

One of the consequences of producer group dominance is that
policy-making tends to be incremental, characterised by what
Lindblom (1965) has termed 'partisan mutual adjustment'. Bargaining between the DHSS and pressure groups often results in
small changes in the *status quo*, and this tends to be to the
advantage of established interests. A great deal of the activity of
the DHSS is not in fact concerned with policy-making as such.
Rather, it is aimed at the continuation of existing services and
policies and the maintenance of good relationships with key
interests. Policy-making is a comparatively rare occurrence because:

> public resources for dealing with issues are relatively scarce.
> They are scarce in many terms – money and manpower
> obviously since public finance and public servants are finite
> quantities, but scarce also in terms of legislative time, media
> coverage, political will, public concern ... Political systems can
> only cope with a limited number of issues at once and these are
> always subject to displacement by new emerging issues of
> greater appeal and force. (Solesbury, 1976, p. 382)

In Easton's terms, then, gatekeepers reduce the number of
demands competing for the time and attention of policy-makers,
and non-decision-making operates to rule some issues off the
agenda and to prevent others from progressing to the point of
action within the political system. Non-decision-making is a concept which describes the way in which challenges to patterns of
resource allocation and established ways of working can be
resisted. For example, the Report of the Working Group on

Inequalities in Health, mentioned above, was published with a foreword by the Secretary of State, stating that

> additional expenditure on the scale which could result from the Report's recommendations – the amount involved could be upwards of two billion pounds a year – is quite unrealistic in the present or any foreseeable economic circumstances, quite apart from any judgment that may be formed of the effectiveness of such expenditure in dealing with the problem identified. I cannot, therefore, endorse the Group's recommendations. (Black Report, 1980)

Again, a report from the House of Commons Social Services Committee on perinatal and neonatal mortality, published in 1980, although welcomed by the government, was in large part rejected because 'the Government has decided that they would not be justified in according maternity and neonatal services the *overriding* priority recommended by the Committee' (DHSS, 1980e, p. 15). Given the barriers to change, what processes do issues have to pass through before action results, and what are the main sourcs of inputs into the political system?

The policy process

Becker (1967) has examined the means by which situations come to be defined as social problems, and he notes that problems have two components: a set of objective conditions, and the definition of those conditions as problematic. It is not sufficient for the conditions alone to exist, because however serious the conditions are, they will not receive consideration unless an individual or group draws attention to them. What is important is the subjective definition of those conditions as problematic.

An example will help to illustrate this. In the NHS, there has always existed a geographical imbalance in the allocation of resources, yet it was not until a number of civil servants and academics drew attention to this imbalance that the situation came to be identified as a problem. Only when the problem was identified in this way was action taken by the DHSS designed to produce a more equal distribution of funds. A second example would be the relative neglect of hospital services for the mentally ill, mentally handicapped and the elderly. The condition of these services came to be defined as a problem in the late 1960s following enquiries at a number of hospitals, extensive media coverage, pressure group activity and ministerial concern. It could be argued that objectively conditions in these hospitals were worse a decade earlier when, particularly in mental illness hospitals, overcrowding was greater, and staffing levels lower. Here again, it was the definition of the conditions as problematic that placed the issue on the political agenda.

In a similar vein, Solesbury argues that issues must pass three tests if they are to survive. They have to command attention, claim legitimacy, and invoke action. It helps issues to command attention if they have particularity. Part of the reason why long-stay hospitals commanded attention is that they were associated with specific institutions, such as Ely Hospital, which came to symbolise the problems of this area of the NHS. Crises and scandals of this kind are often important in forcing an issue on to the agenda. Issues also need to become generalised. This helps them to claim legitimacy and attract the attention of existing political forces. Thus, a particular interest in Ely Hospital came to be generalised into a wider concern with social justice and humanitarian values, thereby bringing it within the dominant political culture and drawing the interest of established political groupings. An issue which has commanded attention and acquired legitimacy has passed two tests, but it must also invoke action. At this stage, issues run the risk of suppression, transformation into other issues, and token or partial responses.

Also relevant here is the notion of symbolic policy-making, a term developed by Edelman (1971) to refer to action intended to demonstrate that something is being done about a problem, rather than action which is a real attempt to tackle the problem. While there are undoubtedly difficulties in identifying the intentions and motives of policy-makers, in a number of areas it would appear that policies have significant symbolic elements. For instance, successive attempts to give greater priority to groups such as the mentally ill, mentally handicapped and elderly have not been accompanied by the allocation of significant amounts of additional resources, nor have ways been found of achieving a major shift towards these groups within existing budgets. In cases such as this, policies may act primarily as a way of maintaining political support and stability. Support is maintained in that the messages contained in policy statements may satisfy key political groups, thereby forestalling demands for more fundamental reforms. It is in this sense that words may succeed and policies fail (Edelman, 1977).

To return to Solesbury's discussion, what is valuable in his analysis is the examination of the hurdles which issues have to jump before they invoke action, the changing nature of issues, and the importance of subjective definitions in issue emergence. As Solesbury notes, it is too simple to see the policy process as linear or sequential, as is implicit in the systems model discussed in Chapter 3. It is more complex,

> moving forward on many fronts, sometimes concerned with legitimacy, sometimes with attention, the issue itself changing its definition as it goes forward, linking with other issues, splitting from yet others, sometimes becoming totally trans-formed into a new issue altogether. The agenda metaphor provides the best indication of the nature of the process. (Solesbury, 1976, p. 396)

There are similarities between Solesbury's approach and that of Hall, Land, Parker and Webb. Working within Easton's systems framework, Hall and her colleagues advance a number of proposi-tions about what determines the priority of a social policy issue. Like Solesbury, they argue that an issue needs to command legitimacy, but they also suggest that the feasibility of a policy and the support it receives are important variables. Certain issue characteristics are also relevant, including their association with other issues, the development of issues into crises, and the origins of issues. In relation to the last characteristic, they suggest that 'prima facie the closer to government the point of origin the better the prospects' (Hall *et al.*, 1975, p. 500). This leads us into a more detailed consideration of the sources of inputs into the policy process.

The sources of policy inputs

Pressure groups

There are many sources of inputs into the health policy-making system, several of which have already been mentioned. First, there are the inputs which come from pressure groups. As we noted in Chapter 3, the collectivist theory of representation legitimates a much greater role for groups than earlier theories of representation, and increasing state involvement in managing the economy and in the welfare state has led governments to negotiate and consult with pressure groups. A distinction has already been made between producer groups, which are often in a strong position to bargain for what they want, and consumer groups, which are relatively weak. The literature on pressure groups also distinguishes between organisations which have a direct economic or social stake in the decisions of government, and organisations which exist to promote a cause arising out of the shared attitudes of their members. Although various terms are used to describe these organisations, the former may be designated as sectional groups and the latter as cause groups. Producer groups in the health service have a direct stake in what government does, and so can be seen as sectional groups. On the other hand, consumer groups may be sectional groups, cause groups or a combination of the two. For example, Age Concern is both a sectional and a cause group, containing members who will benefit directly from better services for elderly people, as well as members who are active because they take the attitude that these services should be improved. An example of a cause group would be Action on Smoking and Health (ASH), which campaigns for the control of smoking and limitations on advertising by tobacco companies. Yet even ASH has backing from a key producer group, the Royal College of Physicians, which demonstrates the difficulty of making clear distinctions in the pressure group world surrounding the DHSS (Popham, 1981).

A further point to note is that many pressure groups have received financial support from the DHSS. This is true of both Age Concern and ASH. It can be argued that Age Concern is supported because of the services it supplies to elderly people, and the information it makes available, while ASH benefits as a result of its health education work. Nevertheless, the grants given by the DHSS to voluntary organisations, amounting to £15 million in 1983–4, undoubtedly help to enhance the pressure group activities of both organisations, and it is not difficult to see why the existence of active pressure groups may be viewed favourably by ministers and civil servants. Ministers, for example, may find it useful in negotiations with Cabinet colleagues to be pressurised by outside groups to spend more on health services. This much is indicated by the quotation earlier in the chapter from *The Castle Diaries*, concerning the National Association of Health Authorities. Again civil servants in the Services Development Group with responsibility for a particular client group, such as the mentally ill, may welcome pressure from organisations like MIND, as it may strengthen their hand in the competition for resources within the DHSS. On other issues where there may be a difference of view between pressure groups, ministers and civil servants may seek to bolster their own position by stimulating group activities. *The Castle Diaries* show that this was done in the 1974–79 Labour government, when trade union opposition to pay beds was stimulated by ministers as part of the policy of persuading the medical profession to accept limitations on private practice within the NHS. It is important to remember, then, that demands may not always arise autonomously in the community, and that pressure may sometimes be welcomed and encouraged by policy-makers.

Pressure groups make demands on a wide range of issues. These demands may require a change in legislation, a decision by a civil servant, or intervention by ministers. Occasionally, they may involve the Prime Minister, the Cabinet and other government departments. The effectiveness of groups in pressing their demands will depend on a variety of factors: the information they possess, their contacts with policy-makers, their expertise, and the sanctions they have at their disposal. In responding to groups, policy-makers will weigh their own preferences against those of the groups. They will also be alert to the need to secure the compliance of key interests, and to the electoral consequences of their decisions. The exact process of decision-making is difficult to define because, as Solesbury notes, it is at this stage that 'one passes into the relatively closed world of the executive departments of state, and to a lesser extent interdepartmental and Cabinet committees, where the consideration given to issues and possible responses by politicians and officials is largely shielded from the public gaze' (Solesbury, 1976, p. 392).

Despite the difficulties of penetrating the intricacies of decision-making within central government, it can be suggested that the national health policy community is itself fragmented into a series of sub-communities concerned with specific aspects of policy.

These sub-communities are organised around issues such as alcoholism, abortion, policies for elderly people, and so on. As we noted earlier in the chapter, different parts of the DHSS have different characteristics, and in one sense the Department itself can be seen to be made up of pressure groups for particular functions, services and client groups. Outside pressure groups are drawn towards those parts of the Department which have responsibility for the policies which the groups are interested in, and sub-communities are formed from the relationships which develop between these groups and civil servants. In an attempt to analyse these relationships, one study of DHSS policies for elderly people suggested that these policies were worked out in an 'iron triangle' rather than an 'issue network' (Haywood and Hunter, 1982). The terminology is that of Heclo, who has argued, in the context of American federal government, that decision-making has moved away from iron triangles involving a small number of participants in a stable relationship with one another, to issue networks comprising a large number of participants in a less stable relationship (Heclo, 1978). In their examination of policies for elderly people, Haywood and Hunter found that the process was well represented by the iron triangle image. The key participants were DHSS officials, leading medical and nursing professionals, and two key producer groups: the Royal College of Nursing and the British Geriatrics Society. Although the consultative process was later widened to encompass a range of other groups, the crucial decisions at an early stage were arrived at by this small set of interests. However, Haywood and Hunter warn that on other issues, such as pay beds and health service organisation, issue networks may be a more appropriate metaphor. Clearly, further work must be done before the processes occurring in health policy sub-communities can be accurately described.

Parliament and the mass media

Not all the demands made by pressure groups will invoke action, and groups which are unsuccessful in their attempt to influence civil servants and ministers will often turn their attention to Parliament and the mass media. Here, then, are two further sources of inputs into the health policy-making system, and not just as vehicles for pressure group demands, but as originators of demands themselves. In recent years the mass media have played an active role in publicising the low standards of care that exist in the 'Cinderella' services. Ever since the appearance of newspaper reports of cruelty to patients in the mid 1960s, the media have been prominent in the campaign to improve conditions for groups such as the mentally ill and handicapped. Television programmes on Rampton Special Hospital and on hospital services for the mentally handicapped have maintained public attention on this area of the NHS to the extent that journalists and television producers have taken on the appearance of pressure groups for under-privileged sections of the community.

The role of Parliament was discussed in Chapter 3. It will be recalled that parliamentary inputs to health policy-making take the form of MPs' questions, issues raised during debates, private members' bills, and reports from select committees. The significance of these mechanisms is that they are important centralising influences in the NHS. The accountability to Parliament of the Secretary of State for Social Services requires a considerable amount of detailed information about health services to be fed up to the DHSS by health authorities. Equally, demands raised in Parliament may have an influence on health policy-making and on the local operation of health services. An obvious example would be legislation resulting from a private member's bill, such as the Abortion Act. On other occasions, government-sponsored legislation may be amended in the course of its passage through Parliament. The section of the NHS Reorganisation Act 1973 relating to Community Health Councils was a case in point. Not having strong views of its own, the government was prepared to listen to and take account of suggestions made by MPs and peers.

Increasingly, too, the House of Commons Social Services Committee and the Public Accounts Committee are providing an informed contribution to the policy-making process. As we noted in Chapter 3, the Social Services Committee, under the chairmanship of Renee Short, has produced a variety of reports on health service issues. There are currently eleven MPs on the Committee, and support is provided by a small group of full-time staff and specialist advisers appointed for particular inquiries. Select committees tend to have greatest impact when they present unanimous reports and in this respect the choice of topics for investigation is important. In its work, the Social Services Committee has chosen to examine issues which in the main are non-controversial in party political terms and this has helped the Committee to present a united front. For example, in investigating the DHSS's expenditure plans every year the Committee focuses more on the procedures involved in planning and monitoring expenditure than on the amount of money allocated to the services covered by the Department. The Committee's reports in this field have provided a continuing critique of DHSS thinking and it has been argued that 'their cumulative effect has been to make the Department improve its own procedures for reviewing and co-ordinating its policies, as well as preparing and presenting expenditure plans' (Nixon and Nixon, 1983, p. 352). In carrying out its work, the Committee receives written and oral evidence, and the staff of the Committee liaise closely with officials in the DHSS. Reports are usually drafted by the Committee Clerk, although in the case of the public expenditure enquiries this is the task of the specialist adviser. The role of the Committee, in the words of one adviser, 'is to change the climate in which policy is made and to monitor it. This is not to assume rationality but to take rationality on board in a process which is essentially political' (ibid, p. 353). Since its inception in 1979, the Committee can claim to have brought about a number of changes, directly in the case of the establishment of the Maternity Services Advisory Committee, set up after the investigation into perinatal and neonatal mortality, and less tangibly in the approach to policy-making adopted within the DHSS.

The Public Accounts Committee scrutinises government spending as a whole and in recent years has examined a number of different aspects of the NHS, including the use of joint finance, the disposal of surplus land and buildings, the profits of the drug industry, and financial control and accountability. A report published in 1981 which criticised the lack of control exercised by the DHSS over the management of the NHS was one of the factors which led to the introduction of accountability reviews in the NHS in 1982. Nairne has referred to the Public Accounts Committee as 'the premier committee of Parliament' (Nairne, 1983, p. 254) and has described the pressures placed by the Committee on the Permanent Secretary in his capacity as Accounting Officer. Certainly, ministers and civil servants have faced some rigorous questioning from the MPs on the Committee and the Committee has had a demonstrable impact on such issues as premature retirement among NHS staff and manpower control within the Service. A study of Parliament and health policy in the period 1970-5 noted, 'it is very difficult on the gathered evidence to sustain the argument that Parliament had any real influence upon health policy-making in the reviewed period' (Ingle and Tether, 1981, p. 148). The work of the Public Accounts Committee and the Social Services Committee requires this judgement to be modified as quite clearly these Committees have exerted influence in recent years.

Health authorities

Health authorities represent a fourth source of inputs into the DHSS policy-making system. Indeed, as we shall discuss in Chapter 5, health authorities do not simply carry out nationally determined policies, but have important policy-making responsibilities themselves. The NHS Planning System, introduced in 1976, was an attempt to develop an iterative planning process between the DHSS and health authorities. The System was based on national guidelines and local plans, with the content of plans influencing the shape of future guidelines. In a related area, the performance indicators published by DHSS in 1983 were developed initially by staff from the Department and the Northern RHA. To carry the initiative forward, a joint NHS/DHSS Group was set up to advise on the future development, publication and use of performance indicators. In addition, an administrator from a district health authority was seconded to the DHSS to oversee the initiative. There are many other examples of policy proposals developed jointly by the centre and the periphery. The DHSS is dependent on health authorities for information about the local development of services and for actually providing the services, while health authorities are dependent on the DHSS for the resources required to carry out their functions. This mutual dependence helps to explain why it is that national policies are often shaped and influenced by field authorities.

The consultative machinery

A fifth input to policy-making comes from the consultative machinery attached to the DHSS. Earlier in this chapter we distinguished between standing advisory groups such as the Health Advisory Service and *ad hoc* enquiries like the Royal Commission on the National Health Service. These and other bodies provide an almost continuous flow of demands into the DHSS. As with other issues in the political system, demands coming from these sources have to compete for the time and attention of policy-makers. Some may be rejected out of hand, others may be subjected to further discussions, while others may be adopted immediately. It is not unusual for the DHSS response to advisory bodies to be ambiguous or unclear. This applied to the Court Report on Child Health Services, where the DHSS accepted the report's demand for an integrated child health service, but rejected many of the more specific proposals put forward. Similarly, the government agreed in principle with the model of care for the mentally handicapped set out in the Report of the Jay Committee but called for further consideration of various aspects of the report. In this case, the opposition of powerful, established interests in the nursing profession to the Jay Committee's recommendations was one of the factors the DHSS had to consider.

As well as advice provided by standing or *ad hoc* groups such as the Jay Committee, there are the regular rounds of formal consultation with health authorities and pressure groups which have already been referred to. Formal consultation typically occurs when a consultative document on a particular issue is published. Recent examples of consultative documents have included a review of hospitals policy, a statement on moving patients and resources from hospitals into the community, and proposals for the future of family practitioner committees (FPCs). The extent to which these documents are really open to influence varies: in many cases there may be little scope for groups to influence what is decided, but on some occasions a well organised group can have a significant impact. An example was the success of the BMA in achieving autonomy for FPCs. Whether groups are able to exercise influence may depend on the stage during the consultative process that they become involved. Haywood and Hunter (1982) point out that formal consultation is often preceded by informal consultation on draft documents. In some cases informal consultation may itself be foreshadowed by discussions among a small number of key participants, as in the iron triangle which develops policies for elderly people. As a rule of thumb, the earlier a group becomes involved, the more likely it is to influence what is decided.

Ministers and civil servants

Sixth, and most important, there are 'withinputs': demands which come from ministers and civil servants within the DHSS. A new Secretary of State for Social Services is likely to have a number of issues he or she wants to pursue while in office. Many will have developed in Opposition, and may have been included in an election manifesto. Banting (1979) has suggested that politicians are particularly important in making certain issues salient, and in defining the agenda for discussion. There is plenty of evidence of this in relation to health policy. The issue of private health care is a good example. For many years this was not a salient issue. Only in 1974, when Barbara Castle attempted to reduce the number of pay beds in NHS hospitals and limit the growth of private hospitals, did the issue become prominent. Private medicine remained a salient issue when the Conservative government elected in 1979 reversed Castle's policy, and sought to encourage the growth of the private health care sector.

What is interesting about this issue, apart from the role of ministers in getting it on to the agenda, is that private medicine is one of the few aspects of health policy where there have been abrupt changes in direction. Such sudden shifts in policy are comparatively rare, partly because there are many areas in which the main political parties agree on what should be done. A further reason, of course, is the continuity provided by civil servants who, both individually and collectively, will have their own views on what policies should be pursued. A strong minister with a manifesto commitment behind him is in a powerful position, but the need to operate with and through civil servants limits a minister's power. Civil servants know that they have to continue administering the health policy-making system long after ministers have moved on, and this inclines them towards a conservative position in which they are reluctant to antagonise key interest groups. In her diaries, Barbara Castle notes that the Permanent Secretary at the DHSS, Sir Philip Rogers, was 'deeply conventional, instinctively out of line with the far-reaching reforms we want to make' (Castle, 1980, p. 52). A later diary entry records the development of the Labour government's policy of phasing out pay beds from NHS hospitals. On this issue, Rogers had submitted a paper stating that DHSS officials 'feel they would be failing in their duty if they did not let me know how opposed they all were to the phasing of private practice out of NHS hospitals' (Castle, 1980, p. 170). Of course, civil servants are not a homogeneous group, and Castle herself notes that 'the department is split into two different worlds: the conventional, change-nothing world of the top Establishment; the challenging irreverent world of the press office and some of the younger officials' (Castle, 1980, p. 209). And even where conservatism does exist, it may result more from the need to operate in an administrative system in which long-term viewpoints are important than from the personal attributes of individuals. The point remains, though, that ministerial aspirations are likely to be modified by civil service advice.

Of particular interest in this context is the role of doctors in government. As we noted at the beginning of the chapter, there is strong medical involvement in decision-making in the DHSS, and a former Chief Medical Officer, Sir George Godber, has observed that 'the doctor in Government has to be facing two ways: he is a Civil Servant and his Minister must be able to rely on his complete loyalty; but he is also a member of his profession, which must be able to trust him too' (Godber, 1981, p. 2). These dual loyalties create the possibility that conflicts may arise in which professional ties will emerge the stronger. Godber notes that such a possibility arose during Crossman's tenure as Secretary of State for Social Services but did not reach the point where the Chief Medical Officer would have resigned. On another occasion Godber states that 'The Permanent Secretary and I once declined to accept our Civil Service increases so long as the doctors' incomes were frozen' (Godber, 1981, p. 3).

Clearly, then, civil servants have their own loyalties and views, and these views have an influence on policy-making. Further evidence of this point comes from Pater's study of the creation of the NHS. Pater argues that the credit for the establishment of the NHS should be widely shared, but he contends

There is no doubt, however, that the main credit for the emergence of a viable and, indeed, successful service must rest with two ... officers of the ministry: Sir William Jameson, chief medical officer from 1940 to 1950, and Sir John Hawton, deputy secretary from 1947 to 1951 and permanent secretary thereafter until his retirement through ill-health in 1960. (Pater, 1981, p. 178)

In different ways both Godber and Pater, writing as former civil servants, confirm the thesis to be found in the memoirs of ex-ministers, that the civil service has a significant impact on the development of policy.

This need not mean that civil servants pursue their own policy preferences against the wishes of ministers. Nairne acknowledges that civil servants are influential, but maintains that the influence of officials derives from a partnership between ministers and civil servants rather than conflict. In Nairne's view, it is misleading to analyse what happens within government departments in terms of whether ministers or civil servants have power because the reality is that senior civil servants have to share responsibility with ministers for formulating policy (Nairne, 1983; Young and Sloman, 1982). One of the implications of partnership is that there will be occasions when civil servants themselves put forward initiatives to ministers. These initiatives will in many cases stem from a review of existing policies and will take the form of suggestions for improving those policies. The Crossman diaries provide an example, this time in relation to resource allocation. On 15 July 1969 Crossman records:

after lunch I had a fascinating seminar on hospital revenue. Dick Bourton (who was then Under Secretary for Finance and Accountant General at the DHSS) has put up an absolutely first rate paper on how the hospital budgets are fixed. A terrific lot of money goes into the teaching hospitals, most of which are in the South and this shifts the balance even more in favour of the London hospitals, with great unfairness to Sheffield, Newcastle and Birmingham, which are really greatly under-financed. The trouble is that the historical costs are gigantic, with about 85 per cent already committed, and I should be very surprised if we can get even 5 per cent reallocated in any one year, especially a year of appalling constrictions such as this. Nevertheless, it was a really good discussion. (Crossman, 1977, p. 569)

Subsequent work within the DHSS led to the introduction of a new resource allocation formula in 1971–2 intended to even up the distribution of funds between areas. This was followed in 1975 by the appointment of an *ad hoc* advisory committee, the Resource Allocation Working Party (RAWP). The Working Party's report provided the basis for improvements to the formula which were incorporated for the first time in 1977–8. The 1975 RAWP initiative was in large part due to the influence of Dr David Owen, Minister of State for Health between 1974 and 1976. In this case, then, the primary source of policy change was within the DHSS, although the work of a number of outside researchers may also have had an impact.

Another example of a policy where internal factors were important is the Hospital Plan of 1962. This was prepared by hospital boards and committees under the guidance of the Ministry of Health. Although outside interests were pressing for increased spending on hospital buildings, the origins of the Plan owed a great deal to the Minister of Health at the time, Enoch Powell, his Permanent Secretary, Sir Bruce Fraser, and the Deputy Chief Medical Officer, Sir George Godber. These three men effectively transformed a vague idea about the need for an expanded building programme into a detailed plan. The coincidence of interest between the minister and senior civil servants helped to account for the promotion of this development in policy. What is also relevant is that here was a policy which had to be agreed between the Ministry of Health and the Treasury because of the major expenditure implications. Fraser, who had previously been a Treasury official, played a key role in these negotiations (Allen, 1979).

A third example of the influence of civil servants over policy-making is provided by Rudolf Klein (1983) in his analysis of the establishment of the NHS. Drawing on official records, Klein demonstrates how in 1939 civil servants identified the main options available for the future organisation of hospital services unprompted by politicians. Although ministers later played a significant role in the creation of the NHS, in the initial stages it was civil servants who were most influential.

An examination of the processes of policy-making and the various inputs into those processes creates, rightly, the impression of a complex policy system in which those responsible for making policy are subject to numerous competing demands. In the last part of the discussion we have drawn attention to examples of policy change, but it is worth remembering the earlier point that change is the exception rather than the rule. A considerable part of the activity of the DHSS is devoted to the maintenance of existing policies and to the continuation of established routines. Although change is possible, it is difficult to achieve because of the operation of demand regulation mechanisms which limit the number of issues on the agenda at any one time. And even in relation to these issues, incremental changes to the *status quo* are more probable than major shifts in direction. This has been clearly demonstrated in a study of government policy on smoking, where it has been argued that decisions were:

> the outcome of a process in which groups have played a major role ... For many years tobacco interests had no difficulty in keeping the subject off the political agenda; their power took a non decision making form. Forerunners of ASH, such as the National Society of Non-Smokers, encountered indifferent or hostile attitudes from Government ... It took the prestige and evidence of elite medical groups, such as the BMA and the RCP, to break the agenda barrier. Even then Government response was cautious because possible adverse electoral consequences were feared by some Ministers if too rigorous a policy of discouragement was pursued. (Popham, 1981, p. 345)

Industrial and commercial interests

The example of smoking draws attention to the role of industrial and commercial interests in the health policy community. At least three sets of interests need to be considered. First, there are those interests which are involved in the provision of private sector health care services. Private providers include both the provident associations such as BUPA and Private Patients Plan and the private hospital groups. Whilst the growth of the private sector has been well documented (see for example McLachlan and Maynard, 1982) little is known about how private providers attempt to exercise influence over policy-makers. Clearly, the private sector has a direct interest in the health policies pursued by government, and more work is needed to examine the channels of influence through which private interests operate.

A second set of interests consists of those companies supplying goods, equipment and services to the NHS. These include firms seeking to obtain contracts for the provision of services such as catering and laundry; the manufacturers of medical equipment and supplies; and the drugs industry. The last of these is particularly significant in view of the fact that the drugs bill, amounting to £1,390 million in 1982, makes up almost 10 per cent of total NHS expenditure (Office of Health Economics, 1984). Multinational companies dominate the drugs industry. While the industry contributes 70,000 jobs and an estimated £600 million per annum in net exports there has been concern at the level of profits earned. Regulation occurs through the Pharmaceutical Price Regulation Scheme, a voluntary scheme in which the DHSS attempts to control prices and profits in the industry. Despite this, the House of Commons Public Accounts Committee has criticised the DHSS for not doing more to limit profits, and in response to the Committee's criticism action was taken in 1983 to introduce tighter controls.

A third set of interests is represented by companies producing goods which may be harmful to health. The tobacco, alcohol and food-processing industries are included in this category. The influence of the food industry has been examined by Cannon (1984) in an analysis of the response to a report on nutritional guidelines for health produced by the National Advisory Committee on Nutrition Education. The report, which recommended reduced consumption of sugar, salt and fat, and increased intake of dietary fibre, was opposed by the food industry and publication was delayed because of objections from the industry. Cannon demonstrates how government is divided between ministers principally concerned with issues of public health and ministers concerned with economic and employment issues. Changes in eating habits which pose a threat to jobs and profits in the food industry are likely to be resisted not only by the industry but also by politicians and civil servants involved in spheres such as trade, industry and agriculture.

Similar issues arise in the case of tobacco. In a careful and stimulating analysis, Taylor (1984) has investigated why governments have done so little to regulate the tobacco industry in the face of overwhelming medical evidence about the harmful effects of cigarette smoking. As Taylor points out, the tobacco industry is composed of a relatively small number of large and wealthy multinational companies whose power derives not so much from their activity as pressure groups – although this may be important – as from their position in the economy. The industry is significant as an employer and as a source of tax revenues, and while DHSS ministers may want to control the industry on health grounds, ministers in the Treasury are inclined to oppose regulations on economic grounds. As Taylor comments:

> In principle, as guardians of the public health, governments ought to be the tobacco industry's fierce opponents, but in practice they are often its firm ally. Cigarettes provide governments with one of their biggest and most reliable sources of revenue: they create tens of thousands of jobs in hard economic times; they present a healthy surplus on the balance of payments; they help development in Third World Countries where tobacco is grown. In purely economic terms, the political benefits of cigarettes far outweigh their social cost. (Taylor, 1984, p. xix)

For this reason, the introduction of health warnings and changes in advertising practices have been brought about on a voluntary basis, and health ministers who have sought changes through legislation have either been defeated or moved on. The examples of food and tobacco lend support to Lindblom's (1977) thesis about the power of business corporations in contemporary politics, and it is this power which helps to account for the predominance of policy maintenance and incremental changes.

The role of ideas

The policy process is not, however, entirely a matter of responding to political demands. An increasingly important part of the process is the attempt to examine a wider range of options, and to subject existing policies to a more thorough analysis. There are two aspects to this. First, there is the contribution which academics and researchers make to policy-making. As Banting (1979) points out, policy-making is both an intellectual activity and a political process. Thus, as well as examining the impact of pressure groups, politicians and other key actors, it is necessary to look at the role of ideas and information in shaping policy. One of the areas of health policy where ideas have had an influence is the organisation of the NHS. The administrative structure introduced in 1974, for example, derived from theories of management and organisational behaviour developed by organisational sociologists at Brunel University and management consultants at McKinsey.

A second area where ideas had an impact was in the thinking behind the Black Report on inequalities and health. The Report was the outcome of the deliberations of an expert working group whose most influential member was Peter Townsend, Professor of Sociology at Essex University. Townsend's previous work on the nature and causes of poverty and deprivation clearly contributed much to the analysis and recommendations of the Black Report. What is interesting is that Townsend's work is very much in the LSE social administration tradition which Banting found had had a strong influence in other areas of social policy (Banting, 1979). It is apparent, though, that this tradition, of which Brian Abel-Smith, a political adviser to a number of Secretaries of State for Social Services, is also a part, has had a greater impact on Labour governments than Conservative governments. The rejection of the Black Report by a Conservative government is evidence of this.

Academics and researchers apart, there have been a number of attempts within the DHSS to develop a more 'rational' approach to policy-making. In varying degrees, these mechanisms have sought to introduce a greater measure of analysis into the policy process, and in the final part of this chapter we review the recent experience of policy analysis in the DHSS.

Policy analysis in the DHSS

In 1970 the Conservative government published a White Paper setting out proposals for increasing the policy analysis capabilities of central government. Among the innovations to follow from the

White Paper were the Central Policy Review Staff, established to provide advice on government policies independent of that offered by existing departments, and Programme Analysis and Review, involving an in-depth study of specific topics within departments. Both innovations affected central government as a whole. At around the same time, and reflecting the spirit of the White Paper, a number of specific developments were taking place in the DHSS designed to improve the Department's capacity for reviewing its policies and priorities. Two developments in particular merit consideration: the introduction of programme budgeting, and the creation of a planning system for the Department.

Programme budgeting was developed in the United States in the 1960s, and its use was first considered within the DHSS in 1971. The aim of programme budgeting is to provide a framework for linking policies with resources, thus enabling priority decisions to be made within an overall strategy. The programme budget originally developed within the DHSS covered both health and personal social services and grouped these services under seven main headings: primary care; general and acute hospital and maternity services; services mainly for the elderly and the physically handicapped; services for the mentally handicapped; services for the mentally ill; services mainly for children; and other services, for example social work. Expenditure on each of these services can be compared through the programme budget, enabling a comprehensive analysis to be undertaken. As well as allowing policy-makers to examine the costs of their policies and giving them a more sophisticated means of reaching decisions on service development, the programme budget helps to communicate DHSS priorities to health authorities and outside interests. Much of the work behind the programme budget contributed to the consultative document on *Priorities* issued in 1976, which contained the first published information about the methods used.

In the words of one of those involved in developing the approach within the DHSS, the programme budget is 'a tool of systematic planning', with the alternative being 'piecemeal planning and unplanned drift' (Banks, 1979, p. 170). Put another way, it is an attempt to counter the incremental mode of policy-making which we argued earlier is dominant within the DHSS. This does not mean that values are excluded from the system. Rather, it is claimed that programme budgeting assists policy-making by making explicit the values on the basis of which judgements are made.

Alongside the programme budget was developed the DHSS planning system. This was started on an experimental basis in 1973 following the reorganisation of the Department referred to earlier in the chapter. The intentions behind the system were to link policy development with resource availability, to provide the Department with information on objectives which could be used in the PESC negotiations (see Chapter 3) and to form the basis of national guidance to health authorities and local authorities. The system was based on planning statements prepared by branches within the DHSS which were then grouped under a number of main headings such as primary care, the mentally handicapped, children, and manpower. A central planning unit within the DHSS prepared a consolidated document on the basis of these grouped statements. This document was submitted to the Planning Committee, located in the Top of the Office and chaired by a Deputy Secretary, which advised ministers on overall strategy. The results of the planning system eventually found their way into the consultative document on *Priorities*, providing guidance to field authorities on the local development of services (Razell, 1980).

In subsequent years the DHSS planning system benefited from the outputs of the NHS Planning System. Health authorities produced their first plans in 1976, and the regional strategic plans submitted to the DHSS in 1977 indicated the extent to which national guidelines were being followed at the local level and pointed to areas where implementation was proving problematic. The DHSS planning system was able to take account of the information provided in regional strategic plans and this was reflected in subsequent national guideline documents. As we noted in Chapter 2, one of the results was that guidelines were expressed more generally, with less emphasis being placed on quantified targets. Also, health authorities were encouraged to interpret national guidelines in the light of local conditions. In practice, the discretion given to health authorities, and the lack of an effective mechanism for analysing strategic plans and controlling NHS performance within the DHSS, meant that designated priority services did not always receive the increased share of resources intended. Table 4.1, which sets out trends in expenditure in programme budget terms, shows that mental illness and

TABLE 4.1 *Health and personal social services in England: current and capital expenditure programme shares* (%)

	1975–6	1981–2
Primary care	18.3	19.7
General hospital and maternity	40.5	38.1
Elderly and younger disabled	14.1	15.1
Mental handicap	4.4	4.4
Mental illness	7.6	7.5
Children	5.3	5.7
Other	9.9	9.5
Total	100.0*	100.0

* Discrepancies due to rounding

mental handicap services continue to be allocated a low proportion of the overall budget.

Within central government as a whole, the spirit of the 1970 White Paper gave way to a particular concern to increase management efficiency and cut down on bureaucracy after the election of a Conservative Government in 1979. Programme Analysis and Review and the Central Policy Review Staff were terminated, to be replaced by Rayner Scrutinies, reductions in manpower, and an initiative on financial management (Cmnd 9058, 1983). In the DHSS, the planning system was wound down – a victim, like its NHS counterpart, of exaggerated expectations. The programme budget, split into separate programmes for hospital and community health services and personal social services, continued to be used, but more as a tool for monitoring past trends in expenditure than as a mechanism for projecting future growth rates. Not surprisingly the latter became less important in a period of limited growth. Consistent with the spirit of the times, the number of civil servants in the Department was reduced by 20 per cent between 1979 and 1984 (Social Services Committee, 1984a, p. 163) and Nairne has described how the Rayner regime and the drive for efficiency and effectiveness in the civil service forced the pace of Departmental management. The impact of this drive was felt in the NHS in the introduction of accountability reviews, the development of performance indicators, and the experiment with a management advisory service (see Chapters 5 and 6). Reflecting on the change in approach, James has argued 'If currently the emphasis is on tackling specific topics and on efficiency rather than grand strategy, this may well prove to be a necessary adjustment to balance earlier concentration on broader objectives' (James, 1983, p. 60).

Yet alongside the emphasis on efficiency, there was a continuing concern to improve the Department's capacity for strategic policy-making. An important influence in this respect was the House of Commons Social Services Committee whose reports on the public expenditure programmes covered by the DHSS stimulated ministers and civil servants to review the effectiveness of the Department's policy-making procedures. The Committee's first report in this field, published in July 1980, could hardly have been more critical. The Committee commented:

On the basis of the evidence we have heard, we are struck by the apparent lack of strategic policy-making at the DHSS: the failure to examine the overall impact of changes in expenditure levels and changes in the social environment across the various services and programmes for which the Department is responsible. We were not able to elicit any specific information about what assumptions the Department is making about the likely effects on the NHS of the planned cut-back in the personal social services. Neither does the Department appear to know what the likely impact of rising unemployment will be on the NHS or the personal social services, despite the availability of at least one relevant study ... the Committee wishes to record its disappointment – and dismay – at the continuing failure of the DHSS to adopt a coherent policy strategy across the administrative boundaries of individual services and programmes. We do not underestimate the difficulty of this task and acknowledge that a considerable investment of effort, and perhaps research, will be needed. We recommend that the DHSS should give high priority to developing its capacity for devising coherent policy strategies for all the areas for which the Secretary of State is responsible. (Social Services Committee, 1980, p. viii)

The Department's reply was robust. After pointing out that 'In a number of cases (for instance on policy analysis and research, monitoring and the information base) the Committee appear to have expressed views on matters on which (perhaps because of shortage of time) they sought little or no detailed evidence' (DHSS, 1980f, p. 1), the Department gave details of a number of committees and groups which existed to undertake strategic policy analysis. These included the Health and Personal Social Services Strategy Committee, chaired by the Permanent Secretary and meeting quarterly to review overall policy developments; and the Cross Sector Policy Review Group, established in 1979 to look at issues of cross sector policy and wider social policy. The DHSS added in its reply that ministers were considering how to strengthen arrangements for policy-thinking across administrative boundaries.

By the time of the Social Services Committee's second investigation into public expenditure in 1981, the Department was able to point to the Policy Strategy Unit, set up to replace the Policy and Planning Unit, as a further example of a group concerned with policy in the round. Working under the leadership of an Assistant Secretary, the Policy Strategy Unit prepared periodic reviews of policy initiatives, identified gaps in policy development, and carried out specific studies usually of a short-term nature. Issues examined by the Unit included ophthalmic services, prescription charges, strategy for the elderly, unemployment and health and the role of voluntary bodies in the field of alcohol misuse (Social Services Committee, 1981, p. 15). In some ways, the Policy Strategy Unit was similar to the Central Policy Review Staff, except that it worked only within the DHSS. Like the CPRS, the Unit had to overcome resistance from entrenched interests and seek to maintain support for its work after its original sponsors had moved on. In practice, the Unit was forced into ever more short-term work, in particular in support of ministers. In the end, the Unit met the same fate as the CPRS, being superseded in 1984. One of those closely involved in this area of work has argued that the Unit's 'co-ordinating role has proved the most durable element, and ... its policy analyses have had only limited impact' (James, 1983, p. 60).

Here, then, are some examples of groups within the DHSS attempting to improve the Department's policy analysis capability.

While we have focused on particular units and committees established specifically to contribute to strategic policy-making, it is useful to bear in mind the point made by Birch (1983), himself a senior official within the DHSS, to the effect that civil servants in the course of their day-to-day work are engaged continously in policy analysis activities. The absence of special policy-planning units should not therefore be taken to indicate that policy analysis is not undertaken. Yet the particular significance of innovations like the programme budget and the Policy Strategy Unit lies in their attempt to bring greater coherence to the Department's work, to enhance the basis on which policy choices are made, and to provide a counter balance to the clamour of political interests. To use a phrase from a slightly different context, these developments seek to challenge the system of 'planning by decibels' (DHSS, 1975b). In practice, of course, political factors cannot be discounted, and the machinery we have described will not necessarily overturn the incremental bargaining processes which are so much in evidence. What it may do, however, is challenge the conservatism inherent in incrementalism, and provide a wider basis for decisions than would otherwise be available.

5
Implementing Health Policy

Considerable attention has been given to issues of policy implementation in recent years. In particular, concern has focused on
the apparent failure to carry out centrally determined policies at
the local level. An example in the health service has been the
difficulty in establishing secure units in each region for groups of
patients who cannot be treated in ordinary psychiatric hospitals.
For many years it has been DHSS policy to set up these units, and
the Department has set aside funds to enable the units to be built.
Yet for a variety of reasons, including public and professional
opposition to the designation of special, secure accommodation,
progress in providing this type of service has been slow. As a
result, pressure groups and parliamentary interests concerned with
psychiatric services have criticised the DHSS and health authorities for failing to implement the policy.

This example leads us back to the definition of policy suggested
in Chapter 3. There we argued that policy involves actions as well
as decisions. Statements by central government are only one part
of the policy process, albeit an important part. It is also necessary
to consider the actions and inactions which follow from central
government decisions. In the health service, actions by health
authorities may be just as crucial in determining patterns of service
provision as pronouncements emanating from the DHSS. An
adequate account of health policy therefore needs to focus on the
means by which national decisions are translated into local action.
Consequently, we will begin our analysis of health policy implementation by examining the administration of the NHS.

The administration of the NHS

The Secretary of State for Social Services has overall responsibility
for health services, and he or she is also responsible for personal

social services and for social security. Different arrangements exist for the administration of these three services outside Whitehall, even though they all come under the umbrella of the DHSS, and it is interesting to compare these arrangements. Social security is essentially a national service provided through regional and local offices of the DHSS. The aim of social security policy is to provide uniform benefits in all parts of the country, and this requires a hierarchical system of administration in which the scope for local variation is reduced as far as possible. Local managers are responsible to regional controllers, who in turn are accountable to DHSS headquarters. The chain of command and accountability is intended to ensure consistency at the local level with central government intentions.

There is a rather different situation in the administration of personal social services, which come under the control of local authorities. The relevant authorities are county councils in shire areas and district and borough councils in metropolitan areas. These authorities have considerable autonomy from central government. Local elections give local authorities an independent power base, while the existence of rates as a source of revenue provides the means by which authorities can determine spending levels. In practice, central government involvement in local affairs has increased in recent years, but local authorities retain considerable freedom to decide on the quality and quantity of services to be provided in their areas. For example, in 1980–81, expenditure on personal social services was 5 per cent above the 1978–79 level in real terms, even though central government recommended a reduction in spending of 6 per cent (DHSS, 1980f). As would be expected, local autonomy also means local variation, and there are wide differences in spending levels and types of services provided.

The administration of health services is different from both social security and personal social services. The Secretary of State discharges his or her responsibility for providing health services through field authorities who are his or her agents. Regional Health Authorities (RHAs) and District Health Authorities (DHAs) administer services at the local level, but these authorities do not simply carry out the Secretary of State's wishes. Health authorities have important policy-making responsibilities in their own right, and they interpret national policies to suit local circumstances. On the other hand, unlike local authorities they lack the legitimacy derived from elections and have no significant independent sources of revenue. Nevertheless, the administration of health services is closer to the administration of personal social services than to the organisation of social security, and there are similar variations in local patterns of service provision. To explore these issues in more detail, it is necessary to examine the operation of health authorities and their functions and responsibilities.

Regional Health Authorities

The need for a regional tier of administration in the NHS has been recognised ever since the establishment of the Service in 1948. In the first phase of the NHS, Regional Hospital Boards played a crucial role in turning a disparate collection of hospitals into a planned and co-ordinated service. In 1974 their functions were extended and their name changed to Regional Health Authorities. Earlier proposals for reorganising the NHS had omitted a regional tier of administration, but the difficulty of establishing direct relationships between the DHSS and a large number of field authorities called for some kind of regional organisation.

There are fourteen RHAs in England, and each has about twenty members appointed by the Secretary of State. In making appointments, the Secretary of State consults with a variety of interested groups, including professional organisations, local authorities and voluntary organisations. All members are unpaid, apart from the chairman who receives a part-time salary. The chairman plays a key role in the work of the authority and DHSS ministers have placed greater emphasis on the role of regional chairmen in recent years. Chairmen operate in close association with their officers, to the extent that they may appear more like officers than members. Indeed, one study of RHAs likened the authority chairman to a local authority chief executive heading a management team (Elcock, 1978).

Each RHA is served by a regional team of officers (RTO). Until 1984, the RTO comprised the regional administrator, the regional medical officer, regional nursing officer, regional treasurer and regional works officer, working together in a system of consensus management. Following the Griffiths Inquiry into NHS Management, RHAs were asked to identify a general manager to take responsibility for the overall managerial performance of the management team and the people under it. The first regional general managers (RGMs) were appointed in July 1984. Those appointed as regional general managers included a number of regional administrators, a regional medical officer, a regional nursing officer and a regional treasurer. Some RHAs decided not to appoint a general manager from existing members of the RTO but to advertise the post and invite applications from within the NHS and from outside.

The RTO is supported by a range of staff, including medical and nursing administrators, personnel officers, architects, engineers and statisticians. These staff contribute to different aspects of an RHA's work. The functions of RHAs include the direct provision of a few services, for example blood transfusion, the employment of senior medical staff in non-teaching districts, allocating resources to DHAs, and preparing plans and policies for health services within the region. The last of these functions involves receiving and interpreting DHSS guidelines on service provision, issuing regional guidelines to DHAs, and preparing detailed plans for service development. It is at this point that there may be departures from centrally determined policies. RHAs may feel that DHSS guidelines are unsuitable for their areas, and that alternative policies are required. For example, authorities may judge that the DHSS policy of running down the large old mental illness hospitals and replacing them with services based around general hospitals in the community is inappropriate. This in fact was precisely the stance adopted in the Leeds region in the 1960s, when the Regional Hospital Board developed its own strategy for mental illness hospitals (Ham, 1981).

The NHS Planning System is intended to show how far health authorities are following central policies, and plans should explain the reason for any divergence from DHSS guidelines. Of particular significance in this context is the accountability review process, introduced in 1982 as an extension of the Planning System. Accountability reviews enable the DHSS to examine in more detail than hitherto the extent to which RHAs are pursuing central policies. Yet there is no guarantee that the review process and the Planning System will result in compliance with those policies. Indeed, regional plans may result in changes in DHSS thinking, as happened in 1977 when, after receiving the first plans submitted by health authorities, the DHSS amended its guidelines on priorities, noting that expenditure on acute hospital services might rise in the short term, rather than decline as had been envisaged in the original guidelines. It is in these sorts of ways that policies are made as they are implemented, and that implementation feeds back into central policy-making.

District Health Authorities

Similar considerations apply to DHAs and their role in the administration of health services. There are 192 DHAs in England, and they were created in 1982 as a result of the abolition of area health authorities. Before 1982 regions were divided into areas, and approximately two-thirds of these areas were themselves divided into health districts. To simplify arrangements, areas and districts were amalgamated to form DHAs supported by district management teams (DMTs). Each DHA comprises between sixteen and nineteen members, some appointed by the RHA after consultation with interested organisations, and some appointed by local authorities. The chairman is appointed by the Secretary of State and receives a part-time salary. Until 1984, the DMT comprised four appointed officers and two elected medical representatives, operating as a consensus management team. The four appointed officers were the administrator, the medical officer, the treasurer and the nursing officer. The two medical representatives were elected by their colleagues in the district – one was a consultant, the other a general practitioner. Following the Griffiths Inquiry into NHS Management, DHAs were asked to identify a general manager to take responsibility for the overall managerial performance of the management team and the people under it. DHAs were requested to submit their proposals for the appointment of a district general manager (DGM) to the RHA in the second half of 1984 after the identification of regional general managers. It was expected that DGMs would be appointed in the first place from existing members of the DMT, although DHAs were able to seek a general manager either from elsewhere in the NHS or from outside the Service.

The main aim of these changes was to strengthen the management process in the NHS, and in particular to speed up decision-making and ensure that decisions were implemented. The system of consensus management which was introduced in 1974, whereby decisions were based on the agreement of all team members, was replaced by the new general management function. This means that where decision-making by consensus is working well it will continue, but where consensus is not working well the DGM will ensure that action is taken. It is hoped that the appointment of general managers will secure effective and timely management action and will promote value for money for patients and high quality care.

As with RHAs, the DHSS has emphasised that DHAs have considerable freedom in deciding how best to implement the Griffiths proposals within the framework for general management set out in official guidance (DHSS, 1984). The appointment of district general managers is likely to result in other changes in management arrangements at district level, including a review of the composition and functions of DMTs. This could mean that chief officers on DMTs who do not become general managers will take on new responsibilities. It could also lead to variations in the membership of DMTs rather than a standard pattern as has existed since 1974. One suggestion put forward is that teams should comprise a director of finance, a director of personnel, a director of planning, a director of operations and a director of marketing, as well as the district general manager (Evans, 1983). It is intended that general managers for units of management should be appointed after the identification of district general managers. The group of general managers within the DHA, once established, is likely to be the key management team in the new arrangements. One possibility is that existing DMTs will be enhanced through the addition of unit general managers (Dyson, 1984).

The appointment of general managers will lead to a change in the relationship between chief officers at district level. The DGM will perform the main role in the management of services within the district and will have personal and visible responsibility for the planning, implementation and control of the authority's performance. Professional chief officers such as district nursing officers will be accountable to the DHA for the provision and quality of professional advice and accountable to the DGM for the day-to-day performance of their management functions on matters relating to the fulfilment of the general manager's responsibility. The distinction between management accountability and professional accountability is not clear-cut and may lead to difficulties.

The functions of DHAs include the provision of services, ensuring effective collaboration between health services and related local authority services, and preparing plans and policies for their districts. DHAs receive and interpret national and regional guidelines, and prepare strategic plans every five years together with annual programmes of action. In the same way that RHAs may choose to adapt DHSS guidelines to suit local requirements, so too may DHAs adapt DHSS and RHA guidelines to fit in with their own preferences. To reduce the scope for local variation, RHAs maintain contact with DHAs through a variety of formal and informal channels. Within each region, there will be regular meetings between the regional chairman and district chairmen; the regional team of officers may visit each district management team from time to time to discuss the problems and needs of a particular district; and officers from the same discipline, for example finance, will meet to discuss common interests. There are also many informal contacts between authority chairmen, members and officers at regional and district levels. In addition, the NHS Planning System will indicate the extent to which DHAs are pursuing central and regional policies, and district review meetings, introduced in 1982 as part of the accountability review process, provide a particular opportunity for the RHA to assess district policies and priorities.

Extensive as the links are between RHAs and DHAs, there is no certainty that regional policies will be implemented. In practice, district services may not match up with the pattern envisaged by the DHSS and RHAs for various reasons: there may be inherited discrepancies between local services and national and regional guidelines; local policy-makers may wish to move in a different direction from the centre and the region; and there may be difficulties in persuading service providers to accept central and local priorities. The last point is particularly significant. It has been argued that:

> It is unusual for a health authority or its senior officers to be in a position to take a decision on an important matter and to have effective executive control over its implementation. The organisation is diffuse, loyalties centrifugal. To be effective most

important decisions require at least the acquiescence of a large number of individuals or interest groups whose first loyalty is not to the health authority or its senior officers. (Malone-Lee, 1981, p. 1448)

This highlights the fact that there may be an implementation problem within districts, particularly if the DHSS wishes to modify the actions of professional groups. We explore this issue more fully later in the chapter. Here we may note the importance of dissecting the different layers of implementation within the NHS: between the DHSS and RHAs; RHAs and DHAs; and between DHAs and service providers.

Family Practitioner Committees

While DHAs are responsible for hospital and community health services, Family Practitioner Committees (FPCs) administer the contracts of general practitioners, dentists, pharmacists and opticians. FPCs relate to one or more DHAs, and their members are appointed by the Secretary of State. Half the members are professional and half are lay. Eight of the lay members are appointed from nominations received from DHAs and local authorities. The remaining seven members are appointed from among people suggested by other organisations and individuals. Under the Health and Social Security Act 1984, FPCs were given independĕnt status with effect from 1 April 1985. Unlike RHAs and DHAs, FPCs are not management bodies. The reason for this is that family practitioners are independent contractors who contract with the FPC to provide a service to the local population. They are not salaried employees, and as a result FPCs have no managerial authority over family practitioners. The payments which FPCs make to practitioners for the provision of services are funded by the DHSS, and FPCs are accountable to the Department for the use of these funds. As well as paying practitioners, FPCs monitor arrangements for deputising services, investigate complaints, provide advice and guidance to contractors and patients, maintain lists of contractors and deal with applications to join these lists, and approve doctors' surgery premises and arrangements for improving premises.

There has been some concern that establishing FPCs as authorities in their own right will lead to a further separation of family practitioner services from other health services. In response to this concern a joint working party on collaboration between FPCs and DHAs was set up and reported in April 1984. The working party recommended that FPCs should develop their planning role by compiling a Profile and Strategy Statement every five years and an Annual Programme. The working party also suggested that collaboration might be helped through regular contacts between FPC and DHA chairmen and through links between members. The report was welcomed by ministers and detailed guidance on collaboration was expected to be issued at the end of 1984.

The role of the DHSS

It is apparent, then, that a large number of agencies are involved in the administration of health services. The intentions of the DHSS have to be filtered down through RHAs, DHAs and FPCs before they have an impact on service provision, and these bodies do not simply carry out the Department's wishes. As we have suggested, health authorities are the Secretary of State's agents, but the agency role does not involve merely implementing instructions received from above. Health authorities are semi-autonomous bodies who themselves engage in policy-making, and as such exercise a key influence over the implementation of central policies.

Having stressed the point that health authorities are not simply a means of translating central policy into local action, it is important to note that the health service is a national service for which the Secretary of State is accountable to Parliament. The basis of parliamentary accountability lies in the voting by Parliament of funds for the NHS, and the statutory responsibility of the Secretary of State for the way in which these funds are spent. The existence of parliamentary accountability is a centralising influence, and requires that the Secretary of State is kept informed of local developments. As we noted in earlier chapters, MPs are able to ask questions and raise issues in debates about the operation of the NHS, and the Secretary of State is expected to be in a position to respond to these questions. Also, the investigations carried out into the NHS by the Public Accounts Committee and the Social Services Committee require that ministers and civil servants have available relevant facts about the local organisation of health services. Health authorities therefore have to provide the DHSS with detailed information about specific aspects of service provision, as well as routine statistical returns, to enable the Secretary of State to answer MPs' enquiries.

But what exactly is the balance between the centre and the periphery in the administration of health services and the development of health policy? A number of matters are decided centrally by the Secretary of State. These include appointing the chairmen and members of RHAs and the chairmen of DHAs; dealing with a variety of personnel questions, including salaries and conditions of service for staff; and making regulations for payments by patients. Among the most important of the Secretary of State's powers is the ability to control NHS expenditure. The size of the NHS budget is determined in the PESC process as a result of negotiations between civil servants and ministers from the DHSS and the Treasury. Following formal parliamentary approval of the outcome of these negotiations, the DHSS allocates the budget to RHAs with the help of the RAWP formula, and RHAs allocate their funds to DHAs. Thus, overall spending on health services, and the distribution of funds to regions, are centrally determined, and are strictly controlled by cash limits which have statutory force. Of course, the RAWP formula was prepared by a committee which involved health authority personnel as well as DHSS officials, and to this extent central policies were influenced by local preferences. But the pace at which the formula is implemented is decided by the Secretary of State, giving the centre considerable control over finance. In contrast to local government, health authorities do not have access to significant sources of local income, and this limits their freedom of choice.

Yet the extent of central control should not be overemphasised. RHAs themselves decide how to distribute funds to DHAs, and many have adopted their own resource allocation formula instead of using the RAWP approach (Butts *et al.*, 1981). Equally, the DHSS has limited control over the uses to which funds are put, with the exception of its powers to examine and approve major capital building projects, defined as projects costing over £5 million in 1984. The Department does issue regular guidance to health authorities on how the monies they are allocated should be spent, but this guidance is usually of an advisory nature, and authorities are able to interpret it according to local circumstances. For example, in a foreword to a handbook on policies and priorities for health services issued in 1981 and addressed to the chairmen and members of DHAs, the Secretary of State said, 'We want to give you as much freedom as possible to decide how to pursue these policies and priorities in your own localities. Local initiatives, local decisions, and local responsibility are what we want to encourage'. The foreword continued, 'but a national health service must also have regard to *national* policies and priorities, and I must ask you to take account of them, as set out in this handbook, in making your plans and decisions' (DHSS, 1981c). Ambiguous policy messages of this kind clearly leave scope for local deviations from central policies.

There is one instrument available for controlling the use of funds, and that is earmarking money for specific purposes. Earmarking funds for long-stay hospital services was used in the early 1970s as a means of giving greater priority to these services, and it has also been employed, in the case of joint finance, to encourage collaboration between health authorities and local authorities. In 1984 earmarked funds existed for getting mentally handicapped children out of hospital, for drug misuse services, services for mental illness in old age, primary health care in inner cities and helping the community to care. There is, however, no guarantee that health authorities will actually use earmarked funds, as the example of regional secure units cited at the beginning of this chapter illustrates. In any case, the amount of money allocated through earmarking is small in relation to total NHS expenditure, and by far the bulk of the funds distributed to health authorities continues to take the form of global allocations.

DHSS gives guidelines to health authorities on the use of these allocations in a number of forms. First, circulars are issued on a range of topics: health centre policy, joint planning and financing arrangements, fund-raising by health authorities, and private medical practice. The nature of the guidance contained in circulars varies considerably: some sets out procedures which have to be followed, for example in the use of joint financing, where the period of funding and the kinds of schemes that can be supported are laid down by the DHSS; other guidance draws the attention of authorities to relevant reports which they may wish to consider or powers which they may wish to use, as in the circular on fund-raising which pointed to the powers contained in the Health Services Act 1980 enabling health authorities to raise money themselves. Much of the guidance issued by the DHSS is of the second kind, allowing health authorities to take whatever action they consider appropriate. The fact that circulars are usually discussed in draft form with health authorities enables local influence to be brought to bear on central guidance, and in theory increases the likelihood of local compliance. However, research indicates that circulars are of doubtful effectiveness as a means of central control (Ham, 1981). In any case, the flow of circulars from the DHSS to health authorities has been reduced in recent years. On the other hand, there has been a tendency in some fields to tighten up on guidance, as in the case of competitive tendering where health authorities were not simply advised to consider the idea of tendering but were requested to submit a timetable to enable tenders for all services to be submitted by September 1986.

Second, the DHSS publishes White Papers and consultative documents proposing developments in specific areas of service provision. Examples include the consultative document and White Paper on prevention and health; the White Papers on better services for the mentally handicapped and the mentally ill; and the consultative document and White Paper on services for elderly people. This form of guidance is often used to make a major statement of government policy and is intended to reach a wider audience than health circulars. Consultative documents usually prepare the ground for White Papers, and enable field authorities and other interests to influence the more definitive statements incorporated in White Papers. White Papers set out general directions in which government wishes policy to develop, and may represent a departure from previous intentions. For example, the White Paper *Better Services for the Mentally Handicapped* emerged from the review of policies for mentally handicapped people carried out after the Ely Report, and set out a new pattern of care which health authorities and local authorities were asked to implement. It is then up to field agencies to decide how to carry out the policies, and over what time scale.

Third, in recent years the DHSS has issued regular guidance to health authorities on priorities for service development. This process started in 1976 with the consultative document on *Priorities* (DHSS, 1976b) and was followed by publication of *The Way Forward* in 1977 (DHSS, 1977b) and *Care in Action* in 1981 (DHSS, 1981c). Circulars have elaborated on these guidelines. The aim of these documents has been to inform health authorities of DHSS priorities for the development of health and personal social services. Some of the documents have also set out standards of service provision, or norms, which the DHSS wants health authorities to follow. These norms establish target levels of provision, whether in terms of staffing or accommodation, for authorities to aim at. However, planning guidance issued in 1984 informed health authorities that norms and targets with implications for resource utilisation should be regarded as advisory rather than prescriptive.

DHSS guidance on priorities is part of the more general attempt by central government to influence local patterns of service provision through the NHS Planning System, discussed in Chapter 2. There it was noted that the nature of DHSS guidelines changed between 1976 and 1981, moving away from relatively specific, quantitative targets towards broad, qualitative indications of central government's priorities. This move was associated with a greater emphasis being placed on the local interpretation of national guidelines. The introduction of the accountability review process in 1982 signalled a shift back towards greater central involvement in planning. A key point to note, then, is the way that centre–periphery relationships in the NHS change over time (Ham, 1981; Hunter, 1983). Yet even strong central guidance based on national standards of service provision may not result in local conformity with central priorities. The fact that health authorities actually provide service and have day-to-day management and planning responsibilities means that the DHSS has to work through and with these authorities to achieve its goals (Haywood and Alaszewski, 1980).

The NHS Planning System was intended to reveal cases where health authorities were deviating from central guidelines, and until 1984 it was the Regional Group within the DHSS which was responsible for receiving RHAs' plans. Within the Regional Group, the regional liaison (RL) divisions had the task of discussing plans with RHAs. One of the civil servants involved in this process has indicated that when there was a disparity between the plan of a region and national policies, 'the RL division goes back to the authority and says, "look, you've got this completely wrong". But there won't be many of those instances where the problems are sufficiently clear' (Clode, 1977, p. 1315). There may also be discussions between ministers and RHA chairmen. This was indicated by a former Permanent Secretary, Sir Patrick Nairne, in evidence to the Public Accounts Committee. When asked what the DHSS would do about a recalcitrant region, Nairne stated, 'In my experience the Secretary of State has sometimes had to directly approach a regional chairman and say, "I have been looking at your plans and I really do not feel happy that you are making enough progress", for example, "in the direction of the mentally handicapped"' (Public Accounts Committee, 1981, p. 86).

After hearing this evidence, and after considering the range of mechanisms available to the DHSS, the Public Accounts Committee concluded that the Department should be in a position to control more effectively what was happening in the NHS. This view was shared by the Social Services Committee. Both committees argued that the Department should pay more attention to issues such as manpower control, hospital building and variations in costs. Partly in response to the Public Accounts Committee's report, and partly as a result of changes among ministers and senior officials in the DHSS, the accountability review process was established. The review process involves a scrutiny of plans and performance leading to annual regional and district review meetings. Regional reviews are attended by a minister, the regional chairman, civil servants and regional officers. The purpose of the meetings is to review the long-term plans, objectives, efficiency and effectiveness of the region, and to provide a means of holding the RHA to account. Discussion focuses on an agenda of issues drawn up in advance by officials and agreed by the minister taking the review. These issues are drawn from a number of sources including regional strategic plans and ministerial priorities. At the end of the review meeting, an action plan for the region is agreed and is sent by the minister to the chairman. The fact that the reviews take place on an annual basis is important as it enables the DHSS to assess progress made in achieving agreed objectives. Following the regional review, the RHA holds a series of district review meetings with each of its DHAs. These are usually attended by the regional chairman, regional officers, the district chairman and district officers. The procedure is similar to that followed at regional reviews and an action plan is agreed at the end of the meeting. The accountability review process was described by the Griffiths Inquiry into NHS Management as 'a good, recent development which provides a powerful management tool' (Griffiths Report, 1983, p. 12) and in 1984 it was extended to units of management.

The experience of regional reviews in 1982 and 1983 suggests that participation by ministers and chairmen is crucial in giving prominence to the review process and in ensuring that discussions have real meaning. It has been emphasised that review meetings do not involve a cosy chat but are businesslike occasions which provide a clear focus for accountability to be maintained. As the process has developed, arrangements for the meetings have been improved by limiting the number of issues covered and by concentrating attention on progress made in carrying out plans already agreed. At the same time, specific targets and objectives for action have been identified, as have timetables for implementation. The kinds of issues raised in regional reviews are, first, the development of services for the elderly, the mentally ill and the mentally handicapped; second, arrangements for joint planning between health authorities and local authorities; third, the efficiency of services as measured by performance indicators and other mechanisms; fourth, key ministerial interests such as the control of manpower, the disposal of surplus land and competitive tendering; and fifth, the process of management within the region. An analysis by the DHSS of issues raised at district reviews reveals that many of the same issues arise in discussion between RHAs and DHAs (see Table 5.1).

One point to note is that the focus of accountability between the DHSS and RHAs is much sharper than between RHAs and DHAs because DHA chairmen are appointed by the Secretary of State not by the RHA. This may create difficulties for RHAs in holding DHAs to account.

Two general comments can be made about accountability reviews. First, although reviews were introduced as part of the simplified arrangements for NHS Planning announced in 1982 (albeit as something of an afterthought), in practice the Planning System and the review process have tended to develop separately,

TABLE 5.1   *Main issues discussed at first round of district reviews*

Issue	Number of District Review action plans in which it appears as a major issue
Services for mentally ill	165
Services for mentally handicapped	161
Manpower planning	161
Estate management/review of land holdings	156
Services for elderly	123
Planning: financial outlook	115
Performance indicators	126
Collaboration with local authorities/joint planning	46
Community services	45

NOTE: Broad headings only are indicated. Some issues were discussed under more than one heading.
SOURCE: DHSS.

a point nicely illustrated by the fact that different parts of the DHSS were responsible for NHS planning and accountability reviews in the initial stage of the development of the review process. The effect of this separate development is that the timetables for planning and accountability reviews are often not synchronised, leading to duplication and overlap.

Second, it is unclear what sanctions the DHSS will impose on RHAs who consistently fail to fulfil their action plans and to improve their performance. The main sanction available to the Secretary of State is the power to sack or at least not reappoint the chairmen and members of RHAs and the chairmen of DHAs. It seems likely, however, that influence or persuasion rather than formal sanctions will continue to be the main currency in which the DHSS deals with health authorities. Equally, of course, health authorities will continue to use their links with the DHSS to influence the development of health policy within central government. In this context, accountability reviews may result in changes to government policies rather than action to ensure local compliance with those policies, although as the review process has developed there has been a tendency for ministers to use reviews as a mechanism for ensuring the implementation of central priorities.

The final instrument of control, and potentially most significant of all, is the Secretary of State's power of direction. This power enables the Secretary of State to direct health authorities to comply with his wishes in relation to any aspect of their work. Also, the Health Services Act 1980 gave the Secretary of State for Social Services specific powers to direct health authorities to keep expenditure within income. In addition, the Secretary of State is able to suspend health authorities, and to set up inquiries into their work. In practice, these powers are used sparingly. As Brown explains, they are used 'only when a Minister decides to use them – in other words when he feels that the political or administrative need to wield the big stick outweighs the political and administrative cost that will be incurred. The more drastic powers are about as usable in practice as nuclear weapons. None can be used as an instrument of day-to-day control' (Brown, 1979, pp. 10–11). There is some overstatement here, as the suspension of the Lambeth, Southwark and Lewisham AHA in 1979 indicates. The AHA was suspended by the Secretary of State for threatening to overspend its budget, and a team of commissioners was appointed in its place. Although the courts later ruled that the Secretary of State's action was illegal, in that the commissioners were appointed for an unspecified period and the appropriate procedures were not followed, the fact remains that as a last resort these powers do exist. Nevertheless, Brown's underlying point is valid, and the reason why these powers are used so rarely is that only very occasionally do they need to be invoked. While relationships between the DHSS and health authorities have become more strained as resources for growth have dried up, for the most part health authorities do not have to be controlled through legal mechanisms. The DHSS is able to maintain general oversight of the NHS through the other instruments already described, and through bargaining and negotiation rather than legal sanctions.

It is conceivable that this could change if ministers pursued policies that health authorities refused to implement, and during the course of 1984 there were indications that ministers might have to use more than their powers of persuasion to carry out their policy on competitive tendering. Health authorities who demonstrated what ministers interpreted as a lack of commitment to the competitive tendering policy were reminded of the financial as well as legal sanctions at the disposal of the DHSS. It was suggested that authorities who failed to meet the Department's implementation timetable might be penalised through a reduction in their financial allocations. These developments were important in highlighting that ultimately power lay at the centre. They also served to demonstrate that governments pursuing policies significantly different from their predecessors might have to use new policy instruments to ensure implementation of these policies.

The balance of power between the centre and the periphery in the NHS has been viewed in various ways. Enoch Powell, Minister of Health from 1960 to 1963, argued that the centre had almost total control (Powell, 1966). Richard Crossman, Secretary of State from 1968 to 1970, maintained that the centre was weak and the periphery strong (Crossman, 1972); and more recently, Barbara Castle, Secretary of State from 1974 to 1976, likened Regional Health Authorities to 'a fifth wheel on the coach. They neither speak as elected representatives nor do they have the expertise of their own officials. And their attitude to the Secretary of State and the department is necessarily pretty subservient – they want to keep their jobs! (Castle, 1980, p. 315). The subservience noted by Castle was not much in evidence in a report on the working of the DHSS prepared by three Regional Health Authority chairmen in 1976 (Regional Chairmen's Enquiry, 1976). The report resulted from an invitation by the Minister of State for Health, Dr David Owen, to the chairmen to examine the functions of the DHSS and its relationship with RHAs. The report was highly critical of the DHSS, and argued, perhaps not surprisingly, that more powers should be delegated to health authorities. In the chairmen's view too much control, and too many detailed decisions, were vested in the DHSS. These points were echoed in the Griffiths Inquiry into NHS Management. Griffiths argued 'The centre is still too much involved in too many of the wrong things and too little involved in some that really matter' (Griffiths Report, 1983, p. 12). The establishment of the Health Services Supervisory Board and the NHS Management Board in the DHSS were an attempt to meet these criticisms.

One point made in the regional chairmen's enquiry was that there should be a greater interchange of staff between the NHS and the DHSS as a way of improving understanding and communication. In fact, this has happened on an increasing scale in recent years, with a number of civil servants undertaking secondments as district administrators in the NHS, and a number of district administrators being seconded into the Department. The process was taken a stage further in 1984 with the appointment of a principal from the regional liaison division in the DHSS to a post which involved working part-time in the Department and part-time as a deputy regional administrator. Some commentators saw this move as an attempt to increase central control over the Service, while others argued that it was a useful way of civil servants gaining experience of the workings of the NHS. Shortly after the appointment, a regional administrator and a regional treasurer joined the DHSS to work on the implementation of the Griffiths Inquiry into NHS Management. After an initial assignment focusing on communication between the DHSS and health authorities, the regional administrator joined the Department on a long-term basis as a Deputy Secretary concerned with a number of issues including management information and planning.

It is apparent from this discussion that neither the DHSS nor health authorities can act independently of one another. The reason for this is that underlying the relationship between the different tiers of administration in the NHS is the dependence of one tier on the other for resources of various kinds: finance, manpower, information and so on. As a result of this dependence, a process of exchange develops through which policies are implemented (Rhodes, 1979). An alternative way of viewing the interaction between administrative tiers is not as a system of exchange but rather as a negotiating process in which policy is evolved as it is implemented (Barrett and Fudge, 1981). Whichever conceptualisation is adopted, it is apparent that a key factor in the implementation of health policy is the link between members of the same profession at different levels. Of particular importance is the position of the medical profession, and we now turn to an examination of its influence on the implementation of health policy.

Professional influences on policy implementation

The medical profession is involved in the administration of health services at several different points, a number of which have already been mentioned. First, there is the profession's contribution to policy-making within the DHSS and through the Department's consultative machinery. Second, at RHA level the profession's views are heard through the medical members of the authority and via medical advisory committees. Each RHA is advised by a regional medical committee, which is itself usually supported by a range of sub-committees. Together these committees make proposals for the development of different aspects of service provision. Third, medical advice at district level is filtered mainly through the medical members of the DMT and the DHA. In addition, there may be a district medical committee representing medical opinion in the district. There will also usually be a 'cog wheel' system for organising hospital doctors. This system derives its name from three reports on the organisation of medical work in hospitals which were published between 1967 and 1974 with a cogwheel design on their covers (see Ministry of Health, 1967). The cogwheel system involves clinicians in associated specialities coming together in divisions, and these divisions forming a medical executive committee to examine hospital services as a whole. GPs are organised through the local medical committee, which advises the Family Practitioner Committee. Fourth, and in many ways the most important of all, there is the role of doctors as direct providers of services. We have already discussed the autonomy enjoyed by GPs within the NHS, reflected in their position as independent contractors rather than salaried employees. The DHSS and FPCs have no management control over GPs, apart from certain powers over the distribution of GPs between different parts of the country. These powers, which are exercised by the Medical Practices Committee, involve mainly negative controls preventing GPs practising in areas which are designated as well provided with family doctors. Otherwise, the organisation of general practice is a matter for GPs alone to decide, subject to broad guidance issued by the DHSS. Occasionally, the Department may formulate guidelines for service provision, as in the case of deputising services, and individual doctors may be approached for overprescribing drugs, but for the most part GPs have considerable freedom of action.

Hospital doctors are employees of health authorities, but again their actions cannot be strictly controlled by the managers of services. The reason for this, as the DHSS has explained, is that

At the inception of the NHS, the Government made clear that its intention was to provide a framework within which the health professions could provide treatment and care for patients according to their own independent professional judgement of the patient's needs. This independence has continued to be a central feature of the organisation and management of health services. Thus hospital consultants have clinical autonomy and are fully responsible for the treatment they prescribe for their patients. They are required to act within the broad limits of acceptable medical practice and within policy for the use of resources, but they are not held accountable to NHS Authorities for their clinical judgements. (Normansfield Report, 1978, pp. 424–5)

Consequently, hospital doctors alone determine what is best for their patients, including the place and length of treatment, and the kinds of investigation to be carried out. Medicine is one of the clearest examples of an occupation which has achieved the status of a profession, and a key feature of professions is the autonomy of their members to determine the content of their work. A central issue in the implementation of health policy is therefore how to persuade doctors to organise their work in a way which is consistent with DHSS and health authority policies. Because doctors are the major resource controllers in the NHS, it is ultimately their behaviour which determines patterns of resource allocation and service development. And because doctors are not managed by health authorities, there is no guarantee that national and local policies will be carried out.

Nevertheless, attempts are made to influence medical practices, as in the consultative document on *Priorities* (DHSS, 1976b), which contained a bibliography of reports concerned with alternative ways of providing services. The reports drew the attention of doctors to innovations in clinical practices, including methods of treating patients on an out-patient basis rather than as in-patients, and ways of reducing the number of unnecessary X-rays carried out. As the consultative document noted, 'decisions on clinical practice concerning individual patients are and must continue to be the responsibility of the clinicians concerned. But it is hoped that this document would encourage further scrutiny by the profession of the resources used by different treatment regimes' (DHSS, 1976b, p. 28).

This attempt to influence professional behaviour suggested that more attention might be given to the important part played by doctors in determining the use of resources. In fact, the successors to the consultative document on *Priorities* placed less emphasis on this issue, and *Care in Action*, published in 1981, stressed instead the scope for improving the efficiency of non-medical services (DHSS, 1981c). In practice, most attempts to change professional practices originate within the profession, and indeed one of the characteristics of professions generally is that control is exercised from within. Thus publications in medical journals, conferences organised by professional associations, and discussions with peers through mechanisms like the cogwheel system are the main means by which change is facilitated. In this context, the role of the DHSS and health authorities has traditionally been, wherever possible, to put the profession in the position of moving in the direction desired by both central and local agencies.

The Griffiths Inquiry into NHS Management is likely to lead to a more active attempt to involve doctors in management. Griffiths argued that clinicians should participate fully in decisions about priorities in the use of resources, and suggested that the cogwheel system provided the basis for such participation. More specifically, Griffiths proposed that a system of management budgeting should be developed involving clinicians and relating work-load and service objectives to financial and manpower allocations. Management budgeting is an extension of the clinical budgeting experiments discussed in Chapter 2, and in the wake of the Griffiths Inquiry work was set in hand in four DHAs to develop a system of management budgeting which could be applied in the NHS as a whole. This, together with the appointment of general managers given the task of achieving significant cost improvements and higher levels of efficiency, poses a considerable challenge to hospital doctors. If, as Griffiths argues, it is doctors' decisions that 'largely dictate the use of resources' (Griffiths Report, 1983, p. 18) then changes in those decisions must occur before cost improvements can be achieved.

Policy-making in health authorities

From the point of view of the DHSS and health authorities, clinical freedom may appear to be entirely negative, an obstacle to the implementation of central policies. However, the definition of policy adopted in Chapter 3, emphasising the idea that policy involves actions and decisions, drew attention to what might be called a bottom-up as well as a top-down perspective on policy. From a bottom-up perspective, the local autonomy of both health authorities and the medical profession is a positive feature in that it permits the development of policies which are appropriate to local circumstances, or at least local preferences. Indeed, local autonomy may lead to innovations which might not occur in a highly centralised administrative system. In the final part of the chapter we examine therefore the local sources of policy change and development.

We have argued that subject to broad guidance on policy from the DHSS, health authorities have considerable freedom to determine what policies to pursue in their areas. However, it is important to recognise that health authorities, like the DHSS, are not wholly or even mainly concerned with making new policies or initiating new developments. As studies of policy-making in health agencies have shown, policy maintenance is more prevalent than policy-making, and any changes that do occur are likely to involve marginal adjustments to the *status quo*. The reason for this is that within the NHS various interests are competing for scarce resources, and in the absence of any one dominant group, bargaining between these interests tends to result in incremental change. As the author has argued elsewhere, 'in policy systems where there are many different interests and where power is not concentrated in any individual or group, it is easier to prevent change than to achieve it. Successful policy promotion in such systems is dependent on the winning of a coalition of support by an active individual or interest' (Ham, 1981, p. 153).

With this in mind, what interests contribute to health policy-making at the local level? Hunter, in a study of resource allocation in two Scottish health boards, suggests that decisions were influenced by a policy triad, comprising health board members, officers, and professional and lay advisory bodies (Hunter, 1980).

Hunter argues that the influence of health board members on resource allocation was minimal. This confirms evidence from other sources indicating that the appointed members of health authorities experience difficulties with their role. Studies of DHAs have pointed to the constraints under which members operate (Ham, 1984; Haywood, 1983) and have highlighted the fact that members are often in the position of approving proposals put forward by their officers rather than making decisions themselves. This does not apply to authority chairmen who tend to be much more closely involved than members in the work of their authorities and who are better placed to influence decisions.

Hunter goes on to note that health board officers, although active and visible in the resource allocation process, were not themselves dominant. Like their counterparts in DHAs, officers appeared to be in control of the business of their authorities, but were constrained by inherited commitments and established patterns of service provision. Officers were able to exert some influence but their freedom of manoeuvre was limited by history and, more particularly, by the power of the medical profession. As we noted earlier in the chapter, this power derives as much from the profession's key position as the direct provider of services, as from its political activity through advisory committees. Hunter expresses the point in the following way:

> allocations ... did not always reflect directly the wishes and wants of doctors; nor did they arise from some conspiracy on the part of the medical profession to win for itself the biggest share of available resources, so depriving other groups in need of them. The process was altogether more subtle ... in their present established position as leaders of the health care team and as the primary decision-makers, doctors' decisions to treat patients commit resources ... and impose additional pressures on administrators charged with allocating resources. (Hunter, 1980, p. 195)

The author's own work on policy-making in the Leeds Regional Hospital Board (RHB) came to similar conclusions. Through a variety of channels, medical interests were able to influence what was decided, and overall 'the distribution of power was weighted heavily in favour of the professional monopolists' (Ham, 1981, p.

198). The terminology used here is derived from the work of Alford, who argues that health politics are characterised by three sets of structural interests: professional monopolists, who are the dominant interests; corporate rationalisers, who are the challenging interests; and the community population, who are the repressed interests (Alford, 1975a). Applying these concepts to the Leeds RHB suggested that 'the history of hospital planning between 1948 and 1974 can be seen as the history of corporate rationalisers, represented by regional board planners, trying to challenge the established interests of the medical profession, with the community hardly in earshot' (Ham, 1981, p. 75). A key point to appreciate is that because the medical profession is in an established position, small changes do not seriously threaten professional dominance. In other words, policy maintenance benefits medical interests by preserving the existing pattern of services within which the profession is predominant.

What should also be apparent is that community interests do not carry a great deal of weight in the policy-making processes of health authorities. Certainly, in the period between 1948 and 1974 organisations representing community or patient interests played little part in the deliberations of the Leeds RHB, although since 1974 the introduction of Community Health Councils (CHCs) at district level in the NHS in England and Wales has strengthened the consumer voice in health care. Hunter's study, which was carried out between 1974 and 1976, found that 'the influence of lay advisory bodies on the allocation process was practically non-existent' (Hunter, 1980, p. 198), but at the time Local Health Councils, the Scottish equivalent of CHCs, were in the process of being established. Since then, CHCs have become more in evidence, and in a number of areas have had a demonstrable impact on decision-making. Like consumer interests at central government level, however, CHCs are in a weak position compared with producer interests, and they have to use their limited financial and manpower resources as effectively as possible if they are to influence health authorities. Nevertheless, CHCs have increased the accountability of health service managers (Brown, 1979) and some have helped to bring about policy changes in their areas.

A number of other potential sources of policy change should be mentioned. First, there are producer interests other than the medical profession, including nurses, paramedical staff and ancillary workers. These interests have been increasingly active in recent years, and their influence is likely to be felt on issues such as hospital closures, facilities for private medical care, and competitive tendering. Second, there are external agencies, of which local authorities are the most significant. The importance attached to collaboration between health authorities and local authorities since 1974 has opened up the possibility of mutual policy influence, although evidence indicates that this has proved a difficult ideal to attain in practice (Booth, 1981; Glennerster *et al.*, 1983). In most cases it seems that authorities have continued to provide and plan their services independently, and only exceptionally have health authority policies been influenced by the preferences of local authorities. Third, there are the Health Advisory Service and the National Development Team for Mentally Handicapped People. These are national bodies which visit health authorities to advise on the development of services for the mentally ill, mentally handicapped, the elderly, and children receiving long-term care. Multi-disciplinary teams spend a period of time examining services for these groups, and report on ways in which improvements can be made. Although these team reports are not always accepted, the advice offered does provide a further source of input to the policy process for health authorities to consider.

Conclusion

It can be seen that policy-making in health authorities involves a range of interests each seeking to influence what is decided. From a policy implementation perspective, the guidelines and advice offered by the DHSS are fed into a policy arena where they have to compete with the demands of the various agencies and interests discussed in the preceding paragraphs. In assessing the strength of these agencies and interests, the powerful position occupied by the medical profession is again apparent. DHSS policies which challenge the interests of key groups within the profession are likely to be resisted. An example was Richard Crossman's attempt to shift resources from acute hospital services to the long-stay sector after the Ely Report. Crossman failed in his attempt because of opposition from the medical profession, and he was forced to earmark additional funds in order to give greater priority to long-stay services (Crossman, 1977).

While it is difficult to overemphasise the strength of medical interests, it should be noted that in some areas of service provision other interests may also be important. For example, policies for the mentally ill and handicapped may be more open to lay and community influences than policies for other client groups. It is, of course, particularly in these areas that the medical contribution is at its weakest. Again, for similar reasons innovations in community health services and prevention may arise among consumer groups and may develop through non-medical interests. Granted these qualifications, the general conclusion of this discussion is that centrally determined health policies are mediated by a range of interests at the local level, among which the medical profession is the most influential.

The picture that emerges, then, is of a complex series of interactions between the centre and the periphery, through which each attempts to influence the other. While the existence of parliamentary accountability gives the appearance of centralisation in the NHS, the reality is rather different. Recognising that the stance taken by the centre tends to change over time, it can be said that the DHSS is able to exercise control over total health service spending and its distribution to RHAs, but has much less control over the uses to which funds are put. Circulars, consultative documents and White Papers, and guidelines on priorities are the main instruments the Department uses to attempt to influence the decisions of health authorities, but the advisory nature of these documents, and often their ambiguity, leaves scope for local interpretation of central policy. The NHS Planning System has not been used as a means of central control, and legal powers, although considerable, are rarely employed. The accountability review process is a significant recent innovation and has led to greater central involvement and in some cases central control over policy-making. Overall, though, as a mechanism for influencing health authorities, persuasion is more important than are statutory controls, necessarily so perhaps in a Service where considerable discretion is accorded to those who provide services.

6

The Impact of Health Services

How can we measure the impact of health services? One approach would be to examine the objectives of the NHS, and to assess how far the Service has succeeded in meeting these objectives. The most general aim of the NHS is 'to secure improvement – (a) in the physical and mental health of the people ... and (b) in the prevention, diagnosis and treatment of illness' (Royal Commission on the NHS, 1979, p. 8). To what extent has the NHS been successful in these areas? In attempting to answer this question, we immediately encounter two problems.

First, concepts of health and illness vary. On the one hand, health may be defined in a negative way, as the absence of illness and disease. Alternatively, it may be defined positively, as in the World Health Organisation's definition of health as a 'state of complete physical, mental and social well-being' (World Health Organisation, 1965). There are also, as we discuss in Chapter 7, significant differences between individual and collective concepts of health. Before the impact of health services can be assessed, agreement has to be reached on which definition of health is to be adopted.

In practice, the best available statistics for measuring health concern mortality. Good measures of ill health or morbidity are hard to come by, and indicators of positive aspects of health are even more difficult to obtain. In using mortality indicators, therefore, it should be remembered that they may not reflect accurately the level of morbidity in a community or the quality of life. Bearing this in mind, a comparison of death rates in 1948 and 1983 in England and Wales illustrates the considerable improvements which have occurred. As Table 6.1 shows, there has been a

TABLE 6.1   *Perinatal and infant mortality rates: England and Wales, 1948–83*

	1948	1983	% change 1948–83
Perinatal mortality*	38.5	10.4	73
Infant mortality+	34.0	10.1	70

* The perinatal mortality rate is the number of still births and deaths in the first week of life per 1,000 total births.
+ The infant mortality rate is the number of deaths under 1 year of age per 1,000 live births.
SOURCE ': Royal Commission on the NHS (1979) and OPCS (1984a).

reduction of almost 73 per cent in perinatal mortality, that is still births and deaths in the first week of life. There has also been a reduction of 70 per cent in infant mortality, that is deaths in the first year of life. Similar, though not as impressive, improvements have been made in death rates among the adult population, as Table 6.2 shows. Life expectancy figures have also improved. Table 6.3 shows that the expectation of life for a boy aged 1 in England and Wales in 1950–2 was 67.7 years compared with 71.0 years in 1980–2. Female life expectancy increased from 72.4 years to 76.9 years over the same period. These statistics suggest that considerable improvements in health have occurred since the NHS was established.

However, there is a second problem which has to be faced in measuring the impact of the NHS, and that is disentangling the effects of health services on health from the effects of other changes occurring at the same time. As the Royal Commission on the National Health Service has noted, how far improvements in health can be attributed to the NHS is 'In one sense ... impossible to answer because there is no way of knowing what would have happened if the NHS had not been introduced in 1948' (Royal Commission on the NHS, 1979, p. 21). The argument here, stated at its simplest, is that the organisation of health services may not be as important in determining health as factors such as income, education, nutrition and housing. The evidence on this point is by no means clear cut, but there is an increasing body of work which indicates that historical improvements in health have arisen mainly from advances in water supplies, sewerage systems and nutrition,

TABLE 6.2　*Adult mortality rates: England and Wales, 1948–82*

		1948	1982	% change 1948–82
Mortality*				
aged 35–44	M	3.15	1.8	43
	F	2.45	1.2	51
aged 45–54	M	8.24	5.9	28
	F	5.33	3.6	32
aged 55–64	M	21.60	17.5	19
	F	12.20	9.7	20

* The mortality rate is the number of deaths in that age range per 1,000 population in the age range.
SOURCE : Royal Commission on the NHS (1979) and OPCS (1984b).

TABLE 6.3　*Life expectancy at age 1 year: England and Wales, 1950–82*

Sex	1950–2	1960–2	1970–2	1980–2*	% change 1950–2 to 1980–2
M	67.7	68.8	69.4	71.0	4.87
F	72.4	74.4	75.4	76.9	6.22

* Provisional
SOURCE : OPCS (1984c)

rather than developments in medical science and health services (McKeown, 1976). At the same time, a number of reports have suggested that future improvements in health should be sought first of all through changes outside organised health care systems.

The issue is complicated further by international comparisons of health and health services. These comparisons indicate that there is no clear or simple correlation between the inputs into health care, expressed in terms of spending and staffing levels, and the outcomes, measured in terms of mortality rates and life expectancy. Put another way, it does not seem that a greater investment in health services will necessarily lead to better health. Of course, the statistics used do not tell the whole story, and are unable to show whether higher spending leads to lower rates of morbidity or improvements to the quality of life, or whether the form of organisation of health services is an important variable. Nevertheless, they do demonstrate the need for caution in drawing conclusions about the impact of health services.

Having established this point, let us explore the extent to which the NHS has succeeded in meeting one of its more specific objectives, that of making services available equally to different sectors of the population. This objective was set out in the 1946 National Health Service Bill, which stated that 'All the service or any part of it, is to be available to everyone in England and Wales. The Bill imposes no limitation on availability – e.g. limitations based on financial means, age, sex, employment or vocation, area of residence, or insurance qualification' (Ministry of Health, 1946, p. 3). Has the NHS been successful in achieving this goal?

The availability of health services

One of the main aims of the architects of the NHS was to provide services to everyone in need of care and treatment. Need was to be the sole criterion according to which services were to be provided, and no longer was there to be a financial barrier to obtaining treatment. Although this principle has been modified by the introduction of charges for some services, it has been argued that 'one of the most significant achievements of the NHS has been to free people from fear of being unable to afford treatment for acute or chronic illness' (Royal Commission on the NHS, 1979, pp. 10–11). Despite this achievement, there are a number of outstanding inequalities, both in health and in the use and distribution of health services. First, there are geographical inequalities in mortality rates and in the allocation of NHS facilities and resources. Second, there are social class differences in mortality and morbidity rates and the utilisation of health services. Third, there are inequalities in the standard of care provided for different client groups. We shall examine each kind of inequality in turn, at the same time noting the various attempts by policy-makers to meet the objective of equal availability of services.

TABLE 6.4   *Mortality rates: England, 1982*

	Infant mortality rate*	Perinatal mortality rate*	Standardised mortality ratio† M	F
England	10.8	11.2	99	99
Northern	10.4	11.8	110	109
Yorkshire	11.5	12.5	107	106
Trent	10.5	11.2	101	102
East Anglia	9.4	10.4	89	92
NW Thames	10.2	9.7	93	94
NE Thames	11.0	11.6	98	95
SE Thames	9.8	10.0	94	93
SW Thames	10.7	10.6	89	92
Wessex	10.3	10.0	89	91
Oxford	9.8	9.9	90	94
South Western	10.1	9.1	91	93
West Midlands	12.0	13.8	106	104
Mersey	10.5	10.9	113	111
North Western	12.1	12.5	112	111

* For definitions of *infant mortality rate* and *perinatal mortality rate*, see the notes to Table 6.1.
† The standardised mortality ratio compares the number of deaths actually occurring in an area with those which would be expected if national mortality rates by age and sex were applicable to the population of that area. England based on England and Wales = 100.
SOURCE: Central Statistical Office (1984) and OPCS (1984b).

Geographical inequalities

Let us first consider the variations in mortality rates between the regions of England. Table 6.4 shows that in 1982, the infant mortality rate for England stood at 10.8, and within England the rate varied from 9.4 in East Anglia to 12.1 in the North Western region. In the same year the perinatal mortality rate for England was 11.2. Within England, the perinatal mortality rate varied from 9.1 in the South Western region to 13.8 in the West Midlands. There are also variations between regions in the standardised mortality ratio (SMR), that is the measure of mortality used by statisticians to compare the number of deaths actually occurring in an area with those which would be expected if national mortality rates by age and sex were applicable to the population of that area. In 1982, the male SMR varied from 113 in the Mersey region to 89 in the East Anglia, Wessex and South West Thames regions. Standardised mortality ratios for women varied from 111 in the Mersey and North Western regions to 91 in Wessex. Table 6.5 illustrates the existence of differences in mortality rates between England, Wales, Scotland and Northern Ireland.

There are similar variations in the distribution of health expenditure and health manpower. Tables 6.6. and 6.7 display some of the relevant data. The tables show, for example, that within England in 1981–2, per capita expenditure on health services as a whole ranged from £189.85 in the Oxford region to £251.65 in the North West Thames region. Expenditure per capita on hospital and community health services varied from £118.52 in the Oxford region to £169.88 in the North West Thames region, and expenditure per capita on family practitioner services varied from £45.50 in the Trent region to £53.19 in the South Western region. In the case of manpower, total staff employed per 10,000 population ranged from 153.6 in the Oxford region to 210.5 in the North East Thames region. The variation in staffing is particularly pronounced in relation to dentists, the best provided region, North West Thames, being served by more than twice the number of

TABLE 6.5   *Mortality rates: UK, 1982*

	Infant[*] mortality rate	Perinatal[*] mortality rate	Standardised[+] mortality ratio	
			M	F
England	10.8	11.2	98	98
Wales	10.6	11.1	104	103
Scotland	11.4	11.5	115	115
N. Ireland	13.7	13.4	106	109
UK	11.0	11.4	100	100

[*] For definitions of infant mortality rate and perinatal mortality rate, see the notes to Table 6.1.
[+] For a definition of standardised mortality ratio, see the notes to Table 6.4.
SOURCE: Central Statistical Office (1984) and OPCS (1984c).

TABLE 6.6   *Distribution of health expenditure: UK, 1981–2 (£ per capita)*

	Hospital and community health services	Family practitioner services	Total*
England	146.93	48.31	225.74
Northern	138.81	48.18	217.79
Yorkshire	137.33	48.15	214.59
Trent	127.09	45.50	201.21
East Anglia	125.74	48.19	205.58
NW Thames	169.88	50.66	251.65
NE Thames	169.74	47.29	248.74
SE Thames	166.18	49.44	245.34
SW Thames	156.55	48.91	236.49
Wessex	126.28	48.57	202.23
Oxford	118.52	46.30	189.85
South Western	137.82	53.19	220.87
West Midlands	130.99	46.48	204.18
Mersey	150.88	47.89	229.39
North Western	152.41	49.17	239.47
Wales	152.74	53.27	236.50
Scotland	193.51	50.04	283.70
N. Ireland	192.53	56.03	289.47
United Kingdom	152.76	48.93	233.32

* The total includes spending on headquarters administration, capital expenditure and 'other services' as well as spending on hospital and community health services and family practitioner services.
SOURCE: Central Statistical Office (1984)

dentists per 10,000 population as the worst provided region, Northern. There are again variations between different parts of the United Kingdom. Scotland, Wales and Northern Ireland spend more per capita on health services than England and also employ more staff in relation to the population served. These variations in financial and manpower resources are not necessarily a cause for concern. Different areas have different needs, depending on the age structure of the population and the pattern of illness in the community. A way has to be found, therefore, of taking account of these needs, and of achieving an equitable distribution of funds between different geographical areas. This was the task given to the Resource Allocation Working Party (RAWP), which pro-

TABLE 6.7　*Distribution of health manpower: UK, 1982 (per 10,000 population)*

	All staff (WTE)[*]	Medical and dental staff (WTE)[*]	Nurses and midwives (WTE)[*]	General medical practitioners	General dental practitioners
England	185.7	8.12	83.9	5.29	2.84
Northern	181.5	8.04	84.6	5.14	1.93
Yorkshire	180.7	7.50	83.1	5.28	2.50
Trent	170.4	7.17	76.7	5.00	2.17
East Anglia	164.9	7.31	74.6	5.22	2.61
NW Thames	187.5	8.69	82.0	5.79	4.34
NE Thames	210.5	9.91	91.9	5.35	2.94
SE Thames	199.7	8.37	86.5	5.30	3.34
SW Thames	182.6	7.46	82.5	5.42	3.73
Wessex	167.2	6.84	77.4	5.40	2.88
Oxford	153.6	7.18	70.2	5.07	2.95
South Western	184.4	7.45	84.6	5.83	3.56
West Midlands	171.7	7.33	79.1	5.21	2.31
Mersey	193.8	8.18	91.7	5.32	2.45
North Western	198.0	8.97	91.6	5.22	2.48
Wales	202.3	8.54	92.2	4.98	2.49
Scotland	249.9	11.80	119.8	6.58	2.70
N. Ireland	251.9	10.84	119.3	5.74	2.55
United Kingdom	194.2	8.55	88.65	5.41	2.80

[*] whole-time equivalent
SOURCE: Central Statistical Office (1984)

duced a formula seeking 'To reduce progressively, and as far as is feasible, the disparities between the different parts of the country in terms of opportunity for access to health care for people at equal risk; taking into account measures of health needs, and social and environmental factors which may affect the need for health care' (DHSS, 1975c). The Working Party, in its final report published in September 1976, recommended that resources for hospital and community health services in England should be allocated on the basis of each region's population, weighted for age and sex according to the national utilisation of different services to take account of the heavier demands made on services by groups such as children, elderly people and women. The report also recommended that regional populations should be weighted for morbidity, with standardised mortality ratios being used as a proxy for morbidity. In this way it was suggested that a target revenue allocation should be built up for each region, making allowances for the flow of patients across boundaries and the costs incurred by the NHS in providing facilities in support of medical and dental teaching.

The Working Party found that some regions had revenue allocations around 10 per cent below their target share of resources, while others had allocations more than 10 per cent above. The report recognised that these disparities could be reduced only gradually and recommended that the distribution of the growth money available each year should be in favour of the most deprived regions. These recommendations were accepted by the Secretary of State for Social Services, and a start was made in implementing them in 1977–8. In practice, at a time of limited growth in NHS spending, progress towards achieving targets has been slow. Figure 6.1 shows how the gap between the best- and worst-funded regions narrowed between 1977–8 and 1984–5. Figures for 1984–5 indicate that the distance of regions from their target allocations varied from 9 per cent above target in North East Thames to 4.9 per cent below target in Wessex. Revenue allocations to health authorities in 1984–5 included a planned rate of growth for the NHS as a whole of 1 per cent, with above-target regions receiving no increase in allocations and below-target regions receiving increases of up to 1.9 per cent. The RAWP formula is used in a similar way to guide the distribution of capital resources between regions. Comparable policies are being pursued in Northern Ireland, Scotland and Wales.

As we noted in Chapter 4, the origins of the policy concern with the geographical maldistribution of resources go back to the time when Richard Crossman was Secretary of State. An internal DHSS review of the distribution of funds to hospital regions led to the introduction in 1971–2 of a new method of allocating revenue designed to equalise distribution over a ten-year period. The RAWP report took the process a stage further, encompassing all services apart from the demand-determined family practitioner services, and introducing a new level of sophistication to the attempt to devise criteria of need for use in the resource allocation process. What is perhaps surprising is that it took so long for

FIGURE 6.1 *Regions' distances from revenue resource allocation targets 1977/8–1984/5*[1]

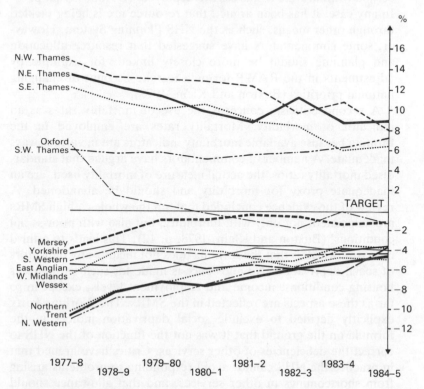

N.W. Thames
N.E. Thames
S.E. Thames
Oxford
S.W. Thames
TARGET
Mersey
Yorkshire
S. Western
East Anglian
W. Midlands
Wessex
Northern
Trent
N. Western

1977–8
1978–9
1979–80
1980–1
1981–2
1982–3
1983–4
1984–5

%
16
14
12
10
8
6
4
2
−2
−4
−6
−8
−10
−12

[1]Distance from targets expressed as percentages of regions' allocations

SOURCE: DHSS (1984b).

central government to take action. The issue of the geographical distribution of resources did not come to be defined as a problem until over twenty years after the NHS had been established. As a former Minister of State for Health has noted, this reflects the fact that 'the department's central responsibility for redressing inequalities has been woefully neglected' (Owen, 1976, p. 8).

The RAWP approach has not been without its critics. First, it has been argued that the Working Party examined only the input of resources and not their deployment or output. In fact, the Working Party deliberately avoided examining the use of resources, stating 'we have not regarded our remit as being concerned with how the resources are deployed' (DHSS, 1976a, p. 8). In any case, it has been argued that resource use is being tackled through other means, such as the NHS Planning System. However, some commentators have suggested that resource allocation and planning should be more closely linked, for example by adjustments in the RAWP formula to take account of changing national priorities (Buxton and Klein, 1978).

A second criticism concerns the use of mortality rates as an indicator of morbidity. Mortality rates are employed in the formula because available morbidity indicators are in various ways inadequate. A number of commentators have argued that standardised mortality ratios, the actual measure of mortality used, are an inadequate proxy for morbidity and should be abandoned. A review of the evidence concluded that 'on the whole ... high SMRs are associated, not only with morbidity, but also with poor social conditions' (Buxton and Klein, 1978, p. 12). This leads to a third criticism, which is that the formula does not include any indicators of social deprivation. No allowance is made for such variables as housing conditions, income and employment levels, except in so far as these aspects are reflected in the SMRs. The Working Party explicitly decided to exclude social deprivation indices in the formula on the ground that it was not the function of the NHS to correct the deficiencies of other services. Critics have argued that in practice the NHS cannot avoid responding to problems arising from shortcomings in other services, and that allowance should have been made for this.

A fourth area of debate has concerned the impact of RAWP within regions. It is at the sub-regional level that the greatest problems have been encountered, particularly in areas such as inner London, which are over-provided in terms of the RAWP formula yet contain pockets of considerable social deprivation. The apparent contradiction here is explained in part by the investment in these areas in expensive teaching hospital services, which may not always be appropriate to the health needs of the local population. These and other difficulties have led some regions to amend the national RAWP formula to take account of specific local circumstances, a move that is in line with the final RAWP report, which suggested that judgement should be used in the local implementation of the policy.

Despite these criticisms, the RAWP policy has won considerable support. The Royal Commission on the NHS, for example, said that 'the RAWP approach is sound in principle' and that 'The introduction of the RAWP formula was an important step towards determining a rational and equitable system of allocating resources to health authorities. It represents a clear commitment to reduce inequalities in health care provision, which have existed since 1948' (Royal Commission on the NHS, 1979, p. 345). While further improvements and modifications may be made to the formula, for example, to make allowances for the increasing importance of private health care provision, the underlying principles seem likely to continue to form the basis of attempts to bring about a greater measure of territorial justice in the NHS.

Social class inequalities

A second major area of inequalities within the NHS concerns social class. Stacey has summarised the position in the following way:

> There is evidence, first, of continuing and perhaps increasing class differentials in death rates; second, of more illness in lower than in higher classes; third, that the health services are more available to the middle classes than to the working classes; fourth, that the middle classes use the health services more than the working classes; and, five, get more out of them when they do use them. (Stacey, 1977a, p. 898)

In this context, class is used in the sense employed by the Registrar General, who divides occupations into five main groupings. These groupings vary from social class 1, which contains professional occupations such as accountants and doctors, to social class 5, which contains unskilled manual occupations like labourers and office cleaners. An analysis of death rates reveals evidence of social class differences in mortality in all age groups. For example, Table 6.8 shows that the infant mortality rate in England and Wales in 1982 varied from 7.0 in social class 1 to 14.5 in social class 5. In the same year, the perinatal mortality rate varied from 8.0 in social class 1 to 14.6 in social class 5. There are similar differences

TABLE 6.8   *Infant and perinatal mortality rates by social class: England and Wales 1982*

Social class	Infant* mortality rate	Perinatal* mortality rate
I	7.0	8.0
II	8.4	9.0
III N	9.1	10.4
III M	9.6	10.9
IV	11.8	13.2
V	14.5	14.6

* For definitions of infant mortality rate and perinatal mortality rate, see note to Table 6.1.
SOURCE: OPCS (1984d)

in childhood, as Table 6.9 demonstrates. To take one example, the death rate among boys aged 1–4 in 1970–2 ranged from 60.58 in social class 1 to 128.72 in social class 5.

These patterns continue into adult life. Table 6.10 shows that the standardised mortality ratio among economically active males (aged 15 to 64) in England and Wales in 1970–2 ranged from 77 in

TABLE 6.9   *Deaths of children by sex, age and social class, England and Wales, 1970–2 (deaths per 100,000 children per year)*

Sex Age group		Social class					
		I	II	IIIN	IIIM	IV	V
Males							
aged 1–4	Rates	60.58	62.02	74.53	75.53	92.89	128.72
aged 5–9	Rates	27.51	31.41	38.93	42.40	44.06	69.10
aged 10–14	Rates	28.32	31.07	34.81	34.64	40.06	56.47
aged 1–14	SMR	74	79	95	98	112	162
Females							
aged 1–4	Rates	57.48	54.02	62.16	61.85	84.21	109.09
aged 5–9	Rates	26.62	23.81	27.46	27.30	32.53	43.42
aged 10–14	Rates	20.83	21.33	19.89	21.29	26.44	32.76
aged 1–14	SMR	89	84	93	93	120	156

SOURCE: OPCS (1978)

TABLE 6.10   *Mortality of men by social class, 1970–2, England and Wales*

		Social class		
I	II	III	IV	V
77	81	104	114	137

NOTE: The measure of mortality used is the *standardised mortality ratio*. This compares the number of deaths actually occurring in each social class with those which would be expected if the death rates for the standard population were applicable to that class.
SOURCE: OPCS (1978)

social class 1 to 137 in social class 5, and the same differences exist among females. Comparisons over time are difficult because of changes in the way in which the Registrar General classifies occupations. However, a special analysis of trends in mortality for men of economically active age carried out by the Working Group on Inequalities in Health (the Black Report, 1980) found that there was greater inequality of mortality between classes 1 and 5 in 1970–2 than in 1949–53. This seems to suggest that although death rates overall are falling, the relative position of people in the lower social groups is deteriorating.

The evidence on morbidity is more problematic to interpret with confidence, mainly because we lack a good measure of ill health. The most commonly used morbidity data come from the *General Household Survey* (GHS) which gathers information about self-reported sickness. The GHS is an annual survey of 15,000 house-holds in Great Britain, and it investigates factors to do with population, housing, employment, education and health. The survey asks questions about long standing illness and restricted activity, which is roughly equivalent to acute illness, and analyses the responses in terms of socio-economic groups which are similar to but not exactly the same as the Registrar General's social classes. The main point to note in interpreting the data from the GHS is that it is self-reported sickness which is being examined, and the evidence may therefore reflect differences between individuals in the propensity to define certain conditions as sickness as well as differences in the actual distribution of ill health.

What the data show is that there are class differences in long standing illness reported to the GHS. The rates of long standing illness are around twice as high for middle-aged males in unskilled manual occupations as for middle-aged males in professional occupations. There are similar differences among females and in other age groups, although inequalities tend to be smaller in childhood, early adulthood and in old age. In contrast, there is no clear pattern of class differences in restricted activity reported to the GHS. Indeed, for boys between birth and 14 there is an inverse gradient, the lower social groups reporting less restricted activity. For other age groups the picture tends to be uneven, showing some class differences, but not the consistent gradient that exists in relation to mortality and long standing illness. As the Working Group on Inequalities in Health noted, a problem in examining these data is 'judging whether the same conditions are as likely to be reported by some occupational groups as others' (Black Report, 1980, p. 58).

If we consider the availability and use of health services by different social classes, there are again indications of important class inequalities. Writing in 1968, Titmuss contended:

> We have learnt from 15 years' experience of the Health Service that the higher income groups know how to make better use of the Service; they tend to receive more specialist attention; occupy more of the beds in better equipped and staffed hospitals; receive more elective surgery; have better maternity care; and are more likely to get psychiatric help and psychotherapy than low income groups – particularly the unskilled. (Titmuss, 1968, p. 196)

Later evidence suggests a rather more complex pattern of usage of health services. For example, GHS statistics on consultations with GPs point to an overall class gradient for males and females in general. However, there are difficulties in drawing straightforward conclusions because for some age groups there is either no class gradient or an uneven gradient. Attempts have been made to combine GHS data on consultation rates and morbidity to construct use–need ratios. These indicate that in relation to reported sickness, the lower social groups make less use of services than other groups (Black Report, 1980, p. 97). Further evidence of class differences is provided by Cartwright and O'Brien (1976) in their study of the nature of GP consultations. Cartwright and

O'Brien found the conversation time with middle-class patients was 6.2 minutes on average, compared with 4.7 minutes for working-class patients. Not only this, middle-class patients discussed more problems than working-class patients, and GPs knew more about the domestic situations of their middle-class patients.

Perhaps the clearest indication of differential usage of services comes from the area of preventive health. Alderson, in his examination of a number of mainly preventive services, found under-usage in the lower social groups in relation to need, and he argued: 'the data presented are compatible with the hypothesis that there is a group in the community who are aware of the provisions of the health service and who obtain a higher proportion of the resources of the health service than would be expected by chance and a much higher proportion in relation to their needs when compared with others in the community' (Alderson, 1970, p. 52). Again, studies of late booking at antenatal clinics have found that late booking is more common in the lower social groups. The relevant statistics are displayed in Table 6.11.

TABLE 6.11   *Late antenatal booking, Scotland, 1971–3*[*]

Occupational class	1971	1972	1973
I	28.4	27.2	27.0
II	35.3	32.3	29.8
III	36.3	33.4	30.6
IV	39.3	37.8	35.3
V	47.1	44.2	40.5

[*] % married women in each occupational class making an antenatal booking after more than twenty weeks of gestation.
SOURCE: Black Report (1980, p. 106).

A further point worth noting is that utilisation may be related to availability. That is, the middle classes may make greater use of services partly because they are more available to them. This is suggested by the inverse care law, formulated by Julian Tudor-Hart, which states that 'the availability of good medical care tends to vary inversely with the need of the population served' (Tudor-

Hart, 1971, p. 412). What Tudor-Hart is arguing is that areas of social deprivation containing high proportions of people from the lower social groups tend to have less good health services. There is evidence to support the inverse care law in a number of services (West and Lowe, 1976; Noyce, Snaith and Trickey, 1974) and clearly this has important implications.

Finally, class differences in the use of services and morbidity can be used with information about the cost of services to analyse which groups benefit most from public expenditure on health care. An analysis by Le Grand on these lines demonstrated that in England and Wales in 1972 the higher social groups comprised some 14 per cent of those reporting ill and received about 17 per cent of expenditure. At the other end of the scale, the lower social groups comprised around 32 per cent of those reporting ill and received only 27 per cent of expenditure. Further analysis showed that 'the upper two SEGs (socio-economic groups) appear to receive at least 40% more expenditure per person ill than the lower two' (Le Grand, 1978, p. 132). Le Grand argued that inequalities reflect different utilisation rates, and advanced a number of reasons why this might be so: the costs in terms of lost wages and time may be greater for lower social groups, and organised health services may be seen as more accessible by higher social groups.

The evidence therefore supports Stacey's summary of the relationship between social class, health and the use of services. Not only are there significant differences between social groups in the use of health services, but also it would appear that the NHS has failed in its aim of making services available· equally to these different groups. Further, the data on mortality differences for adult males, adjusted to take account of changes in classification, indicate that in the period since the establishment of the NHS, inequalities in death rates between the higher and lower social groups have increased. However, as we argued in the discussion of the overall impact of health services on health, it would be too simple to suggest that the reason for the continuation of these inequalities is the failure of the NHS to take appropriate action. The causes of class differentials in mortality and morbidity are both complex and multiple, and it has been argued that underlying these differentials are inequalities in living standards which play an important part in influencing health and welfare. This was the view taken by the Working Group on Inequalities in Health, which was set up to assemble information about the differences in health status among the social classes and about factors which might contribute to these differences. Following a comprehensive review of the available data, the Working Group concluded, 'we wish to stress the importance of differences in material conditions of life' (Black Report, 1980, p. 357) in explaining class inequalities in health. On this basis, the Working Group made a series of recommendations for reducing inequalities, in particular emphasising the importance of factors outside the NHS. Among the proposals were the suggestion that child benefit should be increased, an infant care allowance introduced, housing conditions improved, and free school meals made available to all children.

However, the Working Group also recognised that action could be taken to reduce inequalities in the use of health services. It recommended that attention should be given to the accessibility and facilities of antenatal and child health clinics in order to increase utilisation, and that the quality and coverage of general practice should be reviewed. These and other proposals were based on the premise that while the main influences on mortality and morbidity lay outside the NHS, action to improve the use of services, particularly by the lower social groups, might have some beneficial effect on health.

The Working Group's Report, which was published in 1980, placed the issue of social class inequalities firmly on the health policy agenda. However, the Secretary of State for Social Services rejected the Group's call for additional expenditure to improve the impact of services, although he noted that 'It will come as a disappointment to many that over long periods since the inception of the NHS there is generally little sign of health inequalities in Britain actually diminishing' (Black Report; 1980). The stance taken by the Secretary of State was that extra public expenditure could not be justified, and that in any case the causes of class inequalities were complex and might not be reduced by the kind of proposals made by the Working Group. Working from a different standpoint, Le Grand (1982) has reached a similar conclusion, arguing that little can be done within the scope of the NHS to reduce inequalities in health or health care. In Le Grand's view, the best way to reduce inequalities in health is to reduce inequalities in income. For his part, Peter Townsend, a member of the

Working Group, has responded to the Secretary of State's criticism of the Black Report by maintaining that implementation of the Report's recommendations need not be expensive. Townsend also contends that while more work is needed to identify the precise way in which social and economic deprivation produces inequalities in health, material factors are important causal agents (Townsend and Davidson, 1982). In this respect, Townsend concurs with Le Grand in arguing that action outside the NHS offers the best way of reducing class inequalities in health. These arguments have failed to sway ministers, and firm action on the Black Report is still awaited.

Client group inequalities

The third main area of inequality within the NHS concerns the standard of care provided for different client groups. The comparative neglect of groups such as the mentally handicapped, the mentally ill and elderly people within the NHS is an issue which has received increasing attention since the late 1960s. The issue was brought to prominence in 1967 when a pressure group known as Aid for the Elderly in Government Institutions published a book called *Sans Everything – A Case to Answer*, containing allegations of ill-treatment to elderly patients in psychiatric and geriatric care (Robb, 1967). The Minister of Health asked regional hospital boards to set up independent inquiries into the allegations, and the results were published a year later. The general conclusion of the inquiries was that the allegations were unfounded. Some areas for improvement were identified, but overall the reports from the committees which carried out the inquiries attempted to paint a reassuring picture of the standard of care provided.

As we noted in Chapter 1, a rather different picture emerged from the report of the committee of enquiry set up to investigate conditions at Ely Hospital, a mental handicap hospital in Cardiff. The committee was established in 1967 following newspaper accounts of ill-treatment to patients, and it reported in 1969. The committee found that many of the allegations were true, and that there were serious deficiencies at Ely. A number of recommendations were made for improving standards at Ely and at long-stay hospitals generally, including the setting up of a system of inspection to ensure that the local managers of services were aware of what was required (Ely Report, 1969).

The Secretary of State for Social Services at the time of Ely, Richard Crossman, used the report to give greater priority to long-stay services. The Hospital Advisory Service (HAS) was set up to provide the system of inspection recommended by the committee of enquiry, although it was presented as a means of giving advice rather than an inspectorate. In addition, Crossman earmarked funds to be spent specifically on mental handicap hospitals. These earmarked funds were later extended to other long-stay services, although earmarking came to an end in 1974. At the same time, the DHSS issued advice to hospital boards and committees on measures which could be taken at little cost to raise standards of care.

The momentum provided by Crossman was maintained through the publication of a series of further reports into conditions at hospitals for the mentally ill and the mentally handicapped. Partly in response to these inquiries the DHSS published White Papers setting out the future direction in which services for the mentally ill, mentally handicapped and elderly people should move; and in terms of overall service development, the Department gave priority to these groups. These actions were an attempt to allocate a greater share of resources to an area of the NHS which it was recognised had fallen behind required standards (Martin, 1984).

What has been the impact of these policies? The evidence from a study of hospital services in the Leeds region indicates that in the years immediately after the Ely Report, additional money was spent on long-stay services (Ham, 1981). This resulted in tangible improvements to hospital buildings and the amenities enjoyed by patients, and higher staffing levels. What is more, the visiting teams from the HAS provided a source of outside advice and stimulation, and helped to disseminate good practices. In some cases, the teams were able to engage in more detailed work with hospital staff in an attempt to improve the quality of care provided. The policy of developing community-based services for the mentally ill and handicapped also took the pressure off hospitals, although these services developed only slowly in many areas.

There were, however, limits to the extent to which additional money and visits from the HAS teams could produce long-term improvements in services. This was illustrated by the need to hold enquiries at other long-stay hospitals, and one of the problems revealed in these enquiries was that previous HAS recommendations which might have helped these hospitals had not been implemented. Consequently, when the Health Advisory Service was formed in 1976 out of the Hospital Advisory Service, the importance of the Service following-up reports was stressed. Yet change ultimately depended on the approval of local staff, who were not always sympathetic to the advice given by the HAS. Also, the difficulties encountered in long-stay hospitals often concerned poor communication between staff and entrenched professional positions. These difficulties had to be tackled on a long-term basis, and the resources for doing this were available only in exceptional circumstances. From 1976 onwards the Development Team for the Mentally Handicapped (since renamed the National Development Team for Mentally Handicapped People) supplemented the work of the Health Advisory Service, which concentrated on services for the mentally ill, the elderly and children receiving long-term care, but the pattern of operation of both bodies continued to take the form of relatively short visits rather than in-depth involvement with particular institutions.

The consultative document on *Priorities* published in 1976 stated that priority was to be given to long-stay services. Planned annual growth rates in current expenditure set out in the consultative document were 2.8 per cent for the mentally handicapped, 1.8 per cent for the mentally ill and 3.2 per cent for elderly people, compared with around 2 per cent for health and personal social services as a whole (DHSS, 1976b). These growth rates were intended to increase the share of expenditure allocated to the elderly and the mentally handicapped, and to maintain the position of the mentally ill. By increasing inputs in this way, it was hoped to improve the quality of services. What has happened in practice over the period between 1975–6 and 1981–2 is that the proportion of the health and personal social services budget allocated to services for the mentally ill has fallen, the proportion allocated to services for the mentally handicapped has remained the same, and the proportion allocated to services for the elderly has increased (see Chapter 4). In the case of hospitals for the mentally ill and mentally handicapped, the number of patients cared for has continued to fall while expenditure and staffing levels have increased, leading to some improvements in the quality of care (DHSS, 1983a). Overall, though, progress towards achieving the kinds of priorities set out in 1976 has been slow and uneven. Part of the difficulty of achieving national priorities is that health authorities may not share the objectives of the DHSS. The claims of non-priority groups, particularly in the acute hospital sector, may be pressed strongly at the local level, and may push service development in a different direction from that desired by central government. As we noted in Chapter 5, the implementation of national priorities can therefore be problematic. This point can be illustrated in relation to services for the mentally handicapped, where a review of progress made in implementing the policies set out in the White Paper, *Better Services for the Mentally Handicapped*, noted that the percentage of NHS revenue allocated to services for the mentally handicapped declined between 1974–5 and 1977–8. The review commented:

> the financial data for health services suggests that the constraints since 1974, together with demographic pressures and the need to rationalise acute services in order to release revenue for development, meant that health authorities could do little to sustain the previous increase in expenditure on mental handicap services other than their increasing contribution through Joint Finance. (DHSS, 1980c, p. 62)

Undoubtedly one of the reasons for this is that, despite the priority given by the DHSS, mental handicap and other long-stay services are relatively weak in the struggle for scarce resources that occurs in health authorities.

Monitoring and evaluating services

An examination of different kinds of inequalities in health and health services raises the question of whether the NHS is able to monitor performance and evaluate the effectiveness of service provision in order to identify areas where objectives are not being met. Considerable emphasis was placed on monitoring at the time of health service reorganisation in 1974, and the 'Grey Book' on *Management Arrangements* (DHSS, 1972a) stated that it was the function of health authority officers and members to review the performance of subordinate tiers of administration to see if agreed standards were being achieved. Similarly, referring to the District Health Authorities which came into operation in 1982, the DHSS argued that 'the task of assessing an authority's performance will be a major management responsibility for the authority and its officers. A programme of visits and reviews of district services will help authority members to judge the quality of services provided' (DHSS, 1981c, p. 28). The Department went on to suggest that national policy guidelines would help DHAs to identify what could be achieved, and that comparisons with other authorities would also be valuable. The idea that each DHA should prepare an annual report was put forward as a way of assessing standards.

In practice, the capacity for monitoring and evaluation is not well developed, either within health authorities or in the DHSS. Historically, monitoring has been predominantly local in character, has occurred intermittently and has been a response to crises. The main exceptions to this are bodies like the Health Advisory Service and the National Development Team for Mentally Handicapped People, which are independent of both field agencies and the central department. Also, until it was disbanded in 1980, the National Development Group for the Mentally Handicapped published a series of reports giving advice to health authorities on monitoring standards of service provision. As far as the DHSS is concerned, for many years the central department lacked the means to undertake a sustained review and analysis of health policies. Brown has noted that part of the reason for this was that 'until 1956 the Ministry had no statistician, no economists and no research staff or management experts apart from a small group of work study officers' (Brown, 1979, p. 12).

Although there were moves to make greater use of statistical information and economic analysis during the 1960s, the most significant changes did not occur until the internal reorganisation of the DHSS in 1972 and the parallel development of the Department's policy analysis capability, noted in Chapter 4. A number of innovations have resulted from these developments, including the use of programme budgeting to analyse expenditure on health and personal social services, and the publication of studies of policies on the acute hospital sector (DHSS, 1981f), community care (DHSS, 1981a) and the respective role of the general acute and geriatric sectors in the care of elderly hospital patients (DHSS, 1981g). In addition, reports have been prepared on progress made in implementing policies for mentally handicapped people (DHSS, 1980c), and on NHS capital and buildings (DHSS, 1979b). The DHSS has also published a review of the performance of the NHS over the decade to 1981 (DHSS, 1983a). These are all indications that the Department's monitoring role is being given greater priority.

Yet it remains the case that monitoring and evaluation are difficult tasks to perform within the NHS. This was noted in a memorandum submitted by the DHSS to the House of Commons Expenditure Committee in 1972 on services for the elderly. The Department argued that general aims could be formulated for services, such as 'to enable the elderly to maintain their independence and self respect', but measuring the extent to which these aims were achieved was problematic (Expenditure Committee, 1972, p. 3). Also as we noted earlier in the chapter, disentangling the impact of health services from that of other variables is not easy. Nevertheless, the Department noted that

> this is not to say that the problems are wholly insoluble. It may, for instance, be possible in time to devise means of measuring the condition of individuals against agreed scales of, for example, mobility or social participation and correlating changes in different areas over time with the pattern of services provided; or to establish indicators of the health and social wellbeing of the elderly in particular communities or areas and to undertake similar correlations ... But it will take many years to develop and test agreed measures, to establish a methodology for applying and interpreting them and to collect the necessary information. (Expenditure Committee, 1972, p. 4)

Many of these points apply to other areas of the NHS. The objectives of service provision can often be stated only in general terms, and they may not be entirely consistent with one another. Devising measures in order to assess whether objectives have been met is beset with difficulties, and as a result many of the indicators used concern either inputs into health care, for example expenditure and staffing levels, or activity levels, such as the number of beds occupied or patients treated. Outcome indicators, for example on mortality or morbidity rates, are rarely employed, and it is therefore difficult to judge whether increases in inputs lead to improvements in outcomes. The area of service provision in which performance indicators have been applied most consistently in the past is that of hospital services for the mentally ill and the mentally handicapped. A series of reports published by the DHSS in the 1960s and early 1970s identified those hospitals falling within the lowest tenth of all mental illness and mental handicap hospitals for certain grades of staff and services (see for example DHSS, 1972b). Thereafter, the reports measured progress made in achieving minimum standards of staffing and patients' amenities (see for example DHSS, 1974). The standards for mental handicap services were set out in guidance issued by the DHSS in 1969 and 1972, and the standards for mental illness services were issued in 1972. In this area, then, there has been an attempt to monitor the development of services.

More recently, considerable effort has gone into the production of a set of performance indicators covering the core services provided by district health authorities. The stimulus behind this initiative was an investigation by the Public Accounts Committee in 1981 during which two RHA chairmen acknowledged that there was scope for improving the quality of the information available for comparing the performance of services in different regions. The Committee urged the DHSS to give greater priority to its monitoring role, and subsequently officials from the Department developed an initial set of performance indicators in collaboration with officers of the Northern RHA. These were used on a trial basis in 1982 and a complete set of indicators relating to 1981 was published in 1983 (DHSS, 1983c).

The indicators cover clinical activity, finance, manpower and estate management functions. They draw on routinely available statistical information and enable health authorities to examine their performance in areas such as the length of stay of patients in hospital, the costs per case of treating patients, the costs of providing services such as laundry and catering, and the number of staff employed. The DHSS has emphasised that while comparisons of performance in different authorities may be helpful, the published reports are not intended to be league tables. Rather, they provide a starting point for analysis, and it is expected that exceptional performance as revealed by performance indicators will lead to further investigation. As well as providing a tool for use by local managers, performance indicators are examined during the accountability review process and enable the DHSS to question RHAs, and RHAs to question DHAs on the provision of their services.

Performance indicators form one part of a series of initiatives promulgated by the DHSS in the search for greater efficiency in the NHS (see Chapter 2). The indicators published in 1983 are seen as experimental and a Joint NHS/DHSS Group has been established to advise on future developments. The indicators currently in use have a number of weaknesses and one of the tasks facing the Group will be how to overcome these weaknesses. In part, this means developing indicators for services not covered, such as community services and family practitioner services, and in part it involves devising measures of outcome and quality as well as input and activity. The second of these points is particularly important. As a number of commentators have pointed out, one of the dangers with the performance indicators' exercise is that by focusing primarily on resource inputs and activity levels, it encourages health authorities to reduce costs and increase productivity without providing the means of assessing whether the result is a healthier or more satisfied population (McCarthy, 1983).

Apart from the need to develop a wider range of measures of performance, there is also a need to improve the quality of the current range of indicators. This involves providing data as quickly as possible to local managers, and making sure that data are accurate. The work of the Steering Group on Health Services Information is relevant in this context. The information systems which will be developed as a result of the reports of the Steering Group should provide health authorities with a much more comprehensive picture of their performance than is available through existing data. A final point about performance indicators is the need to involve clinicians in their use. Yates, a researcher who has played a considerable part in developing statistical indices of performance in the NHS, has argued that performance indicators will not be effective unless those who provide services participate fully in debating the indicators and analysing their significance (Yates, 1982).

The importance of monitoring has been emphasised by the House of Commons Social Services Committee as well as the Public Accounts Committee. As the Social Services Committee has commented, 'the DHSS should continue to seek to develop ways of assessing quality independently of the input of resources; this is already the role of the Health Advisory Service and could usefully become a responsibility of any new Management Advisory Service' (Social Services Committee, 1981, p. xiii). The view of the DHSS is that there are two kinds of monitoring: strategic monitoring, which examines whether services are developing in line with agreed policies and strategies; and efficiency monitoring, which assesses whether available resources are being used to the best advantage (DHSS, 1980f). Both types of monitoring are the responsibility of the Management Advisory Service, referred to by the Social Services Committee. Experiments with the Service started in 1982. Originally, it was hoped to undertake three trials in four regions. In the event, two experiments were launched, one in the Wessex region and another covering the Oxford and South Western regions. The MAS, described by Sir Patrick Nairne, a former Permanent Secretary at the DHSS, as 'an external, critical inspectorial eye translated into the NHS' (Public Accounts Committee, 1981, p. 69) has developed in different ways in the two trials. The Wessex approach, known as Performance Review, evolved out of the Regional Monitoring Policy pursued in the late 1970s. In Wessex it has been stressed that Performance Review is a task of everyday management and reviews are undertaken by DHAs themselves. Within a common regional framework, it is the responsibility of district officers to design and implement reviews of services such as catering or maternity services. It is argued that this is more likely to result in effective change than monitoring carried out by a higher tier authority. Participation is therefore voluntary, and the approach used is selective with each DHA reviewing only a part of its services at any one time. The Oxford and South Western version of MAS centres on an independent, multidisciplinary team of experienced NHS officers working under the aegis of a supervisory board. Methods used by the team in promoting change include preparing reports on specific services, disseminating good practices, and working with health authority staff on local management problems and on the development of management processes. Topics examined encompass the management of waiting lists, the development of strategic planning and services for children (Mowbray, 1983). Both MAS trials are being evaluated with a view to deriving lessons for the NHS as a whole.

Notwithstanding the MAS, the development of performance indicators and the range of other mechanisms which exist to monitor and evaluate services, the Griffiths Report commented in 1983 that

> The NHS ... still lacks any real continuous evaluation of its performance ... Rarely are precise management objectives set; there is little measurement of health output; clinical evaluation of particular practices is by no means common and economic evaluation of these practices extremely rare. Nor can the NHS display a ready assessment of the effectiveness with which it is meeting the needs and expectations of the people it serves. (Griffiths Report, 1983, p. 10)

Some of the reasons why monitoring and evaluation are underdeveloped in the NHS are identified by Klein, a former specialist adviser to the Social Services Committee. As Klein (1982) notes, the health policy arena is characterised by complexity, heterogeneity, uncertainty and ambiguity. Complexity is evident in the wide range of occupations involved in providing services; heterogeneity in the variety of services provided; uncertainty in the absence of a clear relationship between inputs and outputs; and ambiguity in the meaning of the information which is available. Given these factors, Klein concludes that performance is inherently a contested notion, and that performance evaluation is most usefully seen as a process of argument.

If this is the case, what territory should the argument cover? As we have noted, most attempts to monitor performance in the NHS have made use of measures of the input of resources and activity levels. Doll (1974) has suggested that these measures of economic efficiency need to be considered alongside indicators of medical outcome and social acceptability. Doll's analysis has been developed by Maxwell (1984) who has identified six dimensions of the quality of health care: access to services, relevance to need, effectiveness, equality, social acceptability, and efficiency and economy. In relation to medical outcome and effectiveness, McCarthy's (1982) work has indicated how health authorities might establish targets in areas such as accidental deaths in children and mortality rates from coronary heart disease as a way of assessing the impact of services on the health of the population. In relation to social acceptability, community health councils provide a means of establishing how well services are performing from the point of view of patients, while *ad hoc* surveys such as those carried out for the Royal Commission on the NHS (Gregory, 1978; Simpson, 1979) are another means of sampling opinion. The work of independent researchers and pressure groups (see, for example, Kitzinger, 1979) offers a further source of data in this area. Nevertheless, as the Griffiths Report observed, health authorities have an imperfect idea of how well their services are being delivered, and the greater use of techniques like market research might help to overcome this.

Conclusion

Monitoring and evaluation provide a means by which information about the impact of services can be assessed and fed back into the policy-making process. In fact, feedback occurs all the time in more or less regular forms. For example, revelations about conditions at long-stay hospitals in the 1960s indicated that not all was well with this part of the NHS, and led to a reformulation of policies. Again, the report of the Working Group on Inequalities in Health, in demonstrating the persistence of class differences in mortality and morbidity, suggested that services should be reorientated in favour of groups with a poor health experience. *Ad hoc* reviews of this kind are supplemented by regular reappraisals of policy within the DHSS. Policy monitoring and evaluation do therefore take place, but the point of the recommendations from the Social Services Committee and the Public Accounts Committee was that these activities should become a more systematic part of the health policy-making process, and that the techniques employed should be developed further. To some extent this has happened in recent years, but a considerable amount of work remains to be done.

　　In this chapter we have examined in some detail the impact of health services in three main areas. We have shown how inequalities exist in relation to the standard of care provided for different client groups; the geographical distribution of mortality rates and resources; and the utilisation of services by social classes, and mortality and morbidity rates between classes. We have also considered the response by policy-makers to evidence about these inequalities. An impressive concern has been shown with client group inequalities, although there have been problems in implementing national policies at the local level; and policies have been devised in the shape of the RAWP formula to even out the allocation of resources to geographical areas. In contrast, social class inequalities have, at the time of writing, not produced a positive policy response. However, we have seen how evidence about client group inequalities was at first largely disregarded and dismissed by policy-makers, and that the issue was forced back on to the agenda with the publication of the Ely Report. The same may apply to social class inequalities, and there may in future be an attempt to prepare a strategy along the lines set out by the Black Working Group on Inequalities in Health. This example notwithstanding, the discussion in this chapter has shown that the experience of implementing policies and reviewing their impact provides an important contribution to the process of policy-making, showing how continuous that process is.

7

Power in Health Services

The examination of the impact of health services in Chapter 6 revealed various inequalities in health and health services. In seeking to explain these inequalities, it is necessary to analyse the distribution of power in health care systems. In other words, explaining the distribution of benefits within health services requires us to ask who controls those services and who influences the allocation of resources? There are a number of theoretical approaches to answering these questions. Three such approaches will be examined here: Marxist, pluralist and what, for want of a better term, we shall call structuralist.

Marxist approaches

Marxists argue that medical care in societies like Britain must be seen as part of the capitalist mode of production (Doyal, 1979). Within capitalism, Marxists contend that there is an important division between the owners of the means of production – the dominant class or the bourgeoisie – and those who have to sell their wage labour – the subordinate class or the proletariat. It is the capitalist mode of production which gives rise to class relations of production, and Marxists go on to argue that the economically dominant class is also politically dominant. The state therefore acts in the long-term interests of the bourgeoisie, and performs a number of functions.

In O'Connor's terms, the state assists in the process of capital accumulation, and also performs the function of legitimation (O'Connor, 1973). State expenditures are directed towards these ends, and are made up of social capital and social expenses. State expenditures on health services comprise partly social capital, in so far as health services involve the reproduction of a healthy labour force, and partly they comprise social expenses, in so far as health services help to maintain non-working groups and promote social harmony. State involvement in the provision of health services stems from two sources: action by the bourgeoisie to reduce the costs of labour power and to prevent social unrest; and action by the proletariat through the class struggle to win concessions from the bourgeoisie. However, Marxists argue that there may develop a fiscal crisis for the state when the demand for expenditure on health services outstrips the ability of the state to fund that expenditure. At this point a restructuring of public expenditure may occur to the disadvantage of state health services. Marxists would interpret this as an attack on the interests of the subordinate class, even though health services are seen as a form of social control (Gough, 1979).

Within this theoretical perspective, inequalities in service provision between client groups are explained in terms of the lack of productivity of the mentally ill, mentally handicapped and the elderly. It is suggested that because these groups cannot make a significant contribution to the development of the economy and of profit, they will receive a lower quality service than productive groups. Similarly, social class inequalities in health are interpreted by Marxists as evidence of the continuing influence of economic factors on health and the persistence of class divisions within society. The distribution of benefits within health services is therefore explained by reference to class conflict and the dominance of the bourgeoisie.

At a macro level of analysis Marxist theory has considerable explanatory value. Yet a convincing theory of power must also be able to explain the processes of policy-making and implementation described in Chapters 4 and 5. Marxist approaches are much weaker at this level of analysis, and Marxist studies of particular decisions, issues or health care organisations are little developed. In contrast, pluralist theories, with their focus on the role of pressure groups and bargaining and negotiation within policy communities, offer a range of insights into the dynamics of health policy-making, and we will now consider the utility of these theories.

Pluralism

The essence of the pluralist democratic theory of power is that the resources which contribute to power are widely distributed among different groups. As we noted in Chapter 3, pluralists argue that no one group is dominant, and each is able to exercise some influence (see for example Dahl, 1961). Power is in fact shared between official groups in governmental agencies and outside interests exerting pressures on these agencies. This helps to ensure there is no consistent bias in the allocation of values, although pluralists would recognise that groups vary in their ability to exercise power. Developments in health services and health policy are explained in terms of the interplay between pressure groups. Since there is no dominant interest, pluralists analyse the distribution of power in relation to particular issues, studying who wins and who loses through often detailed examinations of the preferences of different interests and the extent to which decisions match up with expressed preferences. The question of who has power is for the pluralists an empirical question, to be answered by means of careful case studies of particular policy areas. A range of factors may be important, including party manifestos, key individuals, official reports and the activities of pressure groups, but their relative influence must be studied in specific cases. Examples of studies of the NHS which have their roots in the pluralist democratic tradition are Willcock's (1967) examination of the creation of the NHS and Eckstein's (1960) analysis of the operation of the BMA. Each author analyses the way in which decisions are arrived at in a system of pressure group politics, and each is able to show how the outcomes were the result of compromise between the various interests involved. Professional interests vie with consumer interests, and civil servants with politicians, but alliances change, leading to the fragmentation of power which pluralists observe. The strength of pluralist theory is the richness of detail provided about decision-making and the high degree of sophistication which has often been achieved in the analysis of individual, group and organisational influences on policy processes.

Like Marxism, though, pluralism does not provide a completely adequate theory of power. For example, in earlier chapters we noted the key position occupied by the medical profession in the organisation of health services, and our discussion of how policies

are made and implemented in the NHS suggests certain inade-
quacies in the pluralist position. In particular, the strength of
producer groups and the relative weakness of consumer groups
cast doubt on the pluralists' argument that any group can make
itself heard effectively at some stage in the decision-making
process, and that no group is dominant (Ham, 1977). Accordingly,
as we argued in Chapter 5, attention needs to be paid to the work
of Alford, who has maintained that it is important to analyse the
nature of structural interests within health services. We will now
examine Alford's thesis in greater detail.

Structuralist approaches

Alford argues that structural interests are those interests which
gain or lose from the form of organisation of health services
(Alford, 1975a). There are three sets of structural interests:
dominant, challenging and repressed. Dominant interests are the
professional monopolists; challenging interests are the corporate
rationalisers; and repressed interests are the community population. Dominant interests are served by existing social, economic
and political institutions, and therefore only need to be active
when their interests are challenged. Alford argues that the medical
profession is dominant in health services, but the profession may
be challenged by corporate rationalisers such as health planners
and administrators. Again, patient and consumer groups representing the community population may seek to move out of their
repressed position by organising to articulate their interests. These
struggles between structural interests are not the same as the
competition for power between pressure groups. Pressure group
competition may well take place within structural interests, as
between, for example, different groups of doctors. These conflicts
are important, but they leave unchallenged the principle of
professional monopoly and dominance. Pressure group politics
coexist with struggles between structural interests, and may explain how particular issues are resolved. Structural interests are,
however, more significant in influencing the overall distribution of
benefits, and in shaping the main contours of power relationships.

The value of Alford's framework has been demonstrated in a
study of policy-making in the NHS (Ham, 1981), and the inequali-

ties in power he points to indicate a position close to elitist interpretations of the power structure. In the health sector, professional control of knowledge, recruitment and training, as well as claims to professional autonomy over the content of work, provide the basis of the medical profession's power. Its organisation through powerful pressure groups in continuous contact with governmental agencies, coupled with involvement at all stages in the system of administration, enhance this power. In emphasising elite power based on professional position, the above analysis offers an alternative to both pluralism and Marxism. Structuralist approaches recognise the existence of pressure group politics but contend that studies which remain at the level of groups are incomplete.

Equally, while structuralists acknowledge the importance of economic and class factors, they maintain that class divisions are less important in explaining the development and organisation of health services than divisions between structural interests. The two are by no means synonymous. In particular, the growth of intermediate groups between the bourgeoisie and the proletariat requires some modification of the straightforward Marxist position, and highlights the need for a framework able to take account of the complexities of social divisions within contemporary society. This suggests that what is required is an approach which builds on the strength of each of the theoretical positions discussed here. We have argued that all three positions have some merits, but none provides an adequate account by itself. Rather than seeking to develop one theory to the point where it furnishes a complete explanation in its own right, it may be preferable to attempt to search for links between the different theories. An investment of effort in this direction holds out the prospect of high returns, not least because the three positions we have discussed tend to focus on different levels of analysis.

The key issue, then, is to develop 'mediating frameworks to connect macro-theory with specific policy issues' (Dunleavy, 1981, p. 4). One approach to this is through the examination of dominant value systems in particular policy areas and their influence on policy. More specifically, by analysing the operation of professional ideologies in health services, it may be possible to establish links between the way issues are defined and resources allocated, the nature of structural interests and the distribution of power, and macro theories of the state (Ham, 1980). The difficulties of doing this are considerable, but a start can be made by exploring the role of the medical profession and the way in which the profession's view of health has come to occupy a dominant position.

Concepts of health

There are many different concepts of health. Margaret Stacey has identified three dimensions along which these concepts vary: individual or collective; functional fitness or welfare; preventive or curative (Stacey, 1977b). Stacey notes that in Western societies the individualistic concept of health tends to dominate, and it is usually associated with ideas of functional fitness and curative approaches. This concept seeks the causes of illness within the biological systems of individuals, and it attempts to provide a specific cure for illness in order to make individuals fit for work. Alongside the individualistic concept of health, Stacey notes the existence of a collective concept which emphasises the importance of prevention. The collective concept seeks the causes of illnesses within the environmental, economic and social systems in which people live, and attempts to prevent illness arising by tackling the unhealthy aspects of those systems. Stacey also notes the existence of a welfare concept of health, emphasising the importance of relieving pain and providing care.

While these concepts coexist, it is the individualistic, functional fitness, curative approach which is the most influential. This approach has been characterised as the medical model of health, a model in which doctors have a central role and hospitals play a major part. It has been suggested that the model has two components: a disease component, which holds that illness results from pathological processes in the biochemical functions of the body; and an engineering component, which sees the body as a machine to be repaired by technical means (Illsley, 1977). The medical model emphasises specific, individual causes of illness and searches for specific individual cures for these illnesses.

Acceptance of the medical model is important, first, in justifying the pre-eminent position of the medical profession in health matters, and second, in helping to explain the pattern of investment in health services. Within the NHS, the bulk of resources is allocated to personally orientated, general and acute hospital services. Much less importance has been attached to collective, preventive and welfare approaches to health. However, this may be changing as the medical model comes under increasing attack.

The attack on medical dominance in the health field has been spearheaded by writers such as McKeown, who have questioned the significance of the medical contributioin in bringing about improvements in health. McKeown's work has demonstrated that improved nutrition, purer water supplies, behavioural changes limiting family size and leading to the better spacing of births, and improved methods of sewage disposal, have been mainly responsible for the advances in health which have occurred in the last 200 years. These factors contributed to the decline in infectious diseases, and assisted in reducing death rates and increasing life expectancy. In contrast, medical science had very little impact until the introduction of vaccines and certain drugs in the twentieth century. Yet McKeown argues that even these interventions came at a time when overall death rates were already in decline as a result of earlier environmental and behavioural changes. On the basis of his analysis, McKeown contends that

> medical science and services are misdirected, and society's investment in health is not well used, because they rest on an erroneous assumption about the basis of human health. It is assumed that the body can be regarded as a machine whose protection from disease and its effects depends primarily on internal intervention. The approach has led to indifference to the external influences and personal behaviour which are the predominant determinants of health. (McKeown, 1976, p. xiv)

McKeown's work has had a major influence in the development of the health field concept articulated by Lalonde (1974). The health field concept analyses illness and disease in terms of four elements: human biology, the environment, life-style and health care organisation. Human biology includes aspects of health, such as ageing, which are developed within the body as a result of the basic biology of man. The environment comprises matters relating to health external to the body, over which the individual has little or no control. Life-style refers to the decisions by individuals which affect health and over which they have control. And health care organisation consists of the arrangements made to provide organised health services to individuals. Like McKeown, Lalonde suggests that while most efforts to improve health have centred on medical interventions through health care organisation, it is the other three elements which are more important in identifying the causes of sickness and death. In particular, Lalonde points to the need for people to adopt healthy life-styles in order to prevent illness arising.

This is very much in line with the policy on prevention adopted by the DHSS. As we noted in Chapter 2, the Department has used the work of people like McKeown to argue that greater emphasis should be given to prevention, and that individuals should look after themselves by giving up smoking, adopting an appropriate diet, taking exercise, and so on. This individualistic approach to prevention does not seriously threaten the medical model, and it has been criticised for 'blaming the victim'. A growing body of research indicates that life-style may be less significant than the environment (defined in its widest sense) in influencing illness and disease, and that a collective approach to health is needed if progress is to be made in tackling contemporary health problems. This was the argument of the Black Working Group on Inequalities in Health, and other studies have drawn attention to the industrial and environmental causes of cancer (Doyal *et al.*, 1983), the impact of unemployment on health (Brenner, 1979), and to the various ways in which the processes of production, distribution and consumption contribute to illness and disease (Draper, Best and Dennis, 1977). These studies constitute a significant challenge to the medical model, not least because they imply a much reduced role for doctors. It must be added, though, that medicine has remained remarkably resilient in the face of criticism, and continues to provide the dominant explanation of health problems in contemporary Western societies.

What are the implications of this analysis for the earlier discussion of power in health care systems? What we hope to have shown is that the medical model, as the dominant (though not only) value system in the health field, exercises a key influence on the definition of issues and the allocation of resources. The question this raises is whose interests are served by the medical model? Stacey (1977b) has reminded us that concepts do not stand alone, they must be understood in terms of the power of different groups. Let us then return to the examination of theories of power for help in explaining the dominance of the medical model.

Power, interests and ideology

In the pluralist framework, concepts of health and the role of medicine are not seen as having special significance. The medical profession is viewed as one interest among many, albeit in most studies a key interest; and concepts of health are implicitly assumed to have emerged out of the underlying consensus on which pluralist theories are based. Within this consensus, prevailing concepts of health are no more than a reflection of the shifting balance of power between interests. The fact that they have remained the same over time is seen by pluralists as an indication of the large measure of agreement between these interests on the meaning of health and the manner in which services should be provided. The question that needs to be asked about this interpretation is whether the consensus which pluralists observe is genuine or false. In other words, is the consensus the result of spontaneous agreement among different groups in the population, or does it derive from manipulation by dominant groups?

This question is not easily resolved. Pluralists would argue that people's expressed preferences are the only reliable guide to their interests, and the fact that these preferences demonstrate strong support for the medical profession is in itself sufficient to show that the consensus on values is genuine. In contrast, critics of pluralism would argue that people's real interests may differ from their expressed preferences, in which case the possibility of a false consensus being manipulated by dominant groups cannot be ruled out. The problem with this approach is how to establish the existence of real interests which are different from expressed preferences (Saunders, 1979). One line of analysis in the health field would be to develop McKeown's work, which, as we have noted, has suggested that society's investment in health is not well used because it is based on the medical model. What this indicates is that people's real interests might be better served by an alternative pattern of investment. That is, improved health might result from a reorientation away from personally orientated, hospital-based health care towards a system in which more emphasis was given to the social causes of illness and disease. If this could be demonstrated, then a rather different explanation of the interests served by dominant concepts of health would be needed.

Such an explanation is provided by structuralists. For structuralists, dominant concepts of health serve the interests of the medical profession because they legitimate the profession's claim to control in health services. In other words, prevailing concepts of health are explained by the position of the medical profession as a dominant structural interest and its success in getting individualistic definitions of illness and disease accepted. The dominance of medicine is in turn accounted for historically in terms of the success of physicians, surgeons and apothecaries in winning state approval for their position, and in turning their occupations into professions having exclusive control over their area of work (Wilding, 1982). Medical dominance does not imply a conspiracy against subordinate groups. Rather, it reflects the power of doctors, their control of key resources such as expertise and knowledge, and their ability to achieve acceptance for their own concept of health. This concept of health makes sense to groups in the population other than doctors, but as we have shown, it is not the only concept, and it is not necessarily the concept which best serves the interests of the population.

Like structuralists, Marxists would challenge the pluralists' position that consensus is genuine, but would see dominant concepts of health not as an indication of the power of the medical profession, but as evidence of the dominance of the bourgeoisie. In particular, Marxists argue that the individual, disease-based model of curative medicine helps to maintain the position of the bourgeoisie by masking the real causes of illness which lie within the social and economic system of capitalism. As Navarro has put it:

> the social utility of medicine is measured primarily in the arena of legitimation. Medicine is indeed socially useful to the degree that the majority of people believe and accept the proposition that what are actually politically caused conditions can be individually solved by medical intervention. From the point of view of the capitalist system, this is the actual utility of medicine – it contributes to the legitimation of capitalism. (Navarro, 1976, p. 208)

For Marxists, the medical model is a key linking concept explaining not only how issues are defined and benefits distributed in the policy process, but also highlighting underlying class divisions within society. The conclusion to be drawn from the Marxist analysis is that the dominant concept of health serves bourgeois interests, that power is weighted heavily in favour of those interests, and that doctors, although seemingly in a powerful position, merely administer the health care system on behalf of the bourgeoisie.

It thus emerges that Marxists and structuralists see different interests being served by dominant concepts of health. Structuralists argue that the medical profession has power in its own right, not simply power deriving from its utility to the bourgeoisie. In contrast, Marxists argue that medical power results from class power. The Marxist position is well summarised by Navarro, who criticises writers such as Alford for

> their failure to recognise that those elites (for example medicine) are in reality segments of a dominant class and that, when they are considered in a systemic and not just a sectorial fashion, they are found to possess a high degree of cohesion and solidarity, with common interests and common purposes for transcending their specific differences and disagreements. (Navarro, 1976, pp. 189–90)

The question which needs to be raised about this argument is whether all conflicts are 'in reality' class conflicts, and if so how disagreements between the state and the medical profession can be explained.

It has been suggested, for example, that it cannot be assumed that state expenditure on health services is automatically in the interests of the bourgeoisie. Saunders (1981) has criticised Marxists for ignoring the possibility that such spending may be dysfunctional for capital. The fiscal crisis of the state has illustrated the importance of Saunders's criticism, and has indicated that while expenditure on areas of collective consumption like the NHS may benefit professional interests, it may be against the interests of the bourgeoisie, whose main purpose is to maintain capital accumulation. A similar point is made by Cawson (1982) who argues that the growth of public expenditure has been fuelled by the bargaining processes between the state and producer groups. Cawson explains this in terms of the development of a corporate sector in the British political system in which producer groups like the BMA are intimately involved both in the making of policy and its implementation. Cawson predicts that expenditure cuts will be resisted by producer groups and that governments faced with a fiscal crisis will seek to reduce the burden of public expenditure by privatising services.

It can also be suggested that attempts will be made to curtail professional power. There is evidence that this is happening in the United Kingdom, with the Conservative Government elected in 1979 seeking to limit the restrictive practices of occupations such as solicitors, accountants and architects. In relation to health services, the management reforms initiated since the Griffiths Report can be seen as an attempt to strengthen the hand of planners and administrators in their challenge to medical dominance. The appointment of general managers, and the call for doctors to be more closely involved in management, were both designed to introduce greater control over the activities of the medical profession and to influence the behaviour of consultants in their position as the key controllers of resources in the NHS. What is more, the recommendation in the Griffiths Report that arrangements for consultation on decisions should be streamlined was interpreted by some observers as an attempt to maintain community interests in their repressed position. More important, a number of commentators have argued that what Griffiths was really talking about was a change in management style, with less reliance being placed on administrative and professional values and greater importance being attached to the positive management of the Service (Evans, 1983). As Day and Klein (1983) have noted, one of the implications of this is that conflict between managers and professionals is more likely to occur, particularly if clinical freedom is questioned and challenged. Coincidentally, publication of the Griffiths Report occurred within days of a claim that clinical freedom had died, 'crushed between the rising costs of new forms of investigation and treatment and the financial limits inevitable in an economy that cannot expand indefinitely' (Hampton, 1983, p. 1238). While this obituary appeared premature, the medical profession was not slow to recognise the threat posed by Griffiths and to argue that doctors should take on the general management role whenever possible.

To summarise this argument, it is clear that developments such as the introduction of general management into the NHS, the challenge to the professions and the privatisation of services cannot be explained simply in terms of the internal dynamics of the Service. Policies in the health field are constrained by a wider set of factors, particularly the approach taken by government to the management of the economy and public expenditure. The value of the perspective offered by writers such as Cawson is precisely that it draws attention to the economic context within which social policies are developed. Cawson's analysis of corporatism and welfare is closely linked to the structuralist analysis of power. Both Cawson and Alford recognise the significance of the process of capital accumulation in capitalist society and the role played by the state in promoting profitable economic activity. At the same time, they reject Marxist models of political analysis which reduce all conflicts to class conflicts. Alford in particular maintains that the way in which the accumulation process influences structural interests and policy development in the health field is highly complex. While health policy cannot be adequately understood without reference to economic policy, it cannot be explained solely in terms of class analysis. As Alford has written, 'The translation of class interests (or a cultural consensus) into organisational form and then into action is problematic and contingent' (Alford, 1975b, p. 153). This again points to the need to develop mediating frameworks for linking different levels of analysis.

Conclusion and summary

At first sight, pluralist theories offer a convincing explanation of the distribution of power within health services. After all, the NHS comprises a large number of different groups competing for resources, and most decisions result from bargaining between these groups. Furthermore, health policies tend to involve small adjustments to what has gone before, and a variety of interests are often involved in policy-making. This is in part the picture which has emerged from the discussion of health policy-making and implementation in earlier chapters, and it fits the description of political activity put forward in the pluralist model.

However, Marxist theories challenge the assumptions behind pluralism and provide an alternative explanation. Instead of focusing on immediate conflicts between pressure groups, Marxists seek to relate health care systems to the economic systems within which they are located. By analysing the underlying processes at work, Marxists argue that health services are dominated by the bourgeoisie, whose interests are served by prevailing concepts of health and illness. Health services help to legitimate capitalism and to promote capital accumulation. Pluralists are unable to perceive this because they concentrate on surface struggles and neglect deeper class conflicts. Furthermore, pluralists take dominant concepts of health for granted, and do not question seriously the beneficial impact of medicine or the possibility that conflict may be limited to a narrow range of issues through ideological domination.

In contrast to both approaches, Alford's theory of structural interests looks beyond the surface politics of pressure group conflicts and finds not class struggle but professional dominance. This approach recognises that the world of everyday politics may well approximate to pluralist theories, but it goes further to identify wide discrepancies in power in relation to dominant, challenging and repressed structural interests. Alternative concepts of health are acknowledged to exist, and prevailing concepts reflect the ability of dominant groups to get their definitions accepted. Within this framework, it is possible to encompass both the strengths of pluralist theory, recognising the diversity and variety of pressure group behaviour, and some of the insights of the Marxist analysis, acknowledging that what appears to be going on may obscure underlying conflicts between key interests.

It is suggested, then, that future work might usefully build on this framework and seek to further explicate the 'problematic and contingent' nature of relationships between individual and group action on particular issues of health policy, the role of structural interests, and the characteristics of the state. Our earlier analysis of professional ideologies in the health care system provided some hints on how this might be done, and further empirical studies are required. Above all, it is the interaction of the different levels of analysis which is in need of further investigation. Sophisticated studies of specific policy issues need to be related to the action and inaction of structural interests and the changing role and functions of the state if a complete understanding of the complexities of health policy is to be obtained. Too often in the past, research at one level has occurred in isolation from research at other levels. The challenge now facing students of health policy and politics is to make the links. As we argued at the beginning of the book, individuals and groups may have an impact on policy, but under conditions not of their own choosing. Articulating the relationship betwen action and structure is therefore of the utmost importance, and the discussion in this chapter has pointed to some directions in which work might proceed.

Guide to Further Reading

Chapter 1

Further reading suggestions on the development of health services and health policy must necessarily be highly selective. Useful general accounts of the evolution of the welfare state in Britain are provided by Bruce (1968), Fraser (1973) and Gilbert (1966, 1970). Studies which look more specifically at the history of the medical profession and health services include those by Abel-Smith (1964), Cartwright (1971) and Stevens (1966). Eckstein (1958) and Lindsey (1962) provide a wealth of material on the period before and immediately after the creation of the National Health Service. Levitt (1979) describes the reorganised structure of the NHS introduced in 1974, and Brown (1979) analyses the impact of the 1974 changes. Klein (1983) offers a good overview of the politics of health services in the period since 1939.

Chapter 2

The main sources of further reading on contemporary issues in health policy are the policy documents issued by the DHSS on specific issues or areas of service provision. Most of the relevant documents are referred to in the text. In the main, the documents refer to particular aspects of health services, but general statements can be found in the consultative document on *Priorities* (DHSS, 1976b), *The Way Forward* (DHSS, 1977b), *Care in Action* (DHSS, 1981c), *Health Care and its Costs* (DHSS, 1983a) and the *Health Service in England* (DHSS, 1984b). A summary and review of health service policies was provided by the Royal Commission on the NHS (1979). One of the research studies commissioned by the Royal Commission resulted in the publication of a critical overview of health service planning, priority setting and financing (Bevan, Copeman, Perrin and Rosser, 1980). A further commentary on NHS planning and resource allocation is provided by Butts and his colleagues (Butts, Irving and Whitt, 1981). A summary and analysis of a number of issues in health policy is offered by Allsop (1984).

Chapter 3

More detailed information on the nature of policy and political systems can be found in Easton's work (Easton, 1953, 1965a, 1965b). Jenkins (1978) examines policy analysis using a political and organisational perspective and makes use of an amended systems model. The Crossman and Castle diaries (Crossman, 1975, 1976, 1977; Castle, 1980) give inside views of the organisation of British central government. Beer (1969) provides an important interpretation of the evolution of politics in Britain; and Smith (1976) describes central government from a policy perspective. Brown and Steel (1979) analyse recent changes in the civil service and the machinery of government, while Norton (1981) discusses the role of the House of Commons and Richardson and Jordan (1979) focus on the part played by pressure groups in the policy process. Dunleavy (1983) summarises and assesses the various debates about the distribution of power in the British political system.

Chapter 4

Brown (1975) has written a good, general account of the workings of the DHSS and the part played by the DHSS in the management of the NHS, personal social services and social security. Detailed information on the organisation of the DHSS, particularly in relation to health services, is provided by Butts and colleagues (Butts, Irving and Whitt, 1981) and Razell (1980), although these will become dated when the Griffiths Report (1983) is fully implemented. Griffiths and the Regional Chairmen's Enquiry (1976) indicate some of the reasons why a change in the organisation of the DHSS was necessary. The Crossman and Castle diaries give valuable insights into the politicians' view of health policy-making in central government (Crossman, 1977; Castle, 1980). Studies of policies on hospital planning (Allen, 1979) and smoking (Popham, 1981) have illustrated the role of ministers, civil servants and pressure groups in the policy process. More generally, Solesbury's (1976) work on environmental issues contains material of considerable interest to students of agenda setting in the NHS.

Chapter 5

Brown (1975, 1977) discusses in general terms the relationship between the DHSS and health authorities, while Haywood and Alaszewski (1980) analyse the extent to which the NHS Planning System has been an effective vehicle for the implementation of central policies. Hunter (1980) explores the dynamics of policy-making in health authorities, and identifies a number of phases in centre–periphery relationships (Hunter,

1983). The author's own examination of policy-making in the NHS between 1948 and 1974 (Ham, 1981) covers similar territory. Klein's (1983) work on the politics of the NHS contains much that is relevant to the student of health policy implementation. Recent reports from the Public Accounts Committee (1981) are essential reading in interpreting the changing nature of centre–periphery relationships.

Chapter 6

The *Report of the Royal Commission on the NHS* (1979) contains a general review of the impact of the NHS. The RAWP report (DHSS, 1976a) describes the method used to allocate resources on an equitable geographical basis, and it is summarised and criticised in a research study prepared for the Royal Commission (Buxton and Klein, 1978). The Black Report, *Inequalities in Health* (1980), brings together information on social class differences in health and the use of health services, and makes proposals for reducing these differences. The paperback version of the Black Report (Townsend and Davidson, 1982) includes a response to the Report's critics. The series of inquiries into long-stay hospitals provide powerful evidence of client group inequalities. Examples are the Ely and Normansfield reports (Ely Report, 1969; Normansfield Report, 1978). Martin (1984) has summarised the reports and has analysed the nature of the problems that exist in this area. The reports of the Social Services Committee (1980, 1981) and the DHSS response (1980f) discuss the difficulties of monitoring and evaluating health services. From a different standpoint, Harrison and Gretton (1983) have made an assessment of the strengths and weaknesses of the NHS.

Chapter 7

The Marxist perspective has been most fully developed by Navarro (1976) and Doyal (1979). The structuralist argument has been set out by Alford (1975a), and applied to the NHS by the author (Ham, 1981). Pluralist ideas have been applied in the work of Eckstein (1960) and Willcocks (1967). Stacey (1977b) and Illsley (1977) review different concepts of health and the way these concepts have influenced service provision. Outside the health field, Saunders (1979) has written a major study of theories of power and the role of ideology which is of considerable relevance to the student attempting to understand the complexities of health policy-making.

References

Abel, L.A. and Lewin, W. (1959) 'Report on hospital building', *British Medical Journal Supplement*, 4 April 1959, 109–14.

Abel-Smith, B. (1981) 'Health care in a cold economic climate', *The Lancet*, 14 February 1981.

Abel-Smith, B. (1964) *The Hospitals 1800–1948* (Heinemann)

Alderson, M.R. (1970) 'Social class and the health service', *The Medical Officer*, 17 July 1970, 50–2.

Alford, R. (1975a) *Health Care Politics* (University of Chicago Press).

Alford, R. (1975b) 'Paradigms of relations between state and society', in Lindberg, L.N., Alford, R., Crouch, C. and Offe, C. (eds) *Stress and Contradiction in Modern Capitalism* (Lexington Books).

Allen, D. (1979) *Hospital Planning* (Pitman Medical).

Allsop, J. (1984) *Health Policy and the NHS* (Longman).

Bachrach, P. and Baratz, M.S. (1970) *Power and Poverty* (Oxford University Press).

Bagehot, W. (1963) *The English Constitution*, new edn (Fontana).

Banks, G.T. (1979) 'Programme budgeting in the DHSS', in Booth, T.A. (ed.), *Planning for Welfare* (Blackwell).

Banting, K. (1979) *Poverty, Politics and Policy* (Macmillan).

Barnard, K., Lee, K., Mills, A. and Reynolds, J. (1980) 'NHS planning: an assessment', *Hospital and Health Services Review*, August 1980, 262–5.

Barrett, S. and Fudge, C. (eds)(1981) *Policy and Action* (Methuen).

Becker, H. (ed.) (1967) *Social Problems: A Modern Approach* (Wiley).

Beer, S.H. (1969) *Modern British Politics*, 2nd edn (Faber).

Bevan, G., Copeman, H., Perrin, J. and Rosser, R. (1980) *Health Care Priorities and Management* (Croom Helm).

Birch, R. (1983) 'Policy Analysis in the DHSS: Some Reflections', *Public Administration Bulletin*, no. 43.

Black Report (1980) *Inequalities and Health* (DHSS).

Blackstone, T. (1979) 'Helping ministers do a better job', *New Society*, 19 July 1979, 131–2.

BMJ (1983) 'Trimming fat or cutting bone', vol. 287, 17 September 1983, 780.

Booth, T. (1981) 'Collaboration between the health and social services', *Policy and Politics*, vol. 9, nos 1 and 2.

Brenner, H. (1979) 'Mortality and the national economy', *The Lancet*, 15 September 1979, 568–73.

Brown, R.G.S. (1975) *The Management of Welfare* (Fontana).

Brown, R.G.S. (1977) 'Accountability and control in the NHS', *Health and Social Services Journal*, 28 October 1977, B9–15.

Brown, R.G.S. (1979) *Reorganising the National Health Service* (Blackwell and Robertson).

Brown, R.G.S. and Steel, D.R. (1979) *The Administrative Process in Britain*, 2nd edn (Methuen).

Bruce, M. (1968) *The Coming of the Welfare State*, 4th edn (Batsford).

Butler, J.R. with Bevan, J.M. and Taylor, R.C. (1973) *Family Doctors and Public Policy* (Routledge & Kegan Paul).

Butts, M., Irving, D. and Whitt, C. (1981) *From Principles to Practice* (Nuffield Provincial Hospitals Trust).

Buxton, M.J. and Klein, R.E. (1978) *Allocating health resources: a commentary on the report of the Resource Allocation Working Party*, Royal Commission on the NHS, Research Paper No. 3 (HMSO).

Cannon, G. (1984) 'The cover-up that kills', *The Times*, 12 June 1984, 13.

Cartwright, A. and O'Brien, M. (1976) 'Social class variations in health care', in Stacey, M. (ed), *The Sociology of the NHS*, Sociological Review Monograph 22, Keele.

Cartwright, F. (1971) *A Social History of Medicine* (Longman).

Castle, B. (1980) *The Castle Diaries 1974–76* (Weidenfeld & Nicolson).

Cawson, A. (1982) *Corporatism and Welfare* (Heinemann).

Central Health Services Council (1969) *The Functions of the District General Hospital* (HMSO).

Central Policy Review Staff (1975) *A Joint Framework for Social Policies* (HMSO).

Central Statistical Office (1983) *Social Trends No. 14*, 1984 edn (HMSO).

Central Statistical Office (1984) *Regional Trends*, 1984 edn (HMSO).

Clode, D. (1977) 'Plans aren't worth the paper they are written on', *Health and Social Services Journal*, 16 September 1977, 1314–16.

Cmnd 9058 (1983) *Financial Management in Government Departments* (HMSO).

Court Report (1976) *Fit for the Future*, Report of the Committee on Child Health Services, Cmnd 6684 (HMSO).

Cranbrook Report (1959). *Report of the Maternity Services Committee* (HMSO).

Crossman, R.H.S. (1963) Introduction to *The English Constitution by Bagehot, W.* (Fontana).

Crossman, R.H.S. (1972) *A Politician's View of Health Service Planning* (University of Glasgow Press).

Crossman, R.H.S. (1975) *The Diaries of a Cabinet Minister: Volume One, Minister of Housing 1964–66* (Hamilton and Cape).

Crossman, R.H.S. (1976) *The Diaries of a Cabinet Minister: Volume Two, Lord President of the Council and Leader of the House of Commons 1966–68* (Hamilton & Cape).

Crossman, R.H.S. (1977) *The Diaries of a Cabinet Minister: Volume*

Three, Secretary of State for Social Services 1968–70 (Hamilton & Cape).

Dahl, R. (1961) *Who Governs?* (Yale University Press).

Day, P. and Klein, R. (1983) 'The mobilisation of consent versus the management of conflict: decoding the Griffiths Report', *British Medical Journal*, vol. 287, 1813–6.

DHSS (1971) *Better Services for the Mentally Hendicapped*, Cmnd 4683 (HMSO).

DHSS (1972a) *Management Arrangements in the Reorganised NHS* (HMSO).

DHSS (1972b) *The Facilities and Services of Psychiatric Hospitals in England and Wales 1970*, Statistical and Research Report Series No. 2 (HMSO).

DHSS (1974) *The Facilities and Services of Mental Illness and Mental Handicap Hospitals in England and Wales 1972*, Statistical and Research Report Series No. 8 (HMSO).

DHSS (1975a) *Better Services for the Mentally Ill*, Cmnd 6223 (HMSO).

DHSS (1975b) *Draft Guide to Planning in the NHS*.

DHSS (1975c) *First Interim Report of the Resource Allocation Working Party*.

DHSS (1976a) *Sharing Resources for Health in England* (HMSO).

DHSS (1976b) *Priorities for Health and Personal Social Services in England* (HMSO).

DHSS (1976c) *The NHS Planning System*.

DHSS (1976d) *Prevention and Health: Everybody's Business* (HMSO).

DHSS (1976e) Health Circular (76) 30, *NHS Planning System: Planning Activity in 1976/77*.

DHSS (1977a) *Prevention and Health*, Cmnd 7047 (HMSO).

DHSS (1977b) *The Way Forward* (HMSO).

DHSS (1978a) *A Happier Old Age* (HMSO).

DHSS (1978b) Health Circular (78) 12, *Health and Personal Social Services in England: DHSS Planning Guidelines for 1978/79*.

DHSS (1979a) *Patients First* (HMSO).

DHSS (1979b) *Review of Health Capital*.

DHSS (1980a) Health Circular (80) 8, *Health Service Development Structure and Management*.

DHSS (1980b) *Hospital Services: The Future Pattern of Hospital Provision in England*.

DHSS (1980c) *Mental Handicap: Progress, Problems and Priorities*.

DHSS (1980d) *Organisational and Management Problems of Mental Illness Hospitals* (the Nodder Report).

DHSS (1980e) *Reply to the Second Report from the Social Services Committee on Perinatal and Neonatal Mortality*, Cmnd 8084 (HMSO).

DHSS (1980f) *Reply by the Government to the Third Report from the Social Services Committee, Session 1979–80*, Cmnd 8086 (HMSO).

DHSS (1981a) *Report of a Study on Community Care*.

DHSS (1981b) *Growing Older*, Cmnd 8173 (HMSO).

DHSS (1981c) *Care in Action* (HMSO).

DHSS (1981d) *Care in the Community*.
DHSS (1981e) *Primary Health Care in Inner London* (The Acheson Report).
DHSS (1981f) *Report on a Study of the Acute Hospital Sector*.
DHSS (1981g) *Report on a Study of the Respective Roles of the General Acute and Geriatric Sectors in Care of the Elderly Hospital Patient*.
DHSS (1983a) *Health Care and its Costs* (HMSO).
DHSS (1983b) Health Circular (83) 6 *Care in the Community and Joint Finance*.
DHSS (1983c) *Performance Indicators. National Summary for 1981*.
DHSS (1984a) Health Circular (84) 13 *Implementation of the NHS Management Inquiry Report*.
DHSS (1984b) *The Health Service in England* Annual Report 1984 (HMSO).
Doll, R. (1974) *To Measure NHS Progress* (Fabian Society).
Doyal, L. with Pennell, I. (1979) *The Political Economy of Health* (Pluto Press).
Doyal, L. *et al*. (1983) *Cancer in Britain* (Pluto Press).
Draper, P., Best, G. and Dennis, J. (1977) 'Health and wealth', *Royal Society of Health Journal*, 97, 65–70.
Dunleavy, P. (1981) 'Professions and policy change: notes towards a model of ideological corporatism', *Public Administration Bulletin*, no. 36, 3–16.
Dunleavy, P. (1983) 'Analysing British Politics', in Drucker, H. *et al*. (eds) *Developments in British Politics* (Macmillan).
Dyson, R. (1984) 'Inside View', *Health and Social Service Journal* 16 August 1984, 974.
Easton, D. (1953) *The Political System* (Knopf).
Easton, D. (1965a) *A Systems Analysis of Political Life* (Wiley).
Easton, D. (1965b) *A Framework for Political Analysis* (Prentice-Hall).
Eckstein, H. (1958) *The English Health Service* (Harvard University Press).
Eckstein, H. (1960) *Pressure Group Politics* (Allen & Unwin).
Edelman, M. (1971) *Politics as Symbolic Action* (Markham).
Edelman, M. (1977) *Political Language* (Academic Press).
Elcock, H. (1978) 'Regional government in action: the members of two Regional Health Authorities, *Public Administration*, vol. 56, Winter, 379–97.
Ely Report (1969) *Report of the Committee of Enquiry into Allegations of Ill-treatment of Patients and Other Irregularities at the Ely Hospital, Cardiff*, Cmnd 3975 (HMSO).
Evans, T. (1983) 'Griffiths – The Right Prescription?' (CIPFA–AHST).
Expenditure Committee (1971) Employment and Social Services Sub-Committee, *Minutes of Evidence*, 31 March 1971, Session 1970–1, HC 323ii (IIMSO).
Expenditure Committee (1972) *Relationship of Expenditure to Needs*, Eighth Report from the Expenditure Committee, Session 1971–2 (HMSO).

Forsyth, M. (1982) *Reservicing Health* (Adam Smith Institute).

Fraser, D. (1973) *The Evolution of the British Welfare State* (Macmillan).

Gilbert, B.B. (1970) *British Social Policy 1914–39* (Batsford).

Gilbert, B.B. (1966) *The Evolution of National Insurance in Great Britain* (Michael Joseph).

Glennerster, H., with Korman, N. and Marslen-Wilson, F. (1983) *Planning for Priority Groups* (Martin Robertson).

Godber, G. (1975) *The Health Service: Past, Present and Future* (Athlone Press).

Godber, G. (1981) 'Doctors in government', *Health Trends*, vol. 13.

Gough, I. (1979) *The Political Economy of the Welfare State* (Macmillan).

Gregory, J. (1978) *Patients' Attitudes to the Hospital Service*. Royal Commission on the NHS, Research Paper No. 5. (HMSO).

Griffiths Report (1983) *NHS Management Inquiry* (DHSS).

Guillebaud Committee (1956) *Report of the Committee of Enquiry into the Cost of the National Health Service*, Cmd 9663 (HMSO).

Hall, P., Land, H., Parker, R. and Webb, A. (1975) *Change, Choice and Conflict in Social Policy* (Heinemann).

Ham, C.J. (1977) 'Power, patients and pluralism', in Barnard, K. and Lee, K. (eds) *Conflicts in the NHS* (Croom Helm).

Ham, C.J. (1980) 'Approaches to the study of social policy making', *Policy and Politics*, vol. 8, no. 1, 55–71.

Ham, C.J. (1981) *Policy Making in the National Health Service* (Macmillan).

Ham, C. J. (1984) 'Members in search of an identity', *Health and Social Service Journal*, February, 23, 222–23.

Hampton, J. R. (1983) 'The end of clinical freedom', *British Medical Journal*, vol. 287, 1237–8.

Harrison, A. and Gretton, J. (eds) (1983) *Health Care UK: An Economic, Social and Policy Audit* (CIPFA).

Haywood, S. (1983) *District Health Authorities in Action* University of Birmingham.

Haywood, S. and Alaszewski, A. (1980) *Crisis in the Health Service* (Croom Helm).

Haywood, S. and Hunter, D. (1982) 'Consultative processes in health policy in the United Kingdom: a view from the centre', *Public Administration* vol. 69, 143–62.

Health Advisory Service (1982) *The Rising Tide*.

Heclo, H. (1978) 'Issue networks and the executive establishment', in King, A. (ed.), *The New American Political System* (American Enterprise Institute).

Heclo, H. and Wildavsky, A. (1981) *The Private Government of Public Money*, 2nd edn (Macmillan).

HM Treasury (1984) *The Government's Expenditure Plans 1984–85 to 1986–87*, Cmnd 9143 (HMSO).

Hunter, D.J. (1980) *Coping with Uncertainty* (Research Studies Press).

Hunter, D. (1983) 'Centre–Periphery Relations in the National Health Service: Facilitators or Inhibitors of Innovation?', in Young, K. (ed.) *National Interests and Local Government* (Heinemann).

Illsley, R. (1977) 'Everybody's business? Concepts of health and illness', in Social Science Research Council, *Health and Health Policy – Priorities for Research* (SSRC).

Ingle, S. and Tether, P. (1981) *Parliament and Health Policy: The Role of MPs 1970–75* (Gower).

James, J. (1983) 'Some Aspects of Policy Analysis and Policy Units in the Health Field', in Gray, A. and Jenkins, W. (eds) *Policy Analysis and Evaluation in British Government*

Jay Report (1979) *Report of the Committee of Enquiry into Mental Handicap Nursing and Care*, Cmnd 7468 (HMSO).

Jenkins, W.I. (1978) *Policy Analysis* (Martin Robertson).

Jones, K. (1972) *A History of the Mental Health Services* (Routledge & Kegan Paul).

Kaye, V. (1977) 'The team spirit', *Health and Social Services Journal*, 16 September 1977.

Kitzinger, S. (1979) *The Good Birth Guide* (Croom Helm).

Klein, R. (1982) 'Performance Evaluation and the NHS: A Case Study in Conceptual Perplexity and Organisational Complexity', *Public Administration*, vol. 60, Winter 1982, 385–404.

Klein, R. (1983) *The Politics of the National Health Service* (Longman).

Klein, R. (1984) 'The Politics of Ideology vs. the Reality of Politics: The Case of Britain's National Health Service in the 1980s', *Milbank Memorial Fund Quarterly/Health and Society*, vol. 62, no. 1, 82–109.

Lalonde, M. (1974) *A New Perspective on the Health of Canadians* (Government of Canada).

Le Grand, J. (1978) 'The distribution of public expenditure: the case of health care', *Economica*, vol. 45, 125–42.

Le Grand, J. (1982) *The Strategy of Equality* (Allen & Unwin).

Levitt, R. (1979) *The Reorganised National Health Service*, 3rd edn (Croom Helm).

Lindblom, C.E. (1965) *The Intelligence of Democracy* (The Free Press).

Lindblom, C.E. (1977) *Politics and Markets* (Basic Books).

Lindsey, A. (1962) *Socialized Medicine in England and Wales* (University of North Carolina Press).

Mackintosh, J. P. (1974) *The Government and Politics of Britain*, 3rd revised edn (Hutchinson).

Malone-Lee, M. (1981) 'Where loyalties differ', *Health and Social Services Journal*, 26 November 1981, 1448–9.

Martin, J. P. (1984) *Hospitals in Trouble* (Blackwell).

Maxwell, R. (1984) 'Quality assessment in health', *British Medical Journal*, vol. 288, 12 May 1984, 1470–72.

Maynard, A. (1979) 'Pricing, insurance and the National Health Service', *Journal of Social Policy*, vol. 8 (2), 157–76.

McCarthy, M. (1982) *Epidemiology and Policies for Health Planning* (King's Fund).

McCarthy, M. (1983) 'Are efficiency measures effective?' *Health and Social Service Journal*, 15 December 1983, 1500–01.

McKeown, T. (1976) *The Role of Medicine* (Nuffield Provincial Hospitals Trust).

Health (Nuffield Provincial Hospitals Trust).

Middlemas, K. (1979) *Politics in Industrial Society* (André Deutsch).

Minford, P. (1984) 'State Expenditure: A Study in Waste', *Economic Affairs*, vol. 4, no. 3, April–June.

Ministry of Health (1946). *NHS Bill. Summary of the Proposed New Service*, Cmd 6761 (HMSO).

Ministry of Health (1967) *First Report of the Joint Working Party on the Organisation of Medical Work in Hospitals* (HMSO).

Mowbray, D. (1983) 'Management Advisory Service: the Oxford and South Western Region-wide Experiment', *Hospital and Health Services Review*, September 1983, 207–10.

Nairne, P. (1983) 'Managing the DHSS Elephant: Reflections on a Giant Department', *Political Quarterly*, 243–56.

Navarro, V. (1976) *Medicine Under Capitalism* (Prodist).

Nixon, J. and Nixon, N. (1983) 'The Social Services Committee: a forum for policy review and policy reform', *Journal of Social Policy*, vol. 12 (3), 331–55.

Normansfield Report (1978) *Report of the Committee of Inquiry into Normansfield Hospital*, Cmnd 7357 (HMSO).

Norton, P. (1981) *The Commons in Perspective* (Martin Robertson).

Noyce, J., Snaith, A.H. and Trickey, A.J. (1974) 'Regional variations in the allocation of financial resources to the community health services', *The Lancet*, 30 March 1974, 554–7.

Nuffield Provincial Hospitals Trust (1946) *The Hospital Surveys: The Domesday Book of the Hospital Services* (Oxford University Press).

O'Connor, J. (1973) *The Fiscal Crisis of the State* (St. Martin's Press; also Macmillan, 1981).

Office of Health Economics (1984) *Compendium of Health Statistics*, 5th edn (OHE).

OPCS (1978) *Occupational Mortality Decennial Supplement for England and Wales, 1970–72*, Series D5 No. 1 (HMSO).

OPCS (1984a) *OPCS Monitor Infant and Perinatal Mortality 1983*.

OPCS (1984b) *Mortality Statistics Area* (HMSO).

OPCS (1984c) *Mortality Statistics* (HMSO).

OPCS (1984d) *OPCS Monitor Infant and Perinatal Mortality 1982*.

Owen, D. (1976) *In Sickness and in Health* (Quartet).

Pater, J. E. (1981) *The Making of the NHS* (King's Fund).

Peel Report (1970) *Domiciliary Midwifery and Maternity Bed Needs* (HMSO).

Popham, G. T. (1981) 'Government and smoking: policy making and pressure groups', *Policy and Politics*, vol. 9(3), 331–47.

Powell, J. E. (1966) *A New Look at Medicine and Politics* (Pitman).

Public Accounts Committee (1977) *Ninth Report from the Public Accounts Committee Session 1976–77*, HC 532 (HMSO).

Public Accounts Committee (1981) *Seventeenth Report from the Public Accounts Committee Session 1980–81: Financial Control and Accountability in the NHS*, HC 255 (HMSO).

Razell, E. (1980) *Improving Policy Analysis in the DHSS*, Civil Service College Working Paper No. 19.

Regional Chairmen's Enquiry (1976) *Regional Chairmen's Enquiry into the Working of the DHSS in Relation to Regional Health Authorities* (DHSS).

Rhodes, R. A. W. (1979) 'Research into central–local relations in Britain. A framework for analysis', Appendix 1, in Social Science Research Council, *Central–Local Government Relationships* (SSRC).

Richardson, J. J. and Jordan, A. G. (1979) *Governing under Pressure* (Martin Robertson).

Robb, B. (ed.) (1967) *Sans Everything – A Case to Answer* (Nelson).

Royal Commission on the National Health Service (1979) *Report*, Cmnd 7615 (HMSO).

RIPA (Royal Institute of Public Administration) (1980) *Policy and Practice: The Experience of Government* (RIPA).

Saunders, P. (1979) *Urban Politics* (Hutchinson).

Saunders, P. (1981) 'Notes on the specificity of the local state', in Boddy, M. and Fudge, C. (eds), *The Local State: Theory and Practice* (University of Bristol, School for Advanced Urban Studies).

Short Report (1980) *Perinatal and Neonatal Mortality. Second Report from the Social Services Committee, Session 1979–80* (HMSO).

Simpson, R. (1979) *Access to Primary Care*, Royal Commission on the NHS, Research Paper No. 6 (HMSO).

Smith, B. (1976) *Policy Making in British Government* (Martin Robertson).

Social Services Committee (1980). *The Government's White Papers on Public Expenditure: The Social Services, Third Report from the Social Services Committee, Session 1979–80*, HC 701–2 (HMSO): vol. 1, *Report*; vol. 2 *Minutes of Evidence and Appendices*.

Social Services Committee (1981) *Public Expenditure on the Social Services. Third Report from the Social Services Committee, Session 1980–81*, HC 324–1 (HMSO): vol. I *Report*; vol. II *Minutes of Evidence and Appendices*.

Social Services Committee (1982) *1982 White Paper: Public Expenditure on the Social Services*, Second Report from the Social Services Committee, Session 1981–2, HC 306–1 (HMSO), vol. 1 *Report*; vol. 2 *Minutes of Evidence and Appendices*.

Social Services Committee (1984a) *Griffiths NHS Management Inquiry Report*, First Report from the Social Services Committee, Session 1983–4, HC 209 (HMSO).

Social Services Committee (1984b) *Public Expenditure on the Social Services*, Fourth Report from the Social Services Committee, Session 1983–4, HC 395 (HMSO).

Solesbury, W. (1976) 'The environmental agenda', *Public Administration*, Winter, 379–97.

Stacey, M. (1977a) 'People who are affected by the inverse law of care', *Health and Social Services Journal*, 3 June 1977, 898–902.

Stacey, M. (1977b) 'Concepts of health and illness: a working paper on the concepts and their relevance for research', in Social Science Research Council, *Health and Health Policy – Priorities for Research* (SSRC).

Stevens, R. (1966) *Medical Practice in Modern England* (Yale University Press).

Taylor, P. (1984) *The Smoke Ring* (The Bodley Head).

Titmuss, R. (1968) *Commitment to Welfare* (Allen & Unwin).

Townsend, P. and Davidson, N. (eds) (1982) *Inequalities in Health* (Penguin).

Tudor-Hart, J. (1971) 'The inverse care law', *The Lancet*, 27 February 1971, 405–12.

Ward, L. (1982) *People First* (King's Fund).

West, R. R. and Lowe, C. R. (1976) 'Regional variations in need for and provision and use of child health services in England and Wales', *British Medical Journal*, 9 October 1976, 843–6.

Wickings, I. *et al.* (1983) 'Review of clinical budgeting and costing experiments', *British Medical Journal*, vol. 286, 12 February 1983, 575–7.

Wilding, P. (1982) *Professional Power and Social Welfare* (Routledge & Kegan Paul).

Willcocks, A. J. (1967) *The Creation of the National Health Service* (Routledge & Kegan Paul).

Williams, B. T., Nicholl, J. P., Thomas, K. J. and Knowleden, J. (1984) 'Analysis of the work of independent acute hospitals in England and Wales, 1981', *British Medical Journal*, vol. 289, 18 August 1984.

World Health Organisation (1965) *Constitution Basic Documents*, 10th edn (WHO).

Yates, J. (1982) 'PIG in the middle', *The Health Services*, 1 October 1982.

Young, H. and Sloman, A. (1982) *No, Minister* (BBC).

Index